While Berlin Burns

While Berlin Burns

The Diary of
Hans-Georg von Studnitz
1943–1945

Hans-Georg von Studnitz
Foreword by Andreas von Studnitz
Introduction by Roger Moorhouse

FRONTLINE BOOKS

While Berlin Burns: The Diary of Hans-Georg von Studnitz 1943–1945

This edition published in 2011 by Frontline Books,
an imprint of
Pen & Sword Books Limited,
47 Church Street, Barnsley, South Yorkshire S70 2AS
www.frontline-books.com

Email: info@frontline-books.com or write to us at the above address.

Foreword © Andreas von Studnitz
Introduction © Roger Moorhouse
Copyright © Hans-Georg von Studnitz

ISBN: 978-1-84832-617-0

PUBLISHING HISTORY
While Berlin Burns was first published in the USA by Prentice-Hall,
Inc., Englewood Cliffe, New Jersey in 1964. This edition includes a
new foreword by the author's son, Andreas von Studnitz, and a new
introduction by Roger Moorhouse

CIP data records for this title are available from the British Library

Typeset in 10pt Minion by
Mac Style, Beverley, East Yorkshire

Printed in Great Britain by CPI

Contents

Foreword

My father was the eldest of four brothers, all of whom died during the Second World War, so when I was born I became 'his whole life'. My father was, as you say in German 'dancing on two wedding parties'. One half of him took part in the social life where he came from: aristocracy. The other half broke out, looking for something else. So he became a journalist in his early twenties after some years of hanging around in South America as a banking apprentice. Like many fathers he wanted me to avoid the 'mistakes' he had made in his youth and was very glad about my first intention to become a banker. Great was his disappointment when I had to tell him, 'No Dad, I'm going to study law.' He was shocked when I decided to break up with that too and go to the theatre, first as an actor and then later as a director. On my thirtieth birthday (at that time I was working in a little theatre in Germany, in the middle of nowhere) he asked me whether I was happy with what I was doing, to which I assured him, I was. He responded with, 'Because I think, if you stay mediocre you won't be happy'.

Lucky for him that he had the chance to prove the contrary...

When I first read my fathers' book *While Berlin Burns*, it must have been between 1980 and 1990. He already was older than seventy-five, me in my thirties. The reason was the question coming up in me again: 'How exactly was life for you during the Third Reich and what was your work as a journalist for the press department of the German foreign office during the last years of the Second World War?'

In many conversations about that subject with my father, I always had the impression of a man, to whose attitude towards German fascism the term 'inner emigration' made sense. In the way that he, a *konservative*, patriotically thinking writer (who in his autobiography *Seitensprünge*, wrote: 'I would have preferred to live in the nineteenth than in this barbaric century and I still consider monarchy as the best form of government') was hoping for better times after the war, in which the German people would overcome Hitler and renew itself by own power.

While Berlin Burns is a document of this 'inner emigration' and his loneliness in the years 1943–45. Since he was monitored like everybody in similar positions by the Gestapo, the only place to keep the manuscript safely while he was writing it, was in his office in the ministry of foreign affairs. The only person who knew about it – except him – was his secretary. She kept these lines (which, in their dry way of stating what was happening every day, including the latest Hitler-jokes and the short information that, in the foreign press, for the first time KZ's were mentioned) in the official safe of the press department. There nobody would search them.

While Berlin Burns was my father's first book and the only one which was also published in English. I am very glad about this new edition – in memory of my father.

Rimsting, August 2011
Andreas von Studnitz

Introduction

Hans-Georg von Studnitz was born in Potsdam in 1907. Of old Silesian aristocratic stock, he initially trained as a banker and worked in the Americas in the late 1920s, before returning to Berlin as a young man in 1929. Switching to journalism with the onset of the Depression, he would again travel widely, spending most of the 1930s as a foreign correspondent for the *Berliner Lokal-Anzeiger*, reporting from various European capitals, as well as India and the Middle East, and covering the Spanish Civil War.

Like many other journalists of his era, Studnitz was engaged by the German Foreign Office with the outbreak of war in September 1939, where he was given the task of preparing articles for the domestic press and monitoring the reports of foreign journalists. In the autumn of 1940, he then shifted to the Press Department of the Foreign Office, where he was responsible primarily for writing daily political reports for German embassies and legations abroad. He would remain there until the end of the war.

At some point in those 'interesting times', Studnitz started to keep a diary, to record as he put it; a 'critical survey of a moment of history.' That diary – loyally transcribed and concealed by his Foreign Office secretary – would form the basis of this book: *While Berlin Burns*. Opening with the fall of Stalingrad in February 1943, it is Studnitz's personal account of the final two years of the Second World War; the story of the collapse of Hitler's Third Reich, and of the violent humbling of his once-proud capital city.

Unlike many commentators of the era – such as Ruth Andreas-Friedrich or Missie Vassiltchikov – Studnitz was not what one might describe as an innocent bystander or an opponent of the Nazi regime. Rather, as one of the leading members of the Foreign Office Press Department, he was a man of considerable influence, and a key player in the politics of propaganda within the Third Reich. A Nazi Party member from 1933, Studnitz had quickly proved himself to be an adept propagandist, penning a number of articles and brochures for the Nazi press, usually under a pseudonym, alongside his regular work in the Foreign Office. In this capacity, Studnitz would parrot many of the well-worn Nazi slogans and would wax lyrical in print about the historical perfidy of the British, the wanton materialism of the United States or the 'revanchism' of the French, pausing only to laud those nations that had allied themselves to Nazi Germany, as the shining representatives of 'western Christian culture'.

For all such utterances and allegiances, however, it seems that Studnitz did not quite view himself as a Nazi. He certainly does not come across in his diary as an ideological animal, thereby leaving the reader to wonder whether he was careful with the thoughts that he committed to paper, or whether he assiduously edited himself prior to post-war publication. On this particular point, the wider record is silent, but it is quite possible that the Studnitz revealed in the pages of this diary is the real one, and the pontificating ideologue of the press was a career-driven affectation.

It certainly does not seem that Studnitz came to the Nazi Party through an overt ideological sympathy. He was an arch-conservative rather than a Nazi; one who arrived at support for Hitler through a rejection of democracy – and the equality that it implied – and a misplaced belief that the leadership-principles of Nazism could be equated with the ideas of aristocratic privilege. Thus, it is notable that he writes of 'the Nazis' only in the third person, and is not above quite vehement attacks on his superior – Foreign Minister Joachim von Ribbentrop – describing him in turns as egocentric, arrogant, obstinate and lacking in intelligence. Tellingly, too, Studnitz certainly did not feel it necessary to express any misgivings or remorse for the role that he himself had played in building up the Nazi regime. Any ideological or political identification with Hitler, it seems, had already worn rather thin by 1943.

Rather – as his diary makes clear – Studnitz very obviously identified himself with the traditional élite; ministers, ambassadors and fellow aristocrats. He evidently enjoyed the social whirl of his class; forever breakfasting at the Adlon or enjoying receptions in elegant surroundings. In fact, Studnitz was astonishingly well connected. Those that are familiar with the other great diarists and commentators of the war, will see some of their names mentioned here – Missie Vassiltchikov, for instance, or Lally Horstmann – all of them, it seems, were part of the same set; dining at the same restaurants and coinciding at the same functions. Yet, Studnitz was also an habitual name-dropper, littering his diary with so many Bismarcks, Metternichs and assorted noble titles, that occasionally it almost reads like a nineteenth century court gazette. Indeed, by a strange twist of fate, on the eve of the attempt on Hitler's life on twentieth July 1944, Studnitz was at a society wedding, sharing best man responsibilities with one of those aristocrats later implicated in the plot – Peter Yorck von Wartenburg.

So, on one level at least, *While Berlin Burns* can be read and enjoyed as a traditional society diary; full of functions, weddings and gossip, as Berlin's gilded youth danced away the nightmare of another lost war and the catastrophe of Nazism. In her diary, Missie Vassiltchikov would describe Studnitz as a natural raconteur: 'witty and cruel, [he] loves a good story', she wrote, adding: 'we laughed so much that I got a kind of cramp.'[1] There is precious little humour in Studnitz's own diary, but the storyteller in him nonetheless shines through.

More importantly, however, the book serves as a chilling chronicle of the horrors of aerial bombing during the Second World War. The subject makes its first appearance in the diary in early March 1943, when one of the RAF's earliest heavy raids was reported in rather dry, matter of fact tones: 'Prager Platz reduced to ashes … A dud fell in the Richthofen's garden. Another landed on the Italian Embassy.' It was almost as though the bombing war was something that happened to other people. But Studnitz was already alive to the potential dangers, adding that same day that 'we are sending our little daughter to the country.'

Already by the following winter, those potential dangers had become all too real. In November, Studnitz experienced one of the opening raids of the RAF's 'Battle of Berlin', a vain attempt to batter the German capital into submission and so end the war. He experienced that raid – which would devastate a large swathe of the city's western suburbs and destroy the now-iconic Kaiser Wilhelm Memorial Church – initially from a stationary train, whilst returning from a weekend in the Pomeranian countryside. It was, he recalled, 'an indescribable experience… like the end of the world.' Being forced to continue his journey on foot, Studnitz recalled that the night air was 'polluted with the smell of burning and with the fumes of escaping gas', whilst the roadway was littered with uprooted trees, downed telegraph poles, craters and mounds of rubble. 'Practically all our friends' he wrote in the aftermath, 'have lost everything'.

That sense of loss – both human and material – is one that pervades the remainder of the book. Though the daily diplomatic carousel still dominates Studnitz's account, it is increasingly clear that the war is inching ever closer to the German capital and that its effects were becoming tangible in myriad different ways. Indeed, only when he spent time away from Berlin did he realise how inured he already had become to the everyday horrors of warfare in the capital. On a visit to Vienna in the spring of 1944, for instance, Studnitz described the city as 'a fairyland' where 'nobody talks about the war' and – perhaps more importantly – where the social whirl is still in full swing. Later that autumn, a weekend sojourn in rural Silesia made clear to him what a 'horror-world' he had been inhabiting in Berlin.

By the final weeks of the war, Studnitz's Berlin was a wasteland of dead-eyed refugees and exhausted Berliners, all fearfully awaiting the arrival of the Red Army. Even the newspapers – which he had once overseen and to which he had often contributed – were reduced to single sheets, containing little but empty slogans and bland exhortations to resist. Studnitz himself was by this point in Reelkirchen in Westphalia, where he had taken his family in mid-March 1945. There, he experienced the final collapse of Nazi Germany and made his last diary entry – on Wednesday, 4 April, 1945. 'To look more than fifteen minutes ahead', he wrote, 'is pointless.' One is tempted to muse on how far he had fallen.

While Berlin Burns is engaging on many levels. Beautifully and sympathetically written, it provides insights into the diplomatic world that Studnitz inhabited professionally, as well as illuminating the faltering *demi-monde* in which he moved. As a former journalist, Studnitz was also a well-informed and clear-eyed commentator on the 'moment of history' through which he lived, and he provides much of value for those interested in wider subjects, such as the state of German civilian morale in the final two years of the war.

Yet, Studnitz's greatest contributions, perhaps, are his unsparing descriptions of the material consequences of the war against Berlin – the smashed suburbs, the acrid smoke, the denuded trees in summertime – what he called 'the twisted profile of the great metropolis'. In sparse yet powerful prose, he gave astonishingly vivid first-hand accounts of the bombing raids and of the popular reaction to them: the fatalism, the pessimism and the petty heroism of ordinary Berliners. His is undoubtedly one of the best records of the dying days of the Third Reich.

Roger Moorhouse, August 2011

Note

1. Marie Vassiltchikov, *The Berlin Diaries 1940–1945*, (London, 1985), p. 167.

Preface

Lawrence once said that every man leads a double life – in thought and in deed, that both are equally true and therefore diaries should always be treated as false.

In deciding nevertheless to publish these comments which were jotted down between 1943 and 1945, I have been actuated by two motives, both of which seem to me apposite. In the first place, I imagine that very few other people were in a position to keep a diary during the period under review; and in the second place, any assessment of an epoch based purely on official documents must inevitably lead to false conclusions. Research into the Napoleonic era and the French Revolution has fortunately not been confined to a study of the State archives and the memoirs of the Emperor, but has also been able to draw upon the writings of contemporaries who lived through both eras and made notes about anything which drew their attention. It is often these seemingly unimportant happenings which round off the picture of history and add to it those highlights which sometimes endure longer than the solid facts which they embroider.

Born in 1907, I was a child during the First World War, but faced the outbreak of the Second World War as a man who had acquired a wide and deep knowledge of the world. This circumstance led to my being called up for war service with the Foreign Ministry, and, with one short break, I served in its information and press sections from autumn 1939 until the end of the war. I was entrusted with tasks within the scope of my extensive experience and so was able to follow the events of the war without illusion.

The compilation of this critical survey of a moment of history would not have been possible without the loyal assistance of Fräulein Gisela Albrecht, my secretary in the Foreign Ministry.

It was she who took down these notes and locked the one and only copy of this daily journal safely away in the Foreign Ministry's secret documents strong-room, where it was secure against uninvited scrutiny.

Hans-Georg von Studnitz
Schlaitdorf, February 1963

February 1943

The fall of Stalingrad – Count von Coudenhove's escapades – Ciano: an opponent of the Axis? – Chandra Bose's frustrations – Mission to Italy

Monday, February 1, 1943

Today's communiqué from Supreme Headquarters announces the fall of Stalingrad. The Sixth Army's capitulation has been preceded by a host of rumours. Nearly everybody had some relative or other out there, and many people claim to have met and spoken with officers and men who had been in the 'cauldron' but a few days before. The fate of Adam Baworowski, the tennis champion, my cousin Ernix Studnitz, Dressier, our old school friend from Potsdam and many others remains uncertain. The masses have taken the disaster calmly. Only a very few are capable of appreciating the full implications of the tragedy. The official communiqué is so tersely worded that only those in the know can interpret it correctly. In official Party circles the word has gone round that as far as Stalingrad is concerned the line to be taken is that we must make the best of a bad job. The replacement of Raeder by Doenitz is causing uneasiness in England. Cavallero's relief by Ambrosio is also causing concern here. The former was hand-in-glove with the Ciano coterie. Ambrosio most emphatically is not.

Yesterday I was awarded the Order of Isabella the Catholic as a reward for my services while visiting the German book exhibition in Madrid with Schmidt two years ago. The distinction is as un-merited as are most decorations. But then it is one of the peculiarities of the diplomatic world that people receive decorations for banal trivialities, while genuine services often go unrewarded or are ascribed to the wrong person.

Tuesday, February 2, 1943

Today's communiqué from Supreme Headquarters states: 'The sacrifice of the (Sixth) Army has not been in vain. For weeks on end it broke up the repeated assaults of six Soviet armies and by so doing has given the German High Command the time and opportunity to initiate counter-measures upon which the fate of the whole eastern front depends.' A period of three days of public mourning has been ordered. The communiqué makes no reference to the figure of ninety-one thousand prisoners given out by the Russians. This secrecy as regards the details about Stalingrad will inevitably drive the population into the arms of foreign propaganda sources. What the relatives of some quarter of a million German soldiers want to know is what has happened to their sons, their fathers and their brothers. Not everyone will be able to resist the temptation to try and get news by listening to enemy broadcasts. Those at the top seem to have overlooked the fact that publication of the figures given by the Russians would have allayed anxiety. In the eyes of the simple masses, 'taken prisoner' is very different from 'killed', no matter how many times they are told that the Russians murder all prisoners taken.

Wednesday, February 3, 1943

I have just read an excellent article in the *Frankfurter Zeitung* of February 1 by Irene Seligo on the Beveridge Plan. Had even one of our diplomatic representatives succeeded in compiling such a report it would have been plastered with seals and treated as a state secret. The few remaining good German foreign correspondents are turning in far better-written and more cogent reports than most of those emanating from our diplomatic missions abroad. The truth of Bismarck's dictum that while every journalist is a potential Secretary of State, you can't make a journalist out of every Secretary of State has never been more evident than during these last three years that I have been working in the Foreign Ministry. During this time I have discovered that most journalists are intellectual giants in comparison with the people with whom I am working today. More knowledge, swifter and more logical thinking are demanded of even a modest sub-editor than of many of the high-ranking officials of this Ministry. It is true that German journalism has deteriorated considerably during recent years, but a few first-class brains still remain in the profession. The *Frankfurter Zeitung* devotes three columns to its foreign news. From Lisbon, Irene Seligo submits reports of developments in England while Margret Boveri keeps watch on the United States, and from Tokio Lily Abegg follows the course of events in the Far East. Each of these three women is an outstanding expert in her own field.

A few days ago Friedrich Sieburg, who up to the war had been the Paris correspondent of the *Frankfurter Zeitung,* came and dined with us. His talent as a writer is as great as his skill as a raconteur. On the outbreak of war, Sieburg, Puckler of the *Deutsche Allgemeine Zeitung,* Wirsing of the *Münchner Neueste Nachrichten,* and I myself were ordered to report for duty with the Foreign Ministry. Sieburg himself was given the rank of embassy councillor and was initially sent to Brussels as observer of the situation in France, later visiting Spain and Portugal. After the armistice with France he was posted to the German Embassy in Paris, which had been taken over by Abetz, and was given the task of making contact with leading French figures. But the political influence he exercised on Berlin remained meagre. When he asked to be relieved, the Foreign Ministry wanted to post him to China. This, however, he refused to accept. Now he has succeeded in obtaining his discharge from the Foreign Ministry with effect from July 1, and since February 1 he has been back at his old job with the *Frankfurter Zeitung.*

Thursday, February 4, 1943

The 'Agathe Banquet', arranged for today, first at Horcher's then at the Quartier Latin, will not now take place. In view of the Stalingrad catastrophe the Government has ordered the closing of the last of Berlin's luxury restaurants. Apart from the two named above, the Neva Grill, Peltzer's Atelier and the Tuskulum in the Kurfurstendamm are also affected. Although the more *recherche* dishes have long since disappeared from their menus, these restaurants have nevertheless remained a refuge and an oasis, thanks to the elegance of their appointments and the excellence of their service. Apart from that, one could also count every now and then on getting a coupon-free meal of game or poultry. To be sure of getting a table at Horcher's you have to book days ahead. Most of the tables are permanently occupied by government and other officials, predominantly from the Air Ministry, the aircraft industry, the diplomatic corps and such gentlemen as are entitled to be addressed as *Herr Generaldirektor.* Only rarely does one see a member of the old society set.

As the favourite chef of Hermann Göring, Horcher has risen to become the foremost restaurateur in the Third Reich. Since he has been entrusted with the arrangements for State banquets, he has built up a reserve team of waiters from the leading Berlin restaurants, and it was with their assistance that he organised the banquet held in honour of the Prince Regent Paul of Yugoslavia in the Potsdamer Neuer Palais. With Germany occupying half Europe, Horcher's sphere of activity broadened. From Count Paly Palffy he took over Die Drei Husaren in Vienna, then moved on to Maxim's in Paris and opened branches in Oslo and Belgrade. Before the war he held the concession for the German restaurant at the Paris World Fair, and later he managed a German restaurant in London's Mayfair. His final establishment was in Madrid.

After the closing of his Berlin restaurant, the following story is going the rounds: as the result of an article in *Das Reich,* 'Die Optik des Krieges', by Dr Goebbels, Horcher received a telephone call, ordering him to close his restaurant. The next day a conference was held at the Ministry of Propaganda with Secretary of State Gutterer in the chair to discuss the final measures (among them the closing of Horcher's) to be taken. At the conference it was then found that no one was prepared to admit that he had been responsible for the demise of Horcher's. After much searching, a subordinate 'expert' of the Ministry was discovered who confessed that it was he who had given the order. When asked on what authority he had done so, he admitted that he had acted in accordance with the dictates of his conscience. The news of the closing quickly came to the ears of General Bodenschatz, the *Reichsmarschall's* adjutant, and he at once telephoned to demand why and by whom Horcher's had been closed. With the unfortunate 'expert' repeating again and again that he had acted on grounds of conscience, Bodenschatz had roared: 'To hell with your damn conscience, *Herr Regierungsraf* and slammed down the receiver!

The originator of the 'Agathe Banquet', which is held annually on the name-day of the saint, was Count Hans Coudenhove-Kalergi, son of an Austrian ambassador and a Japanese lady, owner of large estates at Ronspergheim in Bohemia, elder brother of the founder of the Pan-European movement and husband of a woman glider-pilot from whom he is separated. At the outbreak of war, this wealthy aristocrat, succumbing to the lure of Berlin, moved into the

Hotel Kaiserhof, where he regally entertained Berlin society and its hangers-on from the various ministries. He sent invitations to all those he thought might interest him or whom he regarded as influential, and was seldom rebuffed. Before long he was the talk of the town, thanks largely to the eccentric escapades in which he indulged. On one occasion the police surrounded the Kaiserhof, in which Hitler happened to be having tea, preparatory to searching Coudenhove's apartments in connection with two packing-cases which had just arrived from Bohemia and had aroused their suspicions, since a rumour had reached their ears that these crates contained infernal machines. A bomb-disposal squad began dismantling the dangerous crates and eventually found a faience stove shaped in the likeness of a heat-giving Count Coudenhove! The Gestapo retired with red faces, and the Count had the last laugh.

The scene of another of his escapades was the Berlin flat at Lützowufer which he had rented from Captain Wickel. The Bohemian count gave a cocktail party. Scarcely had his guests begun to sip a concoction consisting, for want of better ingredients, of beer and vermouth, than Coudenhove jumped on to a table with a suitcase under his arm and announced that as a surprise for the ladies he had procured an assortment of Parisian perfumes, American stockings and English soap. 'Help yourselves to anything that takes your fancy!' he cried, dumping the contents of the suitcase on the floor. In a flash the room was transformed into a battleground. The wives and daughters of officials, of senior Ministers and Ambassadors fought furiously for possession of the treasures; ladies in mink coats rolled and wrestled about on the floor; crocodile handbags came into play as handy weapons; hats from Paris were trampled underfoot; umbrellas were wielded like swords; and stockings became horribly laddered. The mask of convention dropped to reveal naked greed, pugnacity and tears of rage. But the organiser of this diabolical spectacle stood with folded arms and a Mephistophelean smile on his face, savouring his success at having thus shattered the poise and equanimity of so many fine ladies. The cruel joke reached its climax, however, when a veritable Brunnhilde of a woman, having stuffed her pockets more fully than any of her rivals and then hidden her booty (a bottle of Chanel and several jars of Elizabeth Arden creams and lotions) in her discarded furcoat, found later that it had all been filched and a brick left in its place!

Coudenhove had managed to transform the house in which this scene took place into a sort of Chamber of Horrors. Life-size portraits gazed down from the walls, portraying Coudenhove as Grand Master of a fictitious Order of his own invention; as Europa astride the bull; as the lord of the manor, in evening dress, gazing at a ruined castle, one ring-bedecked hand proffering a goblet of champagne to an ibex; as a Cardinal; and as a judo wrestler. Some of the pseudo-self-portraits had interchangeable faces, so that the observer was confronted by a gaze that was alternatively benevolent and evil. Many of the guests blamed this startling phenomenon on the effects of alcohol. One of the strangest items was a plaster cast of a foot, with the inscription: 'The right foot of Count von Coudenhove-Ronspergheim'.

Coudenhove was the benefactor of many of the fortune-tellers whom the war had swept into Berlin. One of them had prophesied that all women with the name Agathe were destined to bring him good fortune, and it was from this prophesy that the Agathe cult arose. A saint of that name, who had lost her breasts in the torture chamber, inspired Coudenhove with the most extravagant ideas. On her name-day the Count entertained his friends at Horcher's. To all the ladies named Agathe he presented diamond and coral brooches symbolizing the saint's martyrdom, and the same motif was repeated in the silver table decorations. The remaining guests received medallions, portraying Coudenhove in the robes of a Roman Emperor.

Friday, February 5, 1943
Yesterday evening we dined with Ridomi. Lanza was also there. These two diplomats are the brains of the Italian Embassy here. Ridomi, as Press Attaché, keeps the Ambassador informed about everything that is happening in Germany, with particular emphasis on the morale of the people. In this connection his jovial manner and portly figure stand him in good stead, as does his command of German, which, as a native of Trentino, he speaks with a slight south-eastern accent. Ridomi moves with complete self-assurance in all grades of society. He is accepted as a Germanophile, although, like most Italians, he is inclined to be hypersensitive, and his pro-

German sympathies can hardly have been strengthened by recent events. With Ridomi, as with other Italians, the feeling that Italy has backed the wrong horse is growing stronger and stronger. The members of the Embassy here are filled with anxiety regarding the future, and this puts a strain on their attitude towards Germany.

Lanza is the most gifted of the Second Secretaries at the Embassy. He was previously in Moscow and London, and shortly before the war he had been Consul-General in Tunis. He comes from Turin, is married to a rich Milanese and lives in a palatial flat in the Grosse Querallee, belonging to the widow of a Berlin doctor who died in Buenos Aires. The drawing-room of the flat is dominated by a painting of the lady in question depicted as a Greek mythological figure being abducted by Neptune.

Our conversation turned to the Red Army reforms which the Russian radio announced on February 1. Lanza regards the re-introduction of badges of rank, the substitution of 'officer' for 'commander', and the consequent reawakening of the old disciplinarian principles as one of the most important measures since the beginning of the bolshevik revolution. These reforms, he says, denote a return in the Soviet Union to the old, conservative way of life. It was by no means impossible, he thought, that after the Stalingrad victory communist Russia might well remember her national mission and soft-peddle the idea of world revolution.

Lanza regards the situation on the eastern front as extremely serious. If he were the Duce, he said, he would send the Ambassador to the Führer to ask him what forces still remained at his disposal. If Germany did not possess enough reserves to launch a new offensive in the coming spring with greater thrusting power than last year's offensive, then the war was lost. This, he insisted, was a fact that we must face, for only by doing so could we make any preparation for the future. However serious the military situation may be, the political perspectives are still not bad. As before, the Axis still possessed opportunities of bringing the war to a favourable conclusion by means of political manoeuvre. When one's military resources are exhausted, he argued, one must fight on with political weapons. And this would be much easier, because this time the collapse would not come from within, as it did in 1918. If a catastrophe occurs, it will be because the German armies have been defeated in the field. But no one here, he said, seems prepared to admit such a possibility. Lanza confessed freely that he doubted our ability to counteract military failure by political means, and went on to say that the Italians had received information that the Russians had so far not used any of the weapons sent to them by Britain and America, but were apparently accumulating the matériel in a reserve army supply area.

In its last issue the Portuguese newspaper *Acçao* asserts that Great Britain is now manoeuvring with her traditional skill to avoid losing the war – either by herself suffering military defeat, or as the result of a victory by the bolshevist allies, since either of these eventualities would be considered a calamity of equal magnitude.

Saturday, February 6, 1943

The principal event of the day has been the Cabinet reshuffle in Italy. The dismissal of Grandi and Bottai is overshadowed by Ciano's resignation. The Italians have issued the usual declaration about 'a changing of the guard'. Unofficially, there are two versions. One is that Ciano and his supporters are at complete loggerheads with the Duce and that after Ciano's last visit to German Headquarters these differences became acute. In view of the stalemate in the East, Ciano is said to have been instructed to try and persuade the Führer to seek a decision in the Mediterranean theatre. The Italians were in favour of adopting a defensive attitude on the eastern front and of launching a major offensive in the Mediterranean, primarily against Egypt and in Tunis. Ciano, apparently, did not plead his case with the requisite urgency and returned to Rome empty-handed. Since then he and his circle, having come to the conclusion that the war is lost, have been trying to induce Mussolini to accept a reorientation of Italian policy. When, shortly after all this, the situation in south Russia further deteriorated and the Italian Expeditionary Corps suffered severe losses in the process, Cavallero, who is a very close friend of Ciano, resigned, and it was this change in the High Command that was the signal for today's Cabinet reshuffle.

According to the other version, Mussolini fears that Italy will very shortly be faced with a life and death crisis; since Ciano, as the husband of his favourite daughter, is dearer to him than his own sons, he is anxious to relieve Ciano of all responsibility, in order to avoid jeopardising the latter's future and that of his children. In view of Mussolini's strong inclinations towards nepotism, it is quite possible that he is anxious to furnish his son-in-law with an escape route before Italy goes down in defeat.

It is hard to assess what measure of truth there is in any of these rumours. Sudden Cabinet reshuffles have been a quite normal feature of fascism. While I was in Rome in 1935, the Duce one evening dismissed twenty-eight Ministers and Secretaries of State. The reshuffle came so suddenly that the first the victims heard about it was when they read about it in the morning's newspapers. Much the same thing seems to have happened this time.

I first met Count Ciano in the spring of 1941 in Vienna at the official ceremony to mark the accession of Bulgaria and Yugoslavia to the Three Power Pact. At that time he was at the zenith of his career. Here in Germany he was always a controversial figure. His youthful, light-hearted manner jarred on the more stolid Germans. It was an open secret that Ribbentrop and Ciano could not 'get on' together. However, real efforts were made at accommodation with the Italian Foreign Minister's temperament, since he was, after all, the Duce's closest confidant.

When Ciano was in Berlin in 1941 I dined with him at the Italian ambassador's villa in Wannsee. Dinner was supposed to be at 8.00 p.m., but the negotiations in Berlin were so protracted that it was about 11.00 before Alfiero and Ciano reached Wannsee, where we had been waiting in vain for three hours, getting hungrier and more bad-tempered every minute. But when Ciano appeared, the atmosphere changed at once. His charm captivated everyone: he was so very different from the kind of State dignitary to whom people here were used. And thanks to his sparkling good humour, the evening was a great success, in spite of its unfortunate beginning.

About midnight Ciano strolled off into an adjoining room, where he made amorous propositions to one or two ladies. When one of the beauties he was importuning remonstrated: *'Mais non! c'est impossible, Excellence!'* he retorted: *'Impossible! c'est un mot qui n'existe pas dans la langue française!'*

On another occasion I met him at the house of Casardi, the Secretary of the Italian Embassy. There, oblivious to all the other guests, he sat at the far end of a sofa with a blonde, listening eagerly to the mandoline players, who were singing Neapolitan love-songs. He took practically no notice at all of Count Mayalde, the newly arrived Spanish Ambassador – much to the indignation of the other Spaniards present. The young minister was on the best of terms with all the ladies of the Italian Embassy, to all of whom he had presented autographed photographs of himself.

It is still too early to pass judgment on Ciano's political achievements. Whether he made any contributions of his own to Mussolini's foreign policy will be the task of historical research to determine. His greatest mistake was the unfortunate campaign against Greece, the blame for which has been attributed to him. But, catastrophic though the campaign was for Italy, it nevertheless gave the fascists sovereignty over Greece and provided the initial impulse that led to the partition of Yugoslavia, a country that Italy has always regarded as an enemy.

Monday, February 8, 1943
I have been going round the art dealers, who are anxiously waiting to see whether the new regulations mean that they will have to shut up shop. The question of whether or not art dealers may remain open appears at first sight to be of but little importance. In fact, however, the art dealers are at the present moment playing a more important role than one would suppose. They are among the very few whose business has not been affected by the regulations governing price control. Anyone with real knowledge can nowadays make the most astonishing finds. The value of works of art today is on an average about thirty per cent higher than it was in 1939; and even at that time antiques were regarded as a good form of investment. The most striking proof of this can be seen in the auctions conducted by Hans W. Lange, the proprietor of the last of the great Berlin art auction houses, in the Bellevue Strasse, opposite the Hotel Esplanade. As the successor of Lepke, Huldschinsky and others, he is today the only auctioneer in Berlin of international repute. His last auction was held on January 27. In spite of the difficulties of the times, Lange always manages on these occasions to produce a profusely illustrated catalogue, printed on the finest paper. At this auction Freddy Horstmann put up for sale a woodland landscape by the eighteenth century Dutch painter, Koekoek, which he had inherited from his mother-in-law. Its normal value would have been about four thousand Reichsmarks. For the purposes of this auction it was valued at twenty-five thousand; and it was bought by

the Munich art dealer, Almas – for sixty-four thousand marks! The prices of sculpture have risen to an even greater extent.

Among the pieces of furniture at present being offered for sale in Berlin, many are of French origin, with Louis XV and XVI chairs predominating. The art dealers maintain that they bought these pieces at an auction held at the Berlin Finance Office. But it was obvious that they have come from France. Although this French furniture is being eagerly snapped up, the articles do not always afford the buyers unmitigated joy. In some mysterious way the upholstered seat-cushions disappear while the chairs are being transported to Berlin. To obtain new cushions is difficult and to find covers which match the rest of the upholstery is impossible.

At the beginning of the war a number of the Berlin art dealers shut up shop, while others showed no great interest in disposing of the stocks they held, but were content to offer for sale just as much as would keep them going and meet their daily needs. Restocking, in any case, presented very great difficulties. The remaining art dealers will not be very worried if regulations compel them to close, since the State will in that case have to make provision for them. As far as collectors are concerned, it will mean the disappearance of one of the few pleasures in life which remained to them.

Rumours are going around that permanent waving is to be prohibited. One hairdresser told me that as a result of these still unconfirmed reports he has appointments booked for six weeks ahead. The poor fellow is in despair, since he can only cope with a maximum of four clients a day. Permanent waving, he added, was the foundation of his whole business.

The luxury shops, which the régime was anxious to see remain open for the sake of window dressing, have now also been told to close; among them are some of the establishments in the traditionally famous shopping areas, which still display many wonderful things that no one can afford to buy. The shortage of even the most elementary and essential articles has now become so acute, that many of the simplest things can now only be obtained in the black market or by barter. At a press conference, in his address explaining the measures he proposed to introduce, the Minister for Economic Affairs, Funk, told his audience that, recently, scrubbing-brushes had been exchanged for tickets for a Furtwängler concert.

Supreme Headquarters gives the numbers of wounded evacuated

from Stalingrad as forty-six thousand. This is a higher figure than had generally been anticipated. The same authority gave the total strength of the army besieged in Stalingrad as 246,000 men. The Russians claim to have taken ninety-one thousand prisoners. If these figures are accurate, this means that 137,000 of the troops engaged in the operations have survived, either wounded or as prisoners of war, and that the total of killed amounts to 109,000.

The military situation in south Russia continues to be very serious. There is a danger that the Russian armies advancing between the Don and the Donets will wheel southwards, thrust in the direction of Taganrog and surround our forces in the Rostov area. With enemy forces on three sides, Rostov itself is already to all intents and purposes surrounded. If this danger materialises, disaster will not be confined to the southern front alone. It is hoped that the forces cut off in the Krasnodar area in the north Caucasus will be able to withdraw across the Kertch Straits to the Crimea.

Despite the wording of Army communiqués, the mass of the people have no idea of the gravity of the situation. The possibility of military defeat in the east is not taken seriously by the majority, not even by the better-educated. Defeat is something which it is beyond their power to imagine. This may be of help in maintaining morale, for the German, when faced with a difficult situation, is rather inclined to become downhearted. On the other hand, the slogan 'Undefeated in the field' coined at the end of the First World War is now coming home to roost. It gave rise to illusions which have survived to this day.

The civil population is responding very willingly to the appeal for a greater war effort. Everyone seems to be ready to do his utmost, provided he is convinced that the restrictions imposed on him really serve a useful purpose. The closing of restaurants and night clubs is hardly regarded as a measure calculated to win the war. As a waiter said to me a few days ago: 'Do you think the Russians will halt because Horcher's has been closed?'

Ciano has been appointed Italian Ambassador to the Vatican. The potentialities of the Vatican as an intermediary in any peace negotiations are so obvious that Ciano's appointment to the Holy See is a perfectly logical step. Many people, well-informed with regard to the situation in Rome, are convinced that Italian policy is beginning to change and that Ciano, who has for a long time been regarded as an opponent of the Axis, will play an important part in the reorientation. Among the members of the Italian Embassy here the atmosphere of ever-increasing tension is very apparent. They make no secret of their opinion that Italy feels she has been misled by German predictions of favourable developments on the eastern front and that this must inevitably give rise to a reorientation of her policy.

Tuesday, February 9, 1943
The *Frankfurter Zeitung* of February 7 contains a report on the demolition of the ancient harbour district of Marseilles. The article is written in a way which gives the impression that these demolitions are being carried out on the initiative of the Marseilles town council. In fact, they were ordered by the German occupation authorities, the Military Commander, the security forces and so on.

I am not in a position to judge whether these measures are militarily necessary. I am told that a few days ago it came to the Führer's knowledge that the German civil authorities in France had decided to prohibit the publication of pornographic literature in France and to 'reshape' on the German model all periodicals of an erotic nature. Hitler sharply vetoed this typically German attempt to play the schoolmaster towards other nations. In this connection he said: 'The thought that one of these days the German authorities in the East will start scrubbing all the Russians down with soap makes me shudder!' This attempt by our press to assert that the demolition of the old harbour area of Marseilles is being carried out on moral grounds is just as ridiculous. The British have ruled India without ever having interfered with local customs: the beggars, fakirs, *sadhus,* charlatans, the holy cows and apes, the caste system and all the rest of it have been left unmolested. In occupied Europe, National Socialism is as zealous in its worship of the Machiavellian as it is obsessed with its mania to make the world a better place to live in.

In a leaflet which has been dropped over the Russian lines, the 'Russian Committee', in the names of the ex-Soviet Generals Vlassoff and Malyshkin, calls upon the Russians to throw off the yoke of Stalin. As far as I know, this is the first time that we have attempted to create a Russian national movement. A year and a half ago, a leaflet of this kind would have scored a great success. How very different our position in the East would be today, if only we had initiated a constructive policy side by side with our victories! Our soldiers would today be receiving the active support of their respective populations, had we only granted full autonomy to the Baltic States, White Russia and the Caucasian peoples. At the time, many people pointed out the desirability of initiating such a policy; but their proposals went unheeded. Instead, the East has been proclaimed a colonial territory and its population treated as coolies. The result has been the partisan movement which is now giving us more trouble than it would have been possible to imagine at the beginning of the eastern campaign.

Friday, February 12, 1943

The copper roofing is being removed from the Brandenburg Gate. During the last few years the churches have had to surrender most of their bells. Such dismantling operations occur in all wars. Shortly after the invention of gunpowder, church bells were melted down to make cannon-balls. I find it difficult to imagine that this collecting of copper and bronze can be of much importance in modern war. But in England, too, much prominence is being given to the fact that park railings and wrought-iron gates are being dismantled in order to provide 'scrap-iron'.

Excavations – for the construction of air raid shelters – are going on apace in both the Pariserplatz and the Wilhelmsplatz. The face of Berlin becomes increasingly disfigured, and its architectonic form stands under an unlucky star. Since the days of Schinkel no Berlin architect has seen his structures survive his own era. The vast building programme of the Third Reich has been brought to a standstill by the war. In many sectors of the city the new construction plans have not progressed beyond the blueprint stage of the roads. The area in the vicinity of the Potsdam bridges looks as if it had been struck by an earthquake.

No one knows how many air raid shelters Berlin possesses. A little while ago I saw that a fortress-like building had been constructed for this purpose at the corner of Karlstrasse and Schumannstrasse. The underground fortress at the Zoo railway station also contains some shelters. Another huge shelter has been erected at the Kreuzberg. For the rest, bomb-proof shelters are confined to official buildings, like the Foreign Ministry, the Italian Embassy and Schloss Bellevue.

This evening I supped with Federico Diez. Franz Egon, Gloria Fürstenberg, Fia Henschel and Maritza Liechtenstein were the other guests. The gramophone regaled us with Mexican music. After supper we had a shooting match with an air-gun at a target on Federico's writing desk. Gloria won a pair of silk stockings, and Fia a bottle of scent. Diez, one of the most amusing characters of the diplomatic corps, divides his time between Paris and Berlin. He owns some vineyards in Jerez and holds the rank of Secretary in the Spanish Embassy. His delightful manners and generosity have taken Berlin society by storm. He has acquired the pleasing habit of bringing with him from Paris collections of the latest hats, handbags, silk stockings, dress lengths and trinkets, which he distributes to his Berlin lady friends.

Like most diplomats, Diez sends a car to fetch his guests to dinner and sends them home by car afterwards. Although his flat consists of only two rooms, a bathroom and a kitchen, he has a cook and a maid. The cook speaks fluent English, and the Italian maid has a good command of French and Spanish. And, as both of them understand German well, it is not possible to indulge in any conversation which ought not to be overheard by the servants.

Like all the other members of the Embassy staff, Diez groans under the strict discipline of the new Ambassador Vidal, who insists with great pedantry on regular hours of work: one extra reason for the Spaniards here to recall nostalgically Vidal's predecessor, Count Mayalde.

Devoid of any personal ambition, the very personification of simplicity, extremely wealthy and married to the granddaughter of Count Romanones and sister of the Duke of Pastraña, this aristocrat enjoyed tremendous popularity. A friend of the murdered young Primo de Rivera, Mayalde threw in his lot with the Falangists, became Chief of the Madrid Police, then Minister for Internal Affairs, Spanish Ambassador to Berlin and later *Alcalde* (Lord Mayor) of Madrid. His wife, the Countess Casilda Mayalde, is one of the most fascinating women I have ever met. Highly intelligent and widely read, passionate and frank, proud, yet with an aura of melancholy, she enlivened any conversation with the vivacity of her arguments.

With the arrival of Vidal, the social character of the Spanish Embassy changed completely. At the reception which he gave to mark the presentation of his credentials, the refreshments consisted of unbuttered bread spread with cream cheese together with cold red cabbage. Although no one would have taken exception to a simplicity compatible with the times, this very obvious disregard of the gastronomic side of the normal diplomatic reception did arouse a certain amount of comment.

Werner Schicht, the Soap King from Vienna, paid us a visit yesterday evening and told us that forty per cent of all the casualties suffered in Austria had occurred during the last three months of last year.

Monday, February 15, 1943
The Russians have occupied Rostov and Voroshilovgrad. If we are to avoid the danger of another encirclement, we have no option but to straighten out our front; but this, of course, will also enable the enemy to concentrate his own forces. A further problem that has arisen as the result of the withdrawal of the front is the question of our lines of communication into the Crimea, which we must keep open, in order to prevent the cutting-off of the forces retreating from the Krasnodar area across the Kertch Straits.

The question which everybody is discussing is whether we shall be able to launch a fresh offensive in the spring or summer. Some of the senior officers are expressing the opinion that no further offensive in the East will be possible before 1944.

Rosenberg is said to have asserted that we shall not win the war against Russia until we have sent every man to fight at the front and every woman to work in the factories. The maintenance of family life, he is said to have added, is a typical German pipe-dream.

Press reports on sporting events are to be curtailed, if not entirely suppressed. Professional sport is to stop. From March 1 all periodicals, including fashion journals, which are not of importance to the war effort, are to cease publication. Their continued publication would be a farce, anyway, seeing that there is hardly a stitch of clothing to be got anywhere.

In *Das Reich* Goebbels makes the bold assertion that his desk is in the Wilhelmsplatz and that any of his countrymen who so wish can look over his shoulder as he works and can give him advice. This may well apply to the narrow circle of the Ministry of Propaganda, but the other government departments are confident of being free from such uncalled-for collaboration! Public life is now so bound with red tape, the heads of many departments are so firmly entombed in their ivory towers, that they have become unapproachable even to their own assistants, let alone to the ordinary man in the street. If by some happy chance the suggestion of some outsider reaches the ears of those at the top, the wrath of the bureaucrats descends upon him. Many department have with great prudence firmly entrenched themselves against the curiosity of prying eyes. The *Führerprinzip*, far from affording opportunities to the gifted, is now being used to shield the mediocre from the more intelligent.

In the *Frankfurter Zeitung* Margret Boveri writes that in most American households the radio remains turned on from dawn till dusk and that this non-stop listening is so bemusing, that the public has been reduced to a state of radio-deafness. Today the German people seem to be in the same state. The level of uniformity to which the intellectual life has been lowered and the eternal repetition of the same slogans have given rise to a state of lethargic indifference, the degree of which is well illustrated by the nation's reaction to the Stalingrad crisis. For despite the fact that both the official communiqués and the press have stressed the gravity of the crisis and have been unflagging in their efforts to give a realistic picture of the situation on the eastern front, they have not succeeded in breaking through the apathy of the masses. Political commentaries on the radio and in the newspapers go as unheeded as water slipping off a duck's back.

Today Else F. paid us a visit. Since 1939 she has been living apart from her husband in Kitzbühel, where she has rented and furnished a house. On February 2 she received a communication from the Mayor of Kitzbühel, terminating her permission to live there and directing her to leave the house by February 10. Since then the unfortunate woman has been on the move between Berlin, Munich, Salzburg and Innsbruck in an attempt to obtain a postponement of the eviction order. She has approached Hofer, the Gauleiter of the Tyrol, Esser, the Secretary of State in charge of foreign nationals, Goebbels, the Reich Chancellery and the Gestapo, so far without success. No one seems to know who was responsible for the eviction order. She owns a house in Munich, which she had rented to an Air Force major, whom she will now have to turn out – a typical example of the muddles which occur in individual cases as the result of 'wartime measures'.

A few days ago I received a leaflet by post from Warsaw, which called upon me, as the bearer of a Slav name, to learn Czech or Polish. The creation of a Slav State, stretching from Warsaw to Magdeburg, was imminent, the leaflet asserted, and the hour had struck for all bearers of Slav names to join the ranks of the new empire. The leaflet ended with the slogan: *'Heil Slawia!'*

Wednesday, February 17, 1943

Richthofen has been appointed Field-Marshal. He is the fourth officer of the Air Force to be so appointed; the other Field-Marshals are Brauchitsch, Keitel, Rundstedt, Kluge, Bock, Witzleben, Milch, Kesselring, Sperrle, Weichs, Busch, Rommel, Manstein, Kleist, Model and Paulus. Reichenau is dead, and Blomberg has retired. The navy has two Grand Admirals in Raeder and Doenitz. Eleven of these Field-Marshals come from noble families. The continent has not seen so many bearers of a Marshal's baton since the days of Napoleon. The most popular of them is Rommel, though nothing has been heard of him for a long time. In these days of swiftly moving events, names are soon forgotten. Recently a small crowd stood in the cloakroom of the Hotel Eden, gaping at a Field-Marshal's greatcoat and discussing to whom it might belong. Most of them, including the cloakroom attendant, agreed that it must belong to Marshal Mannerberg (who doesn't exist). Eventually they settled for Mannerheim; no one came up with the correct name, Manstein!

In the Soviet Union conscripts for the years 1924, 1925 and 1926 have now been called up, and it is estimated that each category will add some one and a half million recruits to the armed forces. The same categories here would yield only about 420,000 each.

The Russians have announced the fall of Kharkov. According to our information, fighting is still continuing in the outskirts of the city. My brother Rudiger was killed there last year, on January 27, during the defence of that city.

A new regulation has been promulgated, forbidding foreigners and stateless persons to have any contact with prisoners of war within the confines of the Reich. This order, which until now applied only to German nationals, has always led to difficulties.

In rural districts a working relationship with prisoners is unavoidable, particularly in those cases where the farmer himself is on field service and the prisoner has taken his place as a farm hand. The regulation owes its origin to the anger of the Party at the lack of any manifestation of hatred against the enemy. Were the Germans better haters in the past, I wonder? I seem to remember that as school kids during the first war we hated the French, the British and the Russians as our enemies. Nowadays one meets hardly a soul who is imbued with hatred. Even after air raids which have caused great suffering to the population, one seldom hears anything said against the enemy. Such antipathies as the masses feel are of a social, rather than of a national, character. The lower classes are far more ready to inveigh against the British 'plutocrats' than against the Russians. With the more well-to-do the reverse is the case.

It would be interesting to know how this compares with the popular feeling on the other side. As far as one can judge from here, the Germans are hated most violently by the Norwegians, the Dutch and the Poles, followed by the Czechs and the Serbs. Probably more people hate us in Britain than in the United States. The French hate us least of all.

Friday, February 19, 1943

Subhas Chandra Bose is about to cease his activities here. Some two years ago, after an adventurous journey through the Soviet Union he managed to reach Berlin, where at first he lived under a pseudonym. His real identity, however, soon became known, and then he broadcast each week to India. Under his leadership was founded the 'Free India Centre', as a rallying-point for all Indians living in Germany and the occupied territories. He was received once by the Führer and two or three times by the RAM. I have met him frequently, both in the course of official business and socially. It is in his uncompromising enmity towards Britain that he differs from Gandhi, Nehru and other Indian leaders. As a social reformer, too, he has much more radical ideas than they have. For many years he was an ardent communist.

The way in which Bose was treated by the various German government departments confirms the correctness of Tirpitz' prophecy that we were not yet ripe to become a world power. It is true that everything possible was done to make our exotic guest as comfortable materially as we could. He was allotted a villa in the Sophienstrasse, which had previously been occupied by the last American chargé d'affaires. The house was equipped throughout from the Foreign Ministry furniture store, and an office was placed at his disposal in the Lichtensteinallee in the Tiergarten. He was given a car, chauffeur and servants and drew the same rations as were authorised for foreign diplomats. As time passed, Bose gathered around himself a small coterie of Indians and Germans. He maintained contact with the Indian prisoners of war and various government departments in Berlin and also had a hand in the publication of a bi-monthly journal called *Azad Hind* which was published, under my supervision, by Professor Bhatta in English and German.

Bose was greatly influenced by Fräulein Schenkel, whom he had met as a student in Vienna and with whom he later worked in close collaboration.

Responsibility for official liaison with Bose changed hands several times, and German policy towards India was also subjected to a variety of alterations. At first this duty devolved on Under Secretary of State Woermann. He was succeeded by Secretary of State Keppler, an old National Socialist, to whom Adam von Trott zu Solz was attached as assistant. Among the members of the Special Commission for Indian Affairs were Professor Alsdorf, Furtwängler, Dr Werth and Dr Assmann. The closest of Bose's Indian associates were Nambiar, Hassan and Habib ur Rahman.

The value of the use to which Bose's presence as our guest was put by our policy makers is difficult to determine. On several occasions situations arose in India, in which the presence of Bose could have been a trump-card of inestimable value to us. These opportunities, however, were to all intents and purposes ignored. The visit of Sir Stafford Cripps to India presented the Axis Powers with a most favourable opportunity for a declaration of their policy towards that country. Suggestions in this context were by no means lacking, but nothing was ever done. At the last moment all sorts of probable and improbable departments popped up with misgivings, which effectively put a spoke in every plan.

That Bose should very quickly have begun to doubt the sincerity of German intentions is not in the least surprising. From time to time he suffered from fits of depression, which he sought to alleviate by visits to Rome, Paris, Prague and Vienna. All in all, this Indian leader must have come to the firm conclusion that the Germans were as little to be trusted as were the British. The luxury of his material surroundings did nothing to mitigate his keen disappointment at the vacillations of our policy towards India. He felt like a bird in a gilded cage. Added to all that, contact with the leading policy makers in the Reich was made as difficult as possible for him. Whereas in England, Indian politicians enjoy complete freedom and are able at will to confer with British leaders, here Bose and Nambiar are practically ignored.

Saturday, February 20, 1943

The Times summarises its commentary on Goebbels' speech of the day before yesterday by saying: 'This is an attempt to achieve "Strength through Fear".' Unfortunately, it contains more than a little of the truth. Here, too, doubts are being expressed regarding the wisdom of this policy of instilling people with a terror of bolshevism. Is this official panic-rousing the best way, people ask, of raising the nation's morale? Equally inappropriate are the constant threats which Goebbels issues in the Sportpalast and in articles in *Das Reich* against a small clique of loafers. Why doesn't he mention these people by name?

Rome – Monday, February 22, 1943

After a thirty-hour journey, I managed to get a room in the Savoy, an old but not uncomfortable hotel in the Via Ludovici.

As far as Verona I had a German businessman as a travelling companion. Scarcely had we crossed the frontier than he bought himself five bottles of beer, two bottles of Marsala and a bottle of Barolo, all of which he emptied in the space of three hours. When I asked him how he had managed it, he told me that for a day and a half before leaving Berlin he had not touched a drop, so that he would be spared the uncomfortable journey from his sleeping compartment to the lavatory in the middle of the night. Now, he said, he was making up for lost time.

Rome is sparkling in the sunlight of spring. The town is full of bombed-out refugees from Milan and other cities in northern Italy and families from Sicily who have been driven from their homes by the declaration of southern Italy as a theatre of war.

The bars and night clubs are closed. The famous Roman pastries are nowhere to be got, not even at Rosati's, which till 1941 was an oasis for the cake-starved afternoon avenue-strollers. Good tea, however, can still be had. In all the restaurants an excellently cooked, uniform meal is served, at a price of thirty or forty lire. The portions offered, however, are somewhat meagre, and one evening I dined first at Ascensio's and then had a second dinner at Fagiano's before my appetite was satisfied. Travellers are issued with bread and spaghetti cards. By paying a stiff cover charge, you can get all sorts of extras; but that is not allowed, officially. The shop windows are not as full as they used to be, but they still manage to retain an air of peacetime. Foreigners find shopping difficult, as coupons are required for everything. The sale of the famous leather goods has been prohibited, but some very excellent imitations are being offered, which are difficult to tell from the real thing. Even war has not been able to destroy the warmth of the sun, the colours of the houses, ranging from delicate, pastel yellow to deep, vivid ochre, the flower-stalls full of mimosa, magnolia, carnations, tulips and sprigs of peach blossom, the carefree gaiety of the crowds in the streets. Rome is still Rome.

Rome – Tuesday, February 23, 1943

Yesterday I had lunch with Hahn, the representative of the German News Agency, who previously had been in Geneva, Vienna, Budapest, London and The Hague.

In the evening I met Karl Clemm, who lives at No. 11 Piazza della Gensola, in Trastevere, the mansion of the recently deceased protocol chief, Geisser-Celesia. Clemm and his beautiful wife, Veronica, the sister of my friend Fritz Globig, were sent to Rome to give social tone to the German Embassy there. Once the Clemms had acquired the *cachet* of the approval of Princess Colonna, they quickly took their place in Roman society.

The house that Karl and Veronica have rented was once occupied by a German-Syrian named Seyur, who as an attaché in the German Embassy in Buenos Aires had married a lady some twenty years his senior who was a famous hostess in the Argentine capital. The couple were then transferred to Kovno, where Mme Seyur suffered

28

so severely in the inclement winter that Seyur resigned his post and settled in Rome.

Clemm had invited two economic experts, Baron Schmidt-Muller, who, despite his name, is an Italian and is attached to the Italian Embassy in Berlin, and Freiherr von Süsskind, who was in Rome, conducting negotiations with Clodius. Our main topic of conversation was the Italian Government's demand for the return of the two million Italians working in the Reich. The Italians say that their demand is made on account of monetary difficulties. In reality it is of a political character, as Nicki Lanza confirmed. The Italian Government fears that as the war becomes increasingly 'total' in character, disciplinary measures may well be taken against foreign workers employed in Germany, and is anxious to avoid any complications which might ensue. Our standpoint is that Germany has sent her AA batteries unconditionally to Italy and that the latter should adopt the same attitude as regards her workers in the Reich. The German AA divisions protecting Italian industrial installations are even provided with food and ammunition from Germany, at no cost at all to Italy. The Italians further complain that the Germans are refusing Italian industry any participation in developments in the newly-won territories and that this is giving rise to anger in Rome and Milan.

Rome – Wednesday, February 24, 1943

This afternoon I went to see Erda Doertenbach, whose husband works in the German Embassy. The Doertenbachs are members of the Stuttgart patriciate; they own a private bank and are connected by marriage with the Benger textile industry family. Erda herself is a Roedern and so belongs to the aristocracy of Silesia. Before her marriage she was working very successfully as a journalist.

During the Saar plebiscite, thanks to her relationship with the Stumm-Halberg family, she rendered valuable service to the German cause. In the Foreign Ministry Doertenbach upholds the Swabian traditions, established by such names as Kiderlen-Wächter, Marschall, Weizsäcker and Neurath.

In the evening I met Borch, the former representative of the *Deutsche Allgemeine Zeitung* in Rome, who is now employed as assistant to the two Press Attachés, Molier and Leithe-Jaspar. We were supposed to attend a reception given by Ambassador von Mackensen for the new Italian government. But hour after hour went by without the expected invitation from the Embassy materialising. Mackensen is notorious for his pedantry in questions affecting protocol. Two years ago, when I stayed for several days in Rome when accompanying Schmidt, who, as the leader of our delegation ranked as a ministerial director, Mackensen contented himself with inviting Schmidt to take coffee with him. Later he apologised, explaining that he had had to restrict invitations to the reception to ninety. Clodius, too, a Minister, a leading personality in the Foreign Ministry and head of the German Foreign Trade Department, was only invited to come after dinner. He got his own back by turning up at midnight, after most of the guests had already departed.

Rome – Thursday, February 25, 1943
Breakfasting with Otto Bismarck at the Rome Golf Club, I met the entire 'Ciano set'. With us were Princess Bismarck, wearing a sealskin coat, Count Campello, Princess Ruffo, Count and Countess Manolino Borromeo. Also present were Hansi Plessen and Sandro Doernberg – the latter representing Ribbentrop, who was expected that evening.

At a neighbouring table sat the Clemms, Ciano, Marcelino and Cyprienne del Drago, Anfuso, Paolo Borghese, Governor of Rome, and Don Jaime, the deaf and dumb second son of the King of Spain. At breakfast hardly a word of Italian was spoken. English and German were the tongues favoured by this cream of Roman society, many of whose wives are Americans. The high esteem in which the Clemms are held was very obvious. Everyone clustered round them. Whereas in most international circles the Germans are generally accepted on sufferance, here the reverse is the case. This, I think, proves that German missions abroad would have no cause to hang back, provided they were composed of the right type of person. From the political point of view, contacts with leaders of Roman society provide us with much information which would not be obtainable from any other source. Nor has Ciano's downfall made any difference. He and his clique still continue to play an important role in Italian politics, and his position at the Vatican gives him access to many matters which we would like to know about.

During the morning, accompanied by Doertenbach, I visited Prunas, the director of the Oriental Section in the 'Esteri' (the Italian Foreign Ministry). We discussed Bose and a number of questions in connection with the Indian government-in-exile in Berlin. During our conversation with this shrewd man, I could not help comparing him with some of the officials holding similar positions in our own Foreign Ministry. My mind turned to our Indian Committee, in which Melchers, an oriental expert of great experience, and I have vigorously opposed the chairman, Secretary of State Keppler and his general factotum, Adam Trott zu Solz. The latter insists that our propaganda should attack Gandhi and make him look ridiculous in the eyes of the Indian people. As an ex-Rhodes Scholar, he ought to know better, but he is, of course, completely under the influence of Bose, who hates Gandhi. Melchers and I know that any German policy towards India which fails to accept Gandhi as the most potent factor in the Indian independence movement would be devoid of all reality. But Trott is quite incorrigible, and he is supported in his fanatical outlook by Keppler who usually ends our arguments with: 'Let us keep our tempers, gentlemen. No one for a moment believed the *Anschluss* would materialise. But, in his own time, the Führer will solve the Indian question in the same way as he solved the Austrian question.' That any such nonsense should be bandied about in one of the Committees in the Palazzo Chigi is almost inconceivable.

Unfortunately, it is not only in social graces, but also in intelligence that the Italian diplomats are far superior to our own. Among ordinary Italians one seldom comes across a really stupid fellow; but in their diplomatic circle one constantly meets men of exceptional intelligence. Prunas is a case in point.

Dined with Molier, Doertenbach and Megerle at Ascensio's. Megerle arrived very late last night in the Foreign Minister's special train and is staying at the Hotel Ambiascatori. The Minister himself and his entourage are at the Villa Madama. Before arriving at Bologna the special train was involved in an exciting incident. The coach in which the Italian Ambassador Alfieri, who is accompanying Ribbentrop, was travelling suddenly caught fire and in a moment was blazing furiously. The communication cord was pulled, and the train brought to a standstill. The fire then spread to the other carriages; but with everybody including Ribbentrop himself lending a hand, the fire was eventually extinguished. Then a further crisis occurred. The overhead connections were found to have been burnt out, leaving the train without electric current, and the attempt to push the heavy bogies beyond the destroyed sector by hand proved unavailing. Alfieri lost the whole of his luggage, including a new fur coat. He eventually reached Rome wearing Michetti's overcoat. As Alfieri usually changes clothes several times daily, the loss of his resplendent wardrobe was a bitter blow. Doernberg also lost some of his baggage.

Ribbentrop's first conference this morning with Mussolini lasted four hours. The only persons present were the Duce, Mackensen and Alfieri, with Schmidt to take notes and act as interpreter. There are three main topics of discussion – the general situation, the military situation in Russia and the Mediterranean, and the southeastern problems. Well-informed circles fear that neither the German nor the Italian viewpoint is amenable to argument. Our people adhere adamantly to the opinion that the decisive blow can be struck only in the East, while the Italians regard the military situation in Russia as hopeless and consider Britain more important than Russia; they would therefore prefer to enlist our help in forcing a final showdown in the Mediterranean. The realisation that we are the better soldiers and the Italians the better diplomats does nothing to iron out the differences of opinion. The new men with whom Mussolini has surrounded himself are experts in their own spheres, determined to put their own departments in order. But when questions of a political nature arise, they declare that they are not competent to deal with them and turn to the Duce. This adds considerably to the difficulties of our Embassy in the conduct of everyday affairs. With a man like Ciano, one could come to grips with any problem. The new men, like Bastianini, Guariglia and Rosso, are reputed to be calculating diplomats, who regard politics as a business to be conducted without passion.

'Optical' considerations have also insinuated themselves into the Rome conversations. The introduction of the term 'optical' into political affairs originated in an article by Goebbels in *Das Reich*, entitled '*Die Optik des Krieges*'. By this he apparently meant the taking of measures which 'immediately strike the eye', such as the closing of bars and luxury shops.

Yesterday I visited Frau Bergen in her superb Villa Bonaparte.

The Bergens have been representing the Reich at the Vatican for many years. Their house is regarded as one of Rome's most chic establishments, and an invitation to the place confers considerable social prestige. Since the 'black' papal society of Rome takes precedence over the 'white' royalist society, the Embassies accredited to the Vatican enjoy greater distinction than the diplomats accredited to the Quirinal.

Milan – Friday, February 26, 1943

When I climbed into the sleeping-car of the Rome-Milan train, I found myself confronted in my allotted compartment by a bearded gentleman who, with much gesticulation, drew my attention to two parcels which he had deposited on the luggage rack. It then transpired that he had no right to be in my compartment, but he asserted that the parcels contained articles of such great value, that he considered this to be the safest place in which to put them. And the parcels remained there even after the stranger had been herded out into the corridor by the sleeping-car attendant, so that a fellow-traveller and myself could take possession of our berths.

At the Hotel Principe di Savoia in Milan, I found that my bath was filled with water – an air raid precaution which we have yet to introduce in Berlin! Although a fortnight has elapsed since the last air raid on Milan, the population is still in a state of terror. Dense crowds stood watching salvage and demolition operations. Sixty soldiers were buried alive while trying to construct a shaft through to an air raid shelter, in which some survivors were thought to be still alive. Shelters are being constructed under the square in front of the Cathedral. The streets are full of furniture-vans and carts laden with the possessions of people fleeing into the country. The town is said to have lost half its population during the past fortnight as the result of this exodus. The Lombardy peasants are earning fortunes from the hire of carts to remove furniture and the renting of farm buildings. In some districts work on the land has ceased, because the peasants find they can make more money out of the terror-stricken Milanese than they earn from their annual harvest. Thanks to the mass exodus, the food situation in Milan has improved enormously. On the other hand industrial productivity has sunk. Many of the factory workers take three or four hours to get to their work from the places where they have sought refuge.

In the suburbs bullock-carts are being used as a means of transport. Milanese firms, which had granted a separation allowance to those of their employees who had been bombed out, are now offering a bonus to those willing to remain in town.

Breakfasted at Giannino's with Knoche. To get to the restaurant we had to go through the kitchens and past the aquarium, which is still well stocked with succulent varieties of fish. On the other hand the ovens are destitute of chickens. The tables near the fireplace reserved for regular customers are occupied by gourmets, whose gluttony has triumphed over their fear of bombs. We had an excellent meal ('black' – of course). While we were drinking our coffee, the waiter whispered that inspecting officers were in the offing and would we, please, say that we had had nothing but spaghetti to eat? Three men entered, the first of whom kept his hat on his head, while his henchmen followed him bareheaded. They turned out to be 'Foodstuff Secret Police'. The whole thing was a farce. Before they had embarked upon their inspection, the restaurateur had plied the guardians of the law with delicacies, and they looked as well-fed and as satisfied as the public whose meals it was their duty to supervise. Even so, a few restaurants are closed every now and then. Two days before Christmas, for example, Giannino's had to close, despite the fact that twenty-four hours previously he had entertained two hundred and fifty poor children free of charge. Actually, the owners have no complaint if their places are temporarily closed, since a short closure is the best possible advertisement for them. One tavern, which was closed for a few days for having disregarded the food regulations, was crowded out with clients as soon as it reopened; nevertheless, boldly printed on every menu is the sentence: 'He who eats more than his due is betraying the soldiers at the front.'

At Giannino's we met a German who lived in Milan and had been bombed-out. He told us that he was the first victim of an Italo-German treaty under which compensation to German nationals bombed-out in Italy would be paid by the Italian Government, and vice versa. He had waited three months, he said, before the Damage Assessment Committee had visited him, adding that, incidentally, he was required under the treaty terms to leave the house in the state in which the bomb had left it, until it had been inspected. Since then, six further weeks had passed and he had heard no more. On

34

those occasions on which compensation is paid, the amount given is not enough to buy even a pair of sheets. The treaty also applies, he said, to the members of the diplomatic and consular services in Italy.

In the Milan-Turin-Genoa area there is a force of twenty-two thousand German anti-aircraft gunners. I met the divisional commander, Colonel Kuderna, at his Headquarters in Legnano. He told me that when the German Air Force unit arrived the Milanese felt that they were absolutely safe. Their disillusionment was all the greater when the British flew their next sortie over the city and the effectiveness of the German defence unit fell far short of expectations. Their respect for the efficacy of German flak quickly evaporated. In a village near Milan, where a German searchlight section was posted, the local inhabitants rioted because they feared that the searchlights would attract the British aircraft. In the end, *carabinieri* had to intervene to protect the flak unit from the wrath of the crowd. The change of attitude is well illustrated by the fact that Russians conscripted into German flak units who desert are now always given refuge by the local population. Kuderna, an Austrian, has described the difficulty of working with the Italians as very great. A local commander will co-operate only with great reluctance. His field telephone cables are frequently cut and stolen, and as replacements are not available his division, in order to preserve some semblance of efficiency, has no option but to buy back the stolen cables in the black market. Personal relations between the troops and local inhabitants are good. Milan's female beauties are considered more forthcoming than the girls of Sicily, who refused to associate themselves with Kuderna's men. An amicable agreement has been reached regarding the brothels. Our divisional Medical Officer has declared the supervision by the Italian authorities to be excellent, and praises the business-like organisation of these houses of professional pleasure, which enables them to arrange a fortnightly alternative roster of girls.

March 1943

Milan: a rickety Rheingold – Berlin: the raids begin and the diplomats start to scatter – The Scheliha affair – Confusion in Serbia

Milan – Monday, March 1, 1943

I went to see Guido Vanzetti, a young industrialist, whom I had previously known in Berlin. His flat on the second floor of a house exhibiting all the disastrous architectural characteristics of the early years of this century, is one of the sights of the town. For the first time in my life I saw an electrical apparatus designed for use as a bed-warmer. The kitchen and the gymnasium reminded me of the sort of thing one sees on an ocean liner. And all these expensive installations had been completely wrecked by the air-blast from a bomb which had dropped in the vicinity.

In the evening I went to the Scala to see *Rheingold,* conducted by Hosslin and produced by Strohm. The Rhine daughters floating about above the stage swayed violently all over the place, and it looked as though any moment there must be a collision. As Strohm told me afterwards, this was a real danger. A collision would have been a real catastrophe, as it would have brought down the whole of the wiring system and the wings. Each Rhine daughter was suspended by two wires, which were worked by four men. *'Per evitare una confusione in caso d'allarme'*, we were not allowed to leave our coats in the cloakroom. As an air raid precaution, the dress-circle was underpinned by wooden beams. Strohm told me that the production of the *Nibelungenring* had presented great difficulties, because the chorus and the stage-hands were so frightened of a possible air raid that they refused to work in the evenings in the Scala. The performances begin just before five o'clock and end at seven. Then everyone rushes off home as fast as they can. Only on foggy evenings, which the Milanese have canonised as *'Santa Niebla'*, are the rehearsals held in peace and quiet. Fog to the Milanese is what the Pope is to the Romans. In Rome they say the best flak we have is the Holy Father!

Halem, our consul-general, who has a lovely house in the Via Necci, invited me for the weekend to Stresa. I travelled there with Dr Schmitz, the managing director of Ruhrstahl-AG, and Wiesemann, the firm's Milan representative. Schmitz told me that the best of the foreign workers in the Ruhr industry were the Russians and the worst the Italians. The Russian women were outstandingly efficient. Schmitz was full of praise for Saukel, the first man to agitate for a better treatment of the Russians. The *Arbeitsfront* on the other hand vacillates between the two extremes of handing over 'presents from the Führer' and using the firing squad. Ninety-six per cent of all the Russian women workers are unmarried girls. Many of them are now marrying Russian workers, and this is giving rise to fresh problems. These marriages take place without the formality of any ceremony.

Berlin – Wednesday, March 3, 1943
Berlin was severely damaged in the air raid of the night before last. Near us a great number of houses in the Bachstrasse and the Sigis-mundhof were set on fire. Minni Stengel, who lives in the Kaiserallee, lost all she possessed. After the all-clear Marietti and several diplomats hastened to help her rescue what she could. They foregathered in Casardi's house, which was threatened by the fire in the neighbouring barracks. Liveried Italian servants were sent on to the roof with watering-cans to cool the tiles. Such things of Minni's as the flames spared were later plundered, despite the fact that plundering carries the death penalty. The Prager Platz was reduced to ashes, including the home of the parents of Ernst vom Rath, who was murdered in Paris. Only a few days previously the vom Raths had lost their second son. A dud fell in the Richthofens' garden. Another landed on the Italian Embassy. A third is lying in the Tiergarten-strasse, and traffic has had to be diverted. The Foreign Ministry in the Wilhelmstrasse suffered no damage. But our press office on the Karlsbad was burnt down. The Unter den Linden boulevard has suffered greatly. The passage leading to the Friedrichsstrasse is in ruins. People are saying that this raid was laid on deliberately for 'Luftwaffe Day'. The official report puts the number of dead at four hundred and eighty, including six youthful anti-aircraft volunteers. This has been the heaviest attack that Berlin has so far experienced.

We are sending our little daughter to the country. Our silver is going to the bank and we are sorting out our wardrobes, transferring to the country such things as we do not require. More than that we cannot do for the moment. We may perhaps be able to remove some of our furniture to a place of safety. One has to arrange things in such a way that the loss of one's house will not give rise to a struggle for survival. The experience of our friends has made us realise that the first days after losing everything are not the worst. Mutual sympathy and the memory of the dramatic events at first help one to bear up. But the feeling soon passes. Each successive day brings fresh tragedy. Sympathy and succour from one's neighbours are not sufficient to carry one for ever. And suddenly one finds oneself without a roof over one's head, with no clothes and with no idea what to do next.

Thursday, March 4, 1943

Yesterday Schmidt told us about the results of Ribbentrop's visit to Rome. He mentioned that even in the Villa Madama, the official guest-house of the Italian government, the German visitors were given only a minute portion of rancid butter. A neat example of Italian psychological adroitness! A tiny pat of rancid butter is an excellent means of demonstrating Italy's difficult situation to the German negotiators. The German is so used to butter, that he is prone to regard the quantity and quality of this commodity offered to him as a sure yardstick in any situation which confronts him. Goering's slogan of 'guns instead of butter' was based on this butter-mentality.

Tuesday, March 9, 1943

Yesterday Franzi Schmidt-Zabierow came and dined with us. He is a partner in a textile firm which has factories in the Protectorate, Austria and Italy. His factory in Turin was destroyed two months ago in an air raid. His Italian manager advised him not to rebuild, because, he said: 'the British will certainly be here in a few months' time.' The official Italian appraiser, whose job it was to assess compensation, demanded an advance fee of a hundred thousand lire, which Schmidt-Zabierow had to pay him whether he liked it or not.

Thursday, March 11, 1943

Forster, the art historian, told me that, in view of the danger of air raids, he always carries his collection of miniatures in his pockets, whenever he goes out at night.

The Duke of Sotomayor has been accredited to Franco as the representative of the Pretender to the Spanish throne. German policy shows only a purely negative interest in the question of the restoration. This has horrified the Italians. Recently Lanza asked me whether we wished to see the Spanish monarchy restored solely under the aegis of the British. Our ostentatious indifference, he asserted, was driving the Pretender into the arms of the British. If the Spaniards were determined to restore the monarchy, then, he argued, we ought to associate ourselves with the movement. Bismarck told me that he had been meeting the Pretender for several years at the Golf Club, but that in accordance with his instructions, he had made no attempt at establishing any close contact with him. Meanwhile, Don Juan has moved to Lausanne, where the British diplomats make a great fuss of him. Incidentally, Count Rocamora, the Spanish Military Attaché in Berlin, is one of the Prince's closest friends. His wife goes to Switzerland every few weeks to act as occasional lady-in-waiting to the Infanta.

Wednesday, March 17, 1943

On his election as a member of the Spanish Academy, the Duke of Alba made a speech, in the course of which he said: 'We have suffered and survived the ravages of socialism, the penultimate step towards communism. While it would be idle to deny the presence, throughout history, of class warfare, we are, I feel, entitled to claim that civilisation has remained stable only when the reins of government have been in the hands of aristocrats. Thanks to their upbringing, they have been able to fulfil their duties over long periods of time; and to this Rome, Venice, England and, in the epoch of our greatness, we ourselves bear witness.'

It is pleasing to hear this stated thus unequivocally. The European aristocracies are inclined to hide their light under a bushel. While the other classes brag loudly of their achievements and demand an ever-increasing share in the governing of the country, the aristocrats seem content to play the role of onlookers.

They still hold a few positions of importance – in agriculture, in the armed forces and in diplomacy. This very obvious desire to take a back seat is not attributable solely to degeneracy and weariness. It has its roots in the erroneous conviction that this is the best means by which the continued existence of aristocracy can be ensured.

History has repeatedly proved that the nobility has always been better fitted for the business of ruling. Napoleonic France was feared no less than is National Socialist Germany. Despite this, however, the defeat of Napoleon did not bring about the downfall of France. The latter eventuality was averted thanks to two contributory factors – the feeling of solidarity existing between the European dynasties, and the appreciation of their own social status by the European nobles who conducted the negotiations. It is true that Talleyrand went to Vienna in the role of the vanquished, but once there he was in a position to negotiate with his peers. The homogeneousness of their origins was the perfect complement to the intellectual affinity that united the statesmen involved. Metternich, Talleyrand, Hardenberg, Nesselrode and Castlereagh had much in common. They had all been brought up in the same way and with the same interests – women and horses, the arts and hunting, good living and good theatre. They all spoke French as though it were their mother tongue, and they had no need of an interpreter. Their political differences did not affect their personal relations.

Today, the leaders of the belligerent countries hate each other with a violence perhaps without precedent in history. The virulent insults they hurl at each other in their speeches bear eloquent witness to this fact.

When Halifax and Eden came to Berlin before the war, the social chasm between the British aristocrats and the National Socialist 'tribunes of the people' was plain for all to see. Hitler even took exception to Eden's personal appearance, and he still refers to him as 'that perfumed lackey'. Goering felt much the same about Halifax. But then even the Führer and the Duce, statesmen with the same proletarian background, find it difficult to get on well together. The similarity of the political ideologies they support and the fact that their respective parties wear much the same sort of uniform do not suffice to form that bridge which statesmen, like the rest of us, must cross, if they wish thoroughly to understand one another.

It is nevertheless symptomatic that the heads of the smaller European countries now under Axis domination, do their utmost externally to ape the model set by Berlin and Rome. If, in their mimicry, they appear in some sort of fascist-like uniform they greatly enhance their powers of negotiation! When the late Hungarian Foreign Minister Count Csaky visited Berlin, he arrived in a specially ordered diplomatic uniform cut to the German pattern. After he died it was forthwith abolished.

In the past there were no regulations forbidding diplomats to marry foreign women. At the beginning of the nineteenth century good breeding, personality and a thorough mastery of foreign languages were the attributes regarded as prerequisites for entry into the diplomatic service. Today the reverse obtains. Anyone who has personal relations with foreigners is regarded with suspicion.

Thursday, March 18, 1943
Strangely enough, not a soul seems to have taken any particular notice of the fact that the eastern front has been stabilised. The recapture of Kharkov has made little or no impression; the people act as though it was not worth mentioning or was something that they knew was bound to happen. As soon as things at the front become quiet, the East reverts to being that vague concept, exemplified by Goethe's words, 'peoples somewhere beyond Turkey, who are always fighting each other'. In the newspapers the headlines have already disappeared. A few weeks more, and very few will remember that during the winter Germany suffered a military catastrophe without precedent. As long as things are going well, the German is inclined towards boundless optimism. But if we suffer a reverse, he is just as quickly transformed into a pessimist. Once a danger has passed, there is a great tendency to allow things to take their course. A Swedish paper said that nowadays Goebbels dislikes the use of the word 'morale' and would prefer to see it replaced by 'poise'. It is the misfortune of the Germans that 'poise' is just the quality in which they are lacking – in peace as in war, in good fortune as in bad, in love as in hatred.

Friday, March 19, 1943

Four days in the Warthegau. The countryside is not beautiful, but it is fertile. The towns have an old-fashioned Germanic appearance; the public buildings, built of glazed red and yellow bricks, remind me of Altona and Kiel. Many of the estates confiscated from Poles have been handed over to Baits, who, however, have not been installed as the owners, but as lessees, to run them for an unspecified period. The population is Polish, willing to work but without any rights. Churches have been closed. In many districts neither weddings nor baptisms can take place. The German authorities have introduced a completely arbitrary system of administration, under which Germans suffer almost as much as the Poles themselves. I was myself witness of an air raid exercise, carried out, on the order of the Commissar of Pakosch, by the agricultural labourers of Luisenau and Pakosch. The people had been given an entire afternoon off from work to participate in this, but they had to hang about for a whole hour before the commissar appeared in his car. With him, in a gorgeous uniform, came the District Air Raid Precautions Commissar – an erstwhile chimney-sweep. Together they harangued the Polish farm-hands for an hour on end in German. As none of their audience spoke German, not a word of what they said was understood by anybody. One Pole was detailed as a specialist to deal with a broken thigh. Another was told his task would be to gather up the debris from fallen walls. Neither had the slightest idea of what was required of him. The whole of the afternoon was wasted, and we calculated that thanks to this 'exercise' a hundred and fifty-six working hours had been lost. And we're supposed to be fighting a total war! Incidentally, throughout the war not a single bomb has fallen in the Warthegau. But the very idea that British or Russian aircraft might bomb farmsteads has so excited the *Herr Kommissar* that he terrorises the whole district.

In the Wartheland I met Lex Taube, who runs his eighteen-hundred acre estate, Wielitz, very efficiently. At the moment he is serving on the staff of a division at the mouth of the Gironde and has had to leave the day-to-day administration to his wife.

Saturday, March 20, 1943

The heavy air raid of March 1 has resulted in a general flight by local diplomats to country estates in the vicinity of Berlin. Tino Soldati of the Swiss Embassy has rented the Kavalierhaus in Lowenbruch, a Knesebeck property. The Spanish ambassador Vidal and the Oyarzabals are living near Nauen with Frau von Dippe, an Englishwoman by birth, and with Herr von Pfuel-Jahnsfelde. The Rumanians – Valeanu, Popescul and Georgescu – have moved in with Elly Dohna in Buckow. The Italians are moving into Prince Solms' place in Baruth, the Bulgarians have gone to the Kunheims in Wendisch-Wilmersdorf, and the Hungarians have taken the Schaumburgs' house in Kladow. The scarcity of accommodation in which to seek refuge has led to furious altercations among the diplomats. One of the Italians behaved particularly badly. When the Edelstams moved to Oslo, he tried to take over their villa in Dahlem, which they had rented from a Frau Ahlemann. Frau Ahlemann, however, had already leased her house to the Rumanian Attaché, Popescul. The Italian then went the rounds of the various government departments, complaining bitterly. He asserted that the preference given to a Rumanian constituted an insult to the Italian army, of which he was a member. The affair assumed the proportions of a real scandal when the lady in question was suddenly taken into police custody, from which she was eventually released, thanks to the intervention of SS General Wolff.

A similar fracas occurred between the Italians and the Japanese. The Italian Attaché, Benazzo, who occupied a house belonging to Frau Prill-Schlöhmann, was transferred to Rome. Two Italian diplomats and a Councillor of the Japanese Embassy fought so fiercely over the house that Alfieri and Oshima, the respective ambassadors, had to intervene. The underhand methods employed by the diplomats in their fight to obtain accommodation are hardly in harmony with the normal tenets of behaviour on which the diplomatic corps lays such stress.

Yesterday evening Sieburg came over to see us. He is highly delighted at being back once more in the bosom of the *Frankfurter Zeitung* where he finds he has access to more information than in the Foreign Ministry or in our Embassy in Paris. He was particularly enthusiastic about the reports of Dewal from Ankara, Benckiesser from Budapest and Scharp from Berlin. He had the feeling, he said, of being once more among decent people, and his pleasure thereat was accentuated by the thought of the many intriguers whom he had come across in official circles. Sieburg compared his paper to a goldsmith's workshop. Every article was read three times before it was passed for printing. Hours of painstaking endeavour were spent on polishing and improving the style. The editors were doing everything they could to maintain the standard of the paper. The current print order was for three hundred thousand copies, of which only ten thousand were earmarked for Frankfurt. Frankfurt, he said had as little to do with the *Frankfurter Zeitung* as with Frankfurter sausages. Nevertheless, the Gauleiter, Sprenger, and the town itself were both proud that the newspaper took its name from the town. The prestige of the paper, he claimed, was enormous and was growing every day.

Monday, March 22, 1943

The war will end on December 1, 1946! My authority for this startling piece of information is a police regulation regarding the removal of wooden shutters from ground-floor windows. Paragraph 6 reads: 'This regulation comes into force with effect from the date of its publication and will remain in force until December 1, 1946'! As far as I know, this is the first occasion upon which a war regulation with a specified time limit has been promulgated. It obviously took the heavy attack of March 1 to make those responsible realise that wooden shutters on the top floor made ideal fuel for incendiaries. The day before yesterday as early as 7.00 a.m. the air raid warden was round, telling us that the shutters must be taken down by 4.00 p.m.

Moltke's death leaves open once again the post of Ambassador in Madrid. I first met Moltke in 1937 in Warsaw, where he was the Reich's representative. His house there was filled with art treasures, including a Veit-Stoss altarpiece. During the bombardment of Warsaw, the Moltkes' house went up in flames. He lost everything, including, apparently, a portrait of the great Field Marshal by Lenbach, but after the occupation of the city this painting was salvaged from a dustbin. Moltke saw the war coming, but he refused to send his treasures to a place of safety, although he could easily have done so by making use of diplomatic courier privileges. His attitude was typical of the old-time Prussian official, who regarded it as beneath his dignity to put anxiety about personal possessions before the interests of the State.

On completion of his mission in Poland he was posted to the archives section of the Foreign Ministry and placed in charge of the issue of White Papers – a task which afforded him no pleasure. Unsuitably lodged in the Einemstrasse in Edgar Uxküll's house, he led a Spartan existence and finally was granted indeterminate leave, to enable him to join the board of directors of an industrial syndicate in Silesia. Three months later he was recalled and posted to Madrid.

Moltke's wife, *nee* Countess Yorck von Warthenburg of Klein-Ohls, who has borne him eight children, is cast in the same mould as her husband. She was equally admired in Warsaw and in Madrid. In Poland people said of her that Frau von Moltke would only consider that she had her hands full if at one and the same time she was expecting a child, fighting an attack of influenza and had received a message from her husband, regretting that his car had broken down and he would not arrive in time for an Embassy reception, and asking her to entertain a hundred and fifty guests on his behalf.

The Scheliha affair cast a shadow over the last years of Moltke's life.

Scheliha's arrest and sentence to death by hanging struck the Foreign Ministry like a thunderbolt. A Silesian nobleman, the son of a wealthy landowner, married to Maria Luise von Medinger, a Sudeten German, Rudolf von Scheliha had been until the outbreak of war the second senior official in the German Embassy in Warsaw. When war was declared, he was posted to the newly founded Information Section of the Foreign Ministry, of which he was the third senior member, after the director, Dr Gunther Altenburg, and his deputy director, Rudolf Rahn. After the outbreak of war, Scheliha became a close friend of ours, and during our absence in Holland in the first half of 1940 we rented him our house in the Handelallee in the Tiergarten district. Later he moved into a spacious flat in the Sophienstrasse, where he led a gay and sociable life. When we gave a dinner party in the Handelallee house for the Spanish ambassador and Countess Mayalde, he was one of our guests – for the last time. It was also his last evening of liberty. The next morning he was arrested by the Gestapo, and his wife, too, was temporarily taken into custody. Informed by members of his household of what had happened, I hurried immediately to the Sophienstrasse, where, amid the dumbfounded servants and his terrified little daughter, I found half a dozen Gestapo agents who refused to give me any information. Whatever grounds there may have been for the arrest, it must have come as a complete surprise to Scheliha himself. Just recently he had been staying in Switzerland, where he could quite easily have remained and sought refuge. A few months after his arrest, Scheliha was executed. On orders from the Foreign Ministry, Dr Paul Schmidt, the director of the press section, was required to witness the execution.

(Supplementary note, 1948)

In the Foreign Ministry very little was known about the case. Some people hinted darkly at treason, but volunteered no details. It was not until I met Albrecht in Nürnberg in the early summer of 1948 that I was able to glean any further information. As Deputy Director of the Legal Department of the Foreign Ministry, Albrecht had been concerned with the initial investigations, and it was a conversation which he had just had with Roeder that had led him to talk to me about the case.

In the course of that conversation, Roeder, who had been summoned to Nürnberg by the allies and had been the prosecutor in the Scheliha case, had said that in his opinion it was the worst case of treason that had occurred during the whole course of the war. Albrecht had strenuously contested the assertion, which he regarded as an obvious attempt on Roeder's part to clear his own name. He had pointed out, quite rightly, that, despite the 'proofs' submitted by the *Reichsführer SS* to the Führer, no connection whatever had been established between the Scheliha case and the *Rote Kapelle* case (Harnack, Schulze-Boysen, etcetera). Himmler, he contended, had invented this conspiracy in order to provide Hitler with an impressive picture of the efficiency of the police organisations under his command.

Regarding the background of the case, Albrecht gave me the following facts: before the war, while he had been councillor of the German Embassy in Warsaw, Scheliha had drawn his pay not in zloty, but in free currency, a perfectly legal procedure adopted by many of the members of our diplomatic missions abroad. By selling this foreign currency in the Warsaw black market, Scheliha was able to make very handsome profits.

To transact his business he employed, in return for a consideration, the services of a German emigrant living in Warsaw named Herrnstadt, who had previously been a correspondent of the *Berliner Tageblatt*. Part of the proceeds were paid by Herrnstadt on Scheliha's behalf into an anonymous account in Switzerland. On one occasion two hundred pounds sterling were paid in this way into the Swiss bank. Such transactions constituted a contravention of the Polish currency regulations, but were indulged in by most of the foreign diplomats accredited to Warsaw, who were able to supplement their salaries thereby.

When on the outbreak of war Scheliha was transferred to the information section of the Foreign Ministry, he acquired a female secretary named Stübe whom, by chance, he had known in Warsaw, where she had been working for Herrnstadt. The advent of war had not severed the connections between Fräulein Stübe and Herrnstadt, although Scheliha was quite unaware of this fact. One day she brought him a request from Herrnstadt, who at that time was either in Riga or Revel. In a book he was writing on the developments which had led to the war, Herrnstadt was anxious to portray as objectively as possible the attitude adopted by both hostile parties, and he hoped that Scheliha would co-operate with him in the attainment of this object. Would Scheliha be good enough, he asked, to let him have a note on the causes, as the Foreign Ministry saw them, that had led to the declaration of war?

Without giving the matter much thought, Scheliha wrote a paper, into which, for the sake of simplicity and with a complete enumeration of the official sources, he incorporated the propaganda directives issued by the Government through the Foreign Ministry at the beginning of the campaigns in Poland, Norway, Holland, Belgium, etcetera to the German diplomatic missions abroad. Fräulein Stübe, having assumed the responsibility for passing on this document, gave Scheliha, on Herrnstadt's behalf, a fee of eight thousand marks, which Scheliha accepted.

Subsequent investigations revealed that Fräulein Stübe did not deliver this document to Herrnstadt, but to the Soviet Embassy in

Berlin. It must be remembered that the Soviet Union was not yet at war at that time.

In the autumn of 1941 an army patrol inspecting a train from East Prussia to Berlin picked up a Russian agent dropped by parachute into East Prussia, who had been provided with the identification papers of a slain German soldier. By sheer chance, the patrol commander, to whom the man's papers were submitted for scrutiny, happened to be the brother of the dead man who was the real owner of the documents. Realising, of course, that something was wrong, he at once ordered the man's arrest. The agent succeeded in breaking away from his captors, but was shot dead by his pursuers while running along the track. When the body was searched, a notebook was found, containing a number of entries in code, which were eventually deciphered and revealed that the man had been given the names of two contacts in Berlin – Fräulein Stübe and Scheliha. Both were forthwith arrested.

Interrogated by the Gestapo, Fräulein Stübe made a statement revealing the contents of the paper she had received from Scheliha. Among other things her statement contained an extract from the German instructions issued in connection with the advance into Holland and Belgium. The Gestapo then recalled that a portion of the May 10, 1940 plan of attack on Holland and Belgium had been betrayed and that the source of the betrayal had never been discovered. They were pretty sure now that Scheliha must be the culprit.

In court Scheliha was unable to remember details of the currency transactions Herrnstadt had conducted for him – a fact which the judges held against him. The President of the Court, for instance, said: 'If you think you can slip your neck out of the noose and talk yourself out of trouble by vague references to currency malpractices, you are mistaken. That, too, is an offence punishable by death.' Scheliha's fate was sealed when he had to admit that he had received eight thousand marks from Herrnstadt. The court at once condemned him to death.

In a memorandum to Ribbentrop, Albrecht, who was present on behalf of the Foreign Ministry when the verdict was announced, described it as a miscarriage of justice. He pointed out that directives of this kind were not State secrets. It was not their content, but the nature of their source, that was secret. To have named these sources, he said, was undoubtedly an offence, for which Scheliha would have been called to account – regardless of whether it had been committed now, in the era of imperial Germany or under the Weimar Republic. As the distribution of instructions was part of his official duties, he should not have accepted money for his services. Albrecht described Scheliha's action as a dereliction of duty. It could not in any case be described as treason, he asserted, since it had taken place before the outbreak of war with the Soviet Union and Scheliha had not been aware of the fact that Stübe and Herrnstadt were Russian agents.

There had been no lack of efforts to save Scheliha. Moltke himself was asked to intervene with Ribbentrop on his behalf. The President of the Court which had condemned him to death had been Krell, the President of the Senate. The members were Admiral Thomsen, and two Generals, representing the Army and the Air Force respectively. The prosecutor had been the Attorney-General, Roeder.

*   *   *

For weeks on end the Scheliha affair remained the chief topic of conversation in Berlin society. No one could bring himself to believe that Scheliha had been engaged in espionage for money. Most people thought that he had acted from ideological motives, and there were some grounds for this belief. On many occasions Scheliha had made no secret of his hostility towards the régime. At evening parties in his own house he had produced, even in front of guests whom he was meeting for the first time, anti-Hitler caricatures and articles, culled from the foreign press. It was known that after the outbreak of war he had tried to help a large number of Polish aristocrats. For this reason many people took the position that Scheliha had simply acted in a thoroughly unprincipled manner.

Tuesday, March 23, 1943

A current joke claims that at the end of this war the Soviet Union will be a constitutional monarchy, Germany and the United States will be Soviet Republics and Britain will be ruled by a fascist party. There is just a grain of logic in the assertion. At times it looks as though the powers waging war as brothers-in-arms will one day be fighting against each other, while others who are now fighting each other will one day be allies. It is equally obvious that Germany will be able to survive a total war only if she is prepared to adopt Russian methods. On the other hand, many of the wartime measures introduced in the United States and Britain have been adopted from the German or Italian model.

Thursday, March 25, 1943

Yesterday at Dietl's, my tailors, I saw two light grey military greatcoats with bright coloured lapels, the linings adorned with a W and the imperial crown. They were uniforms belonging to Wilhelm II, which his grandson, Prince Franz of Prussia, had inherited and which Dietl was to refashion for him. The father of the Prince, who had fought with distinction on the western front, was Prince Joachim, the Kaiser's youngest son, who had taken his own life in 1918. Previously, old imperial uniforms used to find their way into a museum. Now the undress uniform of a once so mighty monarch finds itself being used to complete the equipment of a grandson, who can count himself lucky to be tolerated as a lieutenant in an army whose Supreme Commander does not take kindly to princes as officers and would, indeed, deny them the privilege of dying on the field of battle. After the death in action of the Crown Prince's eldest son, Hitler issued instructions that members of the former ruling house were not to be allowed to serve at the front, and these instructions are still in force. Since most of the princes have little academic ability and many of them would prefer to be officers, life for them has been robbed of most of its meaning.

Dr Gregoric, the former political editor of the Belgrade *Vreme*, paid me a visit. Gregoric had played an important role at the time of the signing of the Three Power Pact with Yugoslavia. When war broke out between Germany and Yugoslavia, he was lucky enough to be serving with a unit which surrendered to the Germans, otherwise he would certainly have been killed by his compatriots. A southerner endowed with the characteristics of Austrian culture, Gregoric has come to Berlin to pave the way for a visit by the Serbian Prime Minister, General Nedic, who hopes to be able to persuade the German Government to reduce the size of its administrative services in Serbia. At the moment five German and two local governments are ruling a population of something less than four and a half million souls. Of the German governments, that of

Neuhausen, the Consul General, is regarded as the most powerful. Previously Neuhausen had been the representative of the Goering interests in Yugoslavia. Now he occupies a palatial office near the Skuptchina with eight hundred rooms, in which he keeps dozens of 'War Administration Advisers' busy. The second government is that of the Military Commandant, Bader, the third that of the chief of the Military Administration, the privy councillor Thurnau. The fourth German government has been set up by the SD (security services), while the chief of government number five is Minister Benzler of the Foreign Ministry. The last named is, in my opinion, the most efficient, and I cannot understand why Benzler has not been appointed Governor General and the other organisations placed under his orders.

The two local governments are those of the Prime Minister, General Nedic and the rebel leader, General Mihailovic. The latter, who is at the same time War Minister in the Yugoslav Government in exile in London, is regarded by the Serbian people as their national liberator. Apart from this, he is on excellent terms with the German and Italian authorities, who see in him an opponent of the Serbian communists. But Mihailovic is also collaborating with the British, who hope to make use of him as the figurehead of a future invasion of the Balkans.

From what Gregoric told me, the Serbs appear to envisage two possibilities for the future of their nation. In the event of a German victory, they presume they will be incorporated into a Central European confederation of nations, organised on federal fines; if Germany is defeated, they anticipate either the foundation of a Serbian Soviet Republic within the framework of a Balkan federation, or the restoration of the Yugoslav State on a communist basis.

Gregoric considers that the Serbs made a great mistake, historically, in uncompromisingly opposing the Hapsburg monarchy, instead of striving to become incorporated into it. The latter might well have been achieved within the framework of the exploratory policy adopted by the Archduke Franz Ferdinand and was widely discussed in Serbia, until the Sarajevo assassinations put an end to any such possibility. The incorporation of Serbia into the Danubian monarchy, he thinks, would have strengthened the position of the south-eastern Slavonic peoples, and even in the event of the disintegration of the monarchy good would still have come of it, because it would have facilitated the establishment of relations with the Croats and the Slovenes. In that case the mistakes which have led to the end of Yugoslavia might, perhaps, have been avoided.

Monday, March 29, 1943
The State funeral of the late ambassador von Moltke takes place today in Breslau. Half the Foreign Ministry, headed by the Foreign Minister himself, who is to make a speech, has proceeded by special train to Breslau. The dead von Moltke is to be honoured in a manner which he would hardly have deemed possible when he was alive. I cannot help feeling that it is the Spaniards who have inspired this State funeral. The *Völkische Beobachter,* for example, has no hesitation in stating that the Caudillo has issued instructions to the political leaders of the NSDAP in Spain regarding the procession behind von Moltke's cortège. The Spanish Foreign Minister, Count Jordana, has ordered the Spanish Ambassador and the whole of the Spanish colony here to proceed in a body to Breslau. Moltke's death has given the Spaniards the opportunity to demonstrate their friendship for Germany without incurring any political liabilities. As successor to von Moltke the most likely contenders seem to be Dieckhoff, Schulenburg, Bülow-Schwante, Rintelen, Henke and Bismarck. As an outsider *SS-Obergrüppenführer* Lorenz is also mentioned.

Alfieri, the Italian Ambassador, is still highly indignant about the Oertzen scandal. Some six weeks ago Sefton Delmer's British radio transmitter, 'Gustav Siegfried Nr 1', described in great detail an adventure which Alfieri is said to have had at the home of a certain Frau von Oertzen. The report asserted that the Ambassador had been caught *in flagrante delicto* by Frau von Oertzen's husband who had just returned from Africa, and been punched in the face. Little attention was at first paid to the story in Berlin. But in Rome it created a furore. It gave Alfieri's detractors plenty to talk about, particularly when it transpired that there was, in fact, a Frau von Oertzen living at the address given by the 'Gustav Siegfried Nr 1' transmitter. Although the lady in question had no husband, and the Ambassador did not even know her, Alfieri's opponents harassed him unmercifully. Their assault reached its peak when they asserted that the Ambassador was responsible for spreading the story himself, so that a spirited denial might pave the way for his rehabilitation and the cancellation of his imminent recall.

I have just received two new office orders. The first concerns the abolishing of the *Abteilung Deutschland* and the dissolution of the organisation built up by the former Under-Secretary of State Luther.

Unfortunately the opportunity afforded by the closing of *Abteilung Deutschland* and its ancillaries to make a clean sweep of all these 'special units' has not been seized. This is the result of the mistaken policy of General von Unruh's operation *'Heldenklau'*, which merely withdraws individuals from the bureaucracy instead of liquidating the whole bureaucracy itself. Only when this has been done will it be discovered that our reserves of manpower for the prosecution of the war are by no means exhausted. In the politico-cultural section, for example, there is a department called *'Kult Spr.'*, the duty of which is to promote the propagation of the German language abroad and to support the overseas efforts of the German Academy. Seeing that the occupation by German troops of the whole continent from the Arctic to Sicily has rendered superfluous any efforts at propagating the German language, and that in enemy countries no such efforts are possible, it does seem as though we could quite easily dispense with *'Kult Spr.'*.

The second order prescribes an increase in 'the minimum hours of work in public services in wartime'. It would be more to the point if the hours of work were decreased and the officials compelled to work harder and more swiftly!

Last Saturday, while we were celebrating Max Schaumburg's birthday in Cladow, there was an air raid warning. From the house where we were gathered, on the outskirts of the city, we had an excellent view of the whole course of the attack. Flak, searchlights and flares lit up the night sky. Suddenly, quite close to us, something landed with a terrific thud. It was an anti-aircraft 'dud', which plunged into the lawn a few yards from the house and made an enormous crater. Later the sky was lit by the reflection of a gigantic fire. Among Max's guests were two Hanoverian princes, who stood somewhere in the line of succession to the British throne. It certainly looked as though British bombs might quite easily rob them of any chance they may have had!

April 1943

The German press in trouble with the authorities – Bureaucratic muddle and duplicity – The Amery case

Tuesday, April 6, 1943
Details of the great reshuffle consequent upon Luther's resignation and Moltke's death are gradually beginning to seep through. Steengracht becomes Secretary of State, Weizsäcker goes to the Vatican, Woermann to Nanking. Henke, the present chargé d'affaires in Madrid, replaces him. Dieckhoff takes over the Madrid Embassy, Kroll leaves Ankara and goes to Barcelona, Gauss and Hewel become Ambassadors 'on special duty', and Steengracht will add the duties of State Secretary to his existing functions as the Foreign Minister's principal adjutant. There is considerable speculation as to how he will go about his task. Foreign diplomats are wondering whether he will conduct his business from Berlin or from whichever headquarters the Foreign Minister happens to be in.

Yesterday I met Lanza. The Italians are of the opinion that Turkey's attempt to resuscitate the Balkan alliance has been made at Churchill's instigation. They think that Britain would like to see Turkey take over the leadership of an alliance of south-eastern States which would constitute a front against a victorious Russia. Lanza expressed the fear that the British might land in Sardinia, where the Italians have only five divisions. An article by Gayda, which appeared today and which, in the guise of an historical retrospect, seems in reality to be bidding farewell to Sardinia, has been banned by the Ministry of Propaganda in Rome. Lanza asserts that the fighting morale of the Italian troops has never been higher than it is now, a statement which certainly does not tally with the information available to us!

We are worried about the negotiations being conducted by Eisenhower and Clark with General Orgaz in Spanish Morocco regarding a bilateral withdrawal of their respective armed forces. The Americans are anxious to secure their rear, while the Spaniards hope to bring about an easing of tension in their relations with the Anglo-Saxons. Any agreement of this nature would free American troops for employment against Rommel or Arnim. That the Spaniards should have allowed themselves to be drawn into negotiations of this kind is a clear sign of the weakness of our position in Madrid.

On Friday, April 2, 1943 Friedrich Hussong was buried with due solemnity. Sündermann, who was in charge of the funeral arrangements, made a well-phrased speech. Hussong was the kind of journalist who had ink flowing in his veins. From his busy pen flowed a stream of vivid articles, political and otherwise, pamphlets, poems and commentaries. Politically he served several masters, without believing in any one of them. When anyone accused him of cynicism, he was wont to retort: 'You evidently suffer from the misfortune of being unable to rise above your profession.'

Hussong's funeral is being sarcastically described in the Ministry of Propaganda as 'a diversionary offensive'. At the moment the situation in the German press is once again very tense. Four 'bricks' have recently been 'dropped' – two by the *Frankfurter Zeitung*, and one each by the *Deutsche Allgemeine Zeitung* and *Das Reich*, all of them newspapers which have hitherto maintained a certain standard. First the *Frankfurter Zeitung* allowed a 'printer's error' to go unnoticed. One of its articles began with the words: '*Reich-spresseSCHAF* Dr Dietrich ...' [*Schaf* = sheep, fig.: 'fathead', instead of '... *chef*, 'head of ...']. Scarcely had that happened than the same paper in an article on the life and work of Dietrich Eckhardt mentioned the fact that Eckhardt had been a morphia addict. Just previous to this, the editor, Küsel, had written an article on the Ministry of Propaganda which had earned Goebbels' approbation, and this fact proved to be his salvation. Küsel, nevertheless, was at once arrested by Gauleiter Sprenger in Frankfurt, while the assistant editor, Welter, was also held in custody for twenty-four hours. Since these measures had been initiated by the Gauleiter instead of by the Ministry of Propaganda, they constituted a usurpation of the powers of higher authority. The proper initial step would have been the convening of a court of enquiry by the German Press Association. Sprenger, however, refused to accede to the Ministry's request that Küsel be released, and it was only when the Central Security Office in Berlin intervened that he

Tuesday, April 6, 1943

was brought to the capital, interrogated and released. During the
Gestapo interrogation it became obvious that, while the accused
was well informed about Eckhardt's life and work, his accusers
most certainly were not. Furthermore, Küsel was able to show that
the offending passage regarding Eckhardt's addiction had been
taken from a book by Alfred Rosenberg. Finally, he was also able
to quote Eckhardt himself, who had said: 'Posterity must not make
me out to have been better than I was, for to do so would be to go
against National Socialism in both thought and deed.'

Silex, the editor-in-chief of the *Deutsche Allgemeine Zeitung*,
sent in his resignation, informing his readers of his decision at the
end of a leading article. Neither his colleagues nor the proprietors
of the paper had any inkling of his intention. At the Ministry of
Propaganda's press conference Silex was attacked with the remark:
'The sole purpose served by the publication of the *Deutsche Allgemeine Zeitung* is to afford others an example of how not to do
things.' When Silex's assistant, who was present, heard this, he
stalked out of the conference hall and reported what had happened
to his chief. The latter thereupon drew his own conclusions and
joined the Navy.

The fourth 'brick' was dropped by the editor of *Das Reich*, who
as a frontispiece published a photo of a starving *kulak*, tearing flesh
from the corpse of a dead horse. Inside the paper he reproduced
an American illustration, portraying white women being raped by
Japanese soldiers; and to cap it all he published information regarding
certain restrictions that were about to be imposed on the press, the
details of which, however, had not yet been officially released.

Thursday, April 8, 1943
In a new book, *Hitler, King Carol and Lupescu*, an English journalist
named Easterman seeks to prove that Madame Lupescu, Carol IIs
mistress, was not a Jewess, but the natural daughter of Carol I and
a village schoolmistress. It was only after her birth, the author
asserts, that her mother was married to the Jewish chemist, Wolf,
and she thus became legitimised. Only in this way, the book claims,
can one explain the fact that Madame Lupescu received a first-class
convent education and later married an officer of the Rumanian
Guards (Tampeanu). Easterman further asserts that Carol II
succeeded in moving from Seville to Portugal, thanks to the help

56

of the then Spanish Foreign Minister, Serrano Sufier, who was anxious to escape from Hitler's repeated requests for the despatch of the King to Germany.

The Rumanian chargé d'affaires here, Valeanu, says that the Jewish origins of Madame Lupescu have been irrefutably proven. On the other hand he confirms the part played by Serrano Suner in Carol's flight to Portugal. It seems that Germany did, in fact, demand the extradition of Carol to Germany, thereby creating a situation from which Carol's flight to Portugal was the only means of escape.

Valeanu tells an amusing story about the visit paid by Count and Countess Ciano before the war to Warsaw. One evening, after the official programme had come to an end, the colonel of a Polish cavalry regiment asked the Italian Foreign Minister if he and his wife would take supper with him in the regimental mess. The Italian guests accepted the invitation and, accompanied by Beck, the Polish Foreign Minister, proceeded to the mess, where everything had been prepared for their arrival. After supper the colonel asked Countess Ciano whether she would care to dance. When she said that she would, the curtains at the end of the room were drawn aside, to reveal a stage, in the middle of which sat a jazz band with, on each side of it, eighteen Polish officers in full dress uniform. At a sign from the colonel the band began to play and all the officers bowed simultaneously and asked for the pleasure of a dance. For a moment the Cianos were taken aback. Then the Duce's daughter rose splendidly to the occasion and proceeded to dance with each and every one of the thirty-six officers in turn – a programme which kept her pleasantly occupied until the break of day.

Monday, April 12, 1943

Under the title of 'Styria after two years of liberation', today's *Völkische Beobachter* publishes a review of the 'reincorporation and subsequent redevelopment of Lower Styria'. The article describes how a 'German profile' is being restored to a land that has been under foreign rule for a quarter of a century. For this purpose 'cramming schools' and practical units for 'the introduction of wage and tariff reforms' have been set up. The article states that in Lower Styria, with an area of 2,800 square miles and a population of 551,610, no less than 6,625 civil servants, 19,270 group leaders and 11,500 subordinate officials have been appointed. Although in the whole of Lower Styria there are only 177 communities all told, no less than 154 regional groups, 625 cells and 4,208 'blocks' have been set up, in which a total of 37,422 officials are on 'duty'. What a typical example of the German craze for organisation! Just imagine the furious exchange of volleys of memoranda between these 37,422 officials, locked in deadly paper warfare – and all this in the middle of a real war, too! Although every day there are complaints about the bureaucratisation of public life, it would obviously be quite impossible to knock any sense into an organisational maniac of the type of the ruler of Lower Styria.

In British India, with a population of close on four hundred and fifty million, there were, in 1937, only 763 British police officers. There are ten times as many at the headquarters of the Berlin police alone! No wonder that Germany complains of a shortage of man-power. The truth is that here in 'liberated Lower Styria' we have all the manpower we need.

In Hanover I was told of another example of the confusion of thought among our organisers. Among others affected by the closing of superfluous businesses were the confectioners. The object of the closures was to free labour for work of importance to the war effort. The majority of sweetshops in Hanover are kept by little old ladies, who run tiny businesses in their own homes and with a minute turnover manage to make a minute profit. They are far too old and fragile to undertake any other sort of work; but their shops have been closed for all that, and the only one to suffer is the State, which has to assume responsibility not only for the board and lodging of these old ladies, but also for the interest on any debts they may have incurred. Since the beginning of the war some of the confectioners' shops have been transformed into grocers, and their stock now consists of about seventy-five per cent foodstuffs and only twenty-five per cent sweets and confectionery. But, as the closure order has been made applicable with effect from some fixed date in the spring of 1939, all shopkeepers who, on that date, were earning their living as confectioners, have had to close. The net result has been that a large number of shops selling foodstuffs have now had to close down. A man named Schütte, who owns a shop in the Ministerplatz which he had transformed into a grocery and who is regarded as one of the most efficient businessmen in the trade, has now been forced to wind up his business and has been given a job as a liftman in one of the department stores. When he protested, it was suggested that he should take over some other grocer's in a different sector of the city. Schütte went and inspected the shop, came to a financial agreement with the owner, who was due to retire for reasons of health, and thus remained active in the trade in which he was an expert. But at the same time the State had to compensate him for the losses he had sustained as a result of closing his own shop – all, of course, at the taxpayer's expense! When Schütte closed down his own shop, he came across a case of sweets which he had overlooked. As his shop assistant was still with him and he did not want to leave the sweets to rot, he told her to put them up in half-pound packets and offer them for sale coupon-free to passers-by. Immediately he was reported by the Association of Individual Traders for illicit trading. My informant, himself a confectioner from Hanover named Sprengel, added that he, too, occasionally has cases of sweets which go rotten, because the authorities forbid him to offer them to the public. The official who, for good or evil, presides over the fate of the Hanover confectioners is a former drawing-master who, with a sublime disregard of his own ignorance, insists on a rigid adherence to 'the regulations'. Recently Goebbels announced that a family which, as the result of the head of the family's war services, had become entitled to relief allowances, had been informed by the local Welfare Authority that the amount of assistance payable to them would be restricted to the sum they had paid in rent for their house, which had been destroyed by a bomb. This mistake, said Goebbels was an exception which he had immediately rectified. Unfortunately, such cases are the rule rather than the exception.

Wednesday, April 14, 1943

A notice-board appeared some time ago near the entrance to my private office room, upon which slogans are pinned. The slogans are changed every four weeks. The latest one says:

Tüchtiges Schaffen, das hält auf die Dauer kein Gegner aus.
(Strenuous endeavour will beat every opponent in the end.)

In the past few weeks we have had to face:

> *Ich wünscht, Ich wäre ein Elefant,*
> *Dann würd ich jubeln laut.*
> *Es ist nicht urn das Elfenbein,*
> *Nein, um die dicke Haut.*
> (Ah! Had I been an elephant,
> For joy I would have cried.
> Not for my tusks of ivory,
> But for my nice, thick hide!)

and:

> *Alle Halbheit ist taub.*
> (Half-measures are no-measures.)
>
> *Was mich nicht umbringt, macht mich stärker.*
> (What can't kill me strengthens me.)

The incidence of this almost pathological mania for slogans is one of the strangest phenomena of the war. In the Foreign Ministry there is hardly a corridor that is not plastered with slogans like those above. They are changed from time to time by some mysterious agency. At the head of the main staircase the slogan notice-board is crowned with a symbolic national eagle. Beneath it hangs a picture of the sinking of the aircraft-carrier *Ark Royal,* with the caption: 'The Führer's words went unheeded; now the Führer's weapons speak instead.'

This rash of slogans has also manifested itself in another form, to which I may, perhaps, give the name 'tiles'. For a very long time tiles for our bathrooms have not been obtainable. But every bookshop is full of tiles, bearing artistically painted slogans, such as 'To each craftsman his own tools', 'Don't fuss, man!', 'Everyone has one bee in his bonnet!', 'Don't worry, simply marvel', 'Humour means laughing in spite of oneself', which find a ready sale. No banal fatuity is too stupid to achieve immortality in the shape of a painted tile. Recently a caricaturist drew a picture of a bathroom tiled solely with slogan-tiles!

Quite a lot of other rubbish has stubbornly managed to survive, despite wartime restrictions. There is a popular postcard, showing the heads of Hitler and Churchill, the former smiling broadly and the latter grinding his teeth. Another card shows the Führer with two chimney-sweeps and bears the caption: 'A Strange Meeting'. Another singular piece of rubbish is 'Plischke's national wall calendar' depicting the theme: 'I'm still king of the castle!' There also seems to be plenty of paper available for photos of nudes, which are on sale at every street corner.

Monday, April 19, 1943

In the Foreign Ministry there has recently been an increase in the number of desks that have been broken into during the night. When I got to my office one morning about a fortnight ago, I found that I could not open my desk. The locksmith assured me that an attempt had been made to open the desk with a skeleton key, which had broken off in the lock. At first I thought someone must have been trying to steal my store of cigarettes. Later I was told that authorised agents of the Gestapo search through our desks during the night. Three days ago Hepp had the same experience. He, too, was unable to open his desk – and for the same reason. The night before last the Gestapo agents were caught in the act of going through Fräulein Dr Hausmann's desk. When an explanation was demanded of them, they asserted that it was part of their duties to test the security of 'cash-boxes'. Neither in my office nor in those of Hepp and Fräulein Hausmann is there a cash-box! These people also claim that it is part of their duties to ensure that we are not contravening standing orders by keeping in our offices documents which, in view of the danger of air attack, should be lodged in the strong-room. I have had the following notice placed on my desk: 'Snoopers and pilferers are requested to open the desk in such a way that the skeleton key does not break in the lock and the lock remains serviceable for further use.' Interference with one's private correspondence and the tapping of telephone conversations are now accepted as a matter of course.

Every few days I have the opportunity to study in the office of the Head of the Section the 'Brown Friend', the digest of tapped telephone conversation prepared by the monitoring service. Most of its content is mere tittle-tattle. I am regaled, for example, with the details of a very lengthy conversation between some well-known lady and some equally well-known diplomat. The bits that afford me most amusement are the reports of the conversations that Marietti conducts with her friends from our own house; and in the evening when I get home an astounded Marietti wonders how on earth I found out all about something or other which she had arranged with Valdetaro or Lanza and which was to be a surprise for me. The 'Brown Friend', the compilation of which requires the services of a gigantic staff, is the most secret of all secrets. In the Foreign Ministry only the Minister and Schmidt, the Press Chief, see it.

For the rest, I remain undisturbed at the meticulous scrutiny to which my private life is subjected, in fact the methods of the secret police rather amuse me. In the various Embassies I can at once spot nearly all the servants who earn a bit on the side by acting as agents and informers for the Gestapo. They stand very little chance of catching me out, nor, I think, are they particularly anxious to do so, since I am myself an extremely generous tipper. Warnings which one passes on to one's friends are unfortunately seldom of much use. The Germans' predilection for irresponsible chatter, their intense sense of self-importance and, perhaps, their lack of any appreciation of the climate surrounding a dictatorship that is fighting for its very existence have all combined to bring disaster to an ever-increasing number of people. The number of otherwise shrewd people who throw caution to the winds in conversation with some stranger, who later turns out to be an *agent provocateur,* is quite incredible. The net result is usually a long and wearisome interrogation by the Gestapo, followed by a period of detention 'for reasons of security' – if not something much worse.

The meeting of the Führer and the Duce at German Headquarters has not led to any appreciable reconciliation of their respective points of view. The Italian statesmen seem to be very concerned regarding a possible withdrawal from Tunis and the repercussions it would cause. They have again urged us to come to some agreement with the Russians and step up our war effort in the Mediterranean.

I have now taken over the 'Politico-Diplomatic Correspondence' issued by the Foreign Ministry. It has been rechristened 'The German Diplomatic Correspondence'. Had this been done in September 1939, we should have had a much more formidable weapon to hand, from the point of view of publicity. For four years I have been urging the amalgamation of *'Politischen Bericht'* (Political Report), compiled by myself, and *'Diplo'*, written by Braun von Stumm, with the object of creating an instrument analagous to Reuter's *Diplomatic Correspondent*. But the combined opposition of the *Reichspressechef,* the German News Agency and Braun von Stumm was too strong. The news that I had been entrusted with the publication of *'Diplo'* came to me by telephone from the Ministry of Propaganda, which had rung up to complain that no free copies had been received. Next came a call from Fuschl [Ribbentrop's country villa], with the Minister asking for a copy. As compensation, Braun von Stumm has been entrusted with the publication of *'The Daily Political Report'*. As *'The Political Report'* is also still being published, there appears to be no end to the duplication of work in the publicity department of the Press Section.

Thursday, April 29, 1943

Yesterday Teddy Geyr returned from Paris, where he had been dealing with the Amery case. When we marched into unoccupied France, John Amery junior, the son of the British Secretary of State for India, fell into our hands. Much to our surprise, this young man, who had previously been living in Nice and had made no attempt to return to England, declared that he was ready to collaborate with us. The first contacts were established by Wismann, the Press Attaché of the German Consulate-General in Vichy, and these were followed up by Councillor Hesse of the 'England Committee'.

Amery placed his services as a broadcaster at our disposal and was transferred to Berlin, where he was put to work under the supervision of the broadcasting section of the Foreign Office. His first broadcast attracted a great deal of attention in England, where even *The Manchester Guardian* and *The Times* deigned to comment on it. As a result, our people formed an exaggerated opinion of Amery's importance and hit upon the idea of making him the leader of a 'British Legion'.

Admiration for the young man cooled off, however, when rumours of his eccentric way of life began to circulate. He had been permitted to bring his mistress, an intelligent young Frenchwoman, to Berlin with him, and it was apparently the financial demands she made on him that had been the main reason for his coming over to the German side. In Berlin, where his girl friend got a job as a singer of popular songs in the Foreign Press Club, this strange couple actually got married – and cost the Reich a very considerable sum of money in the process. During a fortnight's stay in Paris, for example, Amery ran through no less than thirty-four thousand Marks – at our expense. Three weeks ago, however, this idyll came to an abrupt end, when Mrs Amery died of heart failure in the Kaiserhof Hotel in Berlin as the result of an excessive indulgence in absinthe.

Her last wish was that she should be interred at her own home, a small place in the Pyrenees. The arrangements for this devolved upon Teddy Geyr, who had to interrupt his leave on private business in the Warthegau, where he was inspecting his wife's estate, in order to conduct Amery and the urn containing his wife's ashes to France. His primary duty, he was told, was to ensure that Amery was not abducted by British agents on the way to the Pyrenees.

After the grief-stricken Amery had shut himself up for a fortnight in a Paris hotel, consoling himself with alcohol, and Geyr had found him dead drunk in bed with the urn clasped in his arms, the latter informed the Foreign Ministry that he would have no more to do with the case and returned immediately to Berlin.

May 1943

More raids on Berlin: social life disintegrates – Problems of Franco-German relations

Monday, May 10, 1943

On this, the third anniversary of our great offensive in the West, the fall of Tunis has been announced. How the war situation has changed! Three years ago we freed ourselves from the defensive stalemate of that winter behind the Siegfried Line and in a few weeks rose to the height of our military might. With the beginning of the Russian campaign on June 22, 1941 our luck began to desert us. The fall of Tunis is the last link in a chain of defeats that Africa has cost us.

An invasion of southern Europe has now come within the realms of possibility. August would offer the most favourable weather for a landing in Italy. As worthwhile objectives for an offensive the allies have a choice of Catalonia, where the Spaniards would not be able to offer very much resistance, southern France, Sicily, Corsica and Sardinia. That even big islands can be conquered has been shown in Crete. And that the Italians would defend themselves more stubbornly than the Australians in Crete is most unlikely. A possible third objective would be the Balkan peninsula. A landing on the Albanian and Dalmatian coast might well rob us of our supremacy in the Adriatic, though the Allies would, admittedly, first have to force the straits of Otranto. An attack on Salonica would roll up our Balkan front, as it did in the last war. A measure of guarantee against such developments is afforded by the Russian disinclination to see their allies appear in the Balkans.

Tunis and North Africa have been lost as the result of the British superiority at sea. Only by breaking British supremacy at sea could we have hoped to bring the war in the Mediterranean theatre to a successful conclusion. Our first mistake was that, after Dunkirk, we marched on Paris instead of launching an offensive across the Channel. Our second mistake was to embark on the Russian campaign before the British had been driven out of the

Mediterranean. In the spring and summer of 1941, after the conclusion of the campaigns in Yugoslavia and Greece, this might, perhaps, have been possible. By way of Asia Minor and the Iberian land-bridge we could have seized Gibraltar and Suez and transformed the Mediterranean into an inland sea. Great Britain would presumably still have continued the fight, but under very much less favourable conditions. In addition, possession of Turkey would have greatly facilitated our thrust on the Russian oilfields and have spared us the campaign through south Russia and the Stalingrad disaster. But the importance of sea-power finds no place in Hitler's strategic thinking.

The logical course of action, as a result of the loss of Tunis and North Africa, would be to withdraw all German troops from Italy. But this is a course hardly to be adopted. If we retired to the Brenner instead of standing to defend Italy, we should save a large number of divisions and rid ourselves of the burden of having forty million Italian mouths to feed. On the other hand, against such a withdrawal is the fact that it would provide the allies with air bases on the Italian mainland, from which they could threaten southern France, southern Germany, Austria and Central Europe, and would also compel us to abandon our alliance with Italy, which constitutes the cornerstone of our political system in Europe. But how are we to defend Italy, if the Italians themselves have no stomach for it, and certainly we have yet to see any such signs.

Friday, May 14, 1943
Summer is here. The chestnut trees are in bud and the lilac already in blossom. Never has this doomed world of ours looked so beautiful. The evening air is like velvet. It stirs the blood and saddens and yet gladdens the heart at the same time.

Half an hour before midnight the *Deutschlandsender* went off the air – a sure sign that enemy aircraft are on their way in. We had just gone to bed, when the sirens howled and the guns opened up. The alarm lasted for an hour and a half. Twice we came up out of our shelter to look for incendiaries. A hundred and fifty aircraft reached the edge of the city, where they were dispersed by flak; twelve succeeded in reaching the centre and dropped bombs on Lichtenrade and Steglitz. People in west Berlin were as relieved as though Steglitz and Lichtenrade were separated from the Kurfürstendamm by an ocean.

On Easter Saturday our car broke down on the Pomerania autobahn and we had no alternative but to stop in Stettin, which had been bombed four days previously and was still burning. A third of the houses have been destroyed and forty thousand made homeless. At the railway station four thousand people are waiting for transport. As at the time only those who had suffered bomb damage were allowed on the platforms, we had no chance of getting tickets. It was only with the help of Karl Salm, for whom, as the holder of the Knight's Cross, everyone makes way, that we finally managed to board a train.

The process of the disintegration of Berlin society proceeds apace. During the last six months, house after house has put up its shutters. The Edelstams were the first to go. The Casardis are returning to Rome. The Fürstenbergs, Barros, della Portas, Rocamoras, Laroches, Meinsdorps have all left Berlin. The whole of the diplomatic corps is on the move to new quarters.

The farewell party for the Casardis brought together once again the dwindling circle of friends. Germans now take hardly any part in the social activities of the diplomatic corps. Like the monks of Athos, the local diplomats live on a mountain isolated from the world by a veil of cloud. Even the officials of the Foreign Ministry mix very little with foreigners nowadays, though one would have thought that they, of all people, would have considered it their duty to maintain their contacts. No wonder that so many of them have formed a distorted picture of the mentality of the foreigners in our midst.

Breakfast with Lily Schnitzler and her lovely daughter, Lilo Scholz, whose husband is in our Legation in Budapest. *Née* Mallincktrodt from Antwerp, she is married to Georg Schnitzler, a director of the IG Farben, with houses in west Frankfurt and the Tiergarten district of Berlin. She is a patron of up-and-coming painters, a devotee of the theatre and literature, and endowed with a lively appreciation of public affairs and of humanity in general; still enormously attractive, Lily Schnitzler is one of the brightest stars of German society. In her house in the Graf Spee Strasse are many of the works of artists officially condemned as 'degenerate', including Beckmann's *Triptychon*.

August Spee has just returned from the East. What he has to say is in very sharp contrast to the things one usually hears. The Ukrainian maidservants in his officer's mess, he told us, all possess about eight dresses each, enjoy solving crossword puzzles, play Mendelssohn's *Songs without Words* from memory, and have homes filled with embroidered table-cloths and pot plants.

Paul Metternich paints a very different picture of the Leningrad front. There he found nothing but dirt and the most primitive conditions. But he was very impressed by the inherent energy of the Russians. Burghard Preussen expressed much the same views. He and all the other members of former ruling houses, among them twelve serving officers, have now been told categorically that they must resign from the armed forces.

Tuesday, May 25, 1943
There are two main items of news: Churchill's conference in Washington, and the dissolution of the Third International in Moscow.

Wednesday, May 26, 1943
Reports from the Soviet Union indicate that, as the war continues, the influence of the Red Army steadily increases. Here the reverse is the case. The longer the war lasts, the more the armed forces are being thrust into the background. In all matters of concern to the nation as a whole, the Party regards itself as an instrument not only of equal status with the Wehrmacht, but even superior to it. The role of the *Waffen-SS,* in which many profess to see the embryo of a National Socialist army of the future, has been a contributory factor in diminishing the prestige of the Wehrmacht. The progress of this development has been greatly facilitated by the fact that the German professional soldier went into the war with a feeling of profound scepticism. The army commanders and the troops themselves were surprised at the victories they achieved. The Party, on the other hand, with no military knowledge, was full of confidence. They regarded the victories of the opening years as being but little more than a continuation of their own successes in the struggle for power. The swift victories won in the *Blitzkrieg* seemed to prove that the Party, and not the Wehrmacht, had been right, and this greatly increased the self-esteem of Party members.

The Party was furthermore encouraged to press its claims for absolute authority by the example afforded to it by Headquarters, where the Führer issued orders to the generals, rather than sought their advice. Today the Party leaders think they know more about the war and how to wage it than the soldiers. By the time the two winter campaigns on the eastern front had reversed the military situation, the position of the Party had already become so strong that it had little difficulty in persuading the people that it was the Army that had failed. The prestige of the Army began to sink. The same Party that had claimed the credit for the lightning victories of the opening years now succeeded in dissociating itself from all responsibility for our subsequent series of defeats. The Army feels bewildered and helpless, and while the younger intake of officers are predominantly National Socialist in outlook, the more senior no longer know where they stand intellectually.

In the Army itself there is no outstanding example on which the more senior officers might model themselves. The last of the great soldiers was Fritsch, who to our shame was abandoned to his fate. Blomberg, the 'indiarubber lion', struck a blow at the Army's *esprit de corps* with his marriage, and even the war has failed to heal the scar. Reichenau had few friends. Rommel, whose popularity is regarded somewhat askance by his fellow generals, is dismissed as an 'old campaigner'. Kluge, *'der kluge* (wily) Hans', as he is called, is, characteristically enough, trusted by no one. Rundstedt and Manstein enjoy respect as first-class military experts, but are devoid of any political acumen. Some of the Field-Marshals are discredited in the eyes of the people for having accepted large gifts of money or land from Hitler. To receive a Field-Marshal's baton while the outcome of the war is still uncertain is contrary to Prussian tradition. Conversations with more senior officers are generally unfruitful. As regards the political position, even those in the highest positions show themselves astonishingly uninformed. As a body, the generals seem unable to see the situation as a whole, and one cannot help feeling that they have no desire to do so. One encounters opposition mainly among officers of noble birth, who sense that the régime provokes them because they are aristocrats.

Within the Army itself, the glamour which formerly surrounded the whole Army is now confined solely to the holders of the Knight's Cross. These latter exercise an authority that is not overshadowed even by that of the Party itself. On leave the holder of the Knight's Cross can do exactly as he pleases. At a booking-office he can stalk to the head of a queue without a murmur of protest. In the restaurants he is always the first to be served. In the overcrowded hotels there is always a room for him. The prestige he enjoys is something far more than the admiration normally accorded to a hero, because in the eyes of the people he is not only a man who has proved his worth on the field of battle, but also, in the homeland, the only man not a hair of whose head may be touched. The people attribute to him not only valour but a quality of civil courage – a quality which most Germans lack, but which they admire above all others though they rarely strive to acquire it!

Friday, May 28, 1943
Aga Fürstenberg introduced me to the French Ambassador, Scapini, who is in charge of the welfare of French prisoners of war in Germany. Blinded in the war, he moves about with astonishing certainty. He has one glass eye, and the other eye-socket is hidden by a black monocle. He is accompanied everywhere by his secretary, Princess Dadiani, a Russian refugee of Georgian origin, who was brought up in France; two down-at-heel, bareheaded chauffeurs; and a brown dachshund, from which he never allows himself to be separated.

The Ambassador complains bitterly about the sterility of Franco-German relations. Morale in France, he says, is low. The French do not know where they stand with Germany, which still refuses to transform an armistice of three years' duration into a peace. To my remark that at the end of the first war our situation, too, was a hard one, he retorted that Germany had at least known where she stood. The agreement, under which prisoners of war can be exchanged against volunteer workers, is, he asserts, a thoroughly bad bargain. For every prisoner returning home ill, France has to find four healthy workers. These latter are quite willing to work for Germany, but they do not understand why they must come here, instead of being employed in factories in France, where a considerably higher production could be achieved. The French workers' complaint is that as a result of the laboriously meticulous German methods of production they have too little to do. On a job which any one intelligent man could easily do, they say, anything from four to eight Frenchmen are employed. This robs them of the chance of earning more, as they would like to do. The female workers imported from France, they assert, are completely useless. Most of them are worthless creatures, whose one idea is to jump into bed with a man, and who are a menace to the morals of French and German workers alike. Decent, worthwhile workers do everything they can to avoid being sent to Germany. The Ambassador doubts very much whether the recently introduced leave-system will work, despite the so-called Foreign Police unit, which was set up to supervise the movement to and fro of men on leave. He fears that most of them will not return, once they get to France.

He could not understand, he said, why Germany had failed to appreciate the great issues at stake. The unification of Europe and the consolidation of the New Order might well be wrecked by trivialities. The German army of occupation in France should be transformed into a field army. The French were accustomed to having foreign field armies in their country, and in the ultimate analysis, it made no difference to them whether they were defended by British, American or German troops.

Scapini regards the solution of the Alsace-Lorraine question as a compromise. The present uncertainty, he said, was helping to poison Franco-German relations. France could make no territorial concessions to Italy, for she had not been defeated by Italy. Africa, on the other hand, could well become the subject of negotiation, if one regarded it as a possession that belonged to Europe as a whole. France, he said, could not give Tunis to Italy, because then she would have to surrender Morocco in favour of Spain. But a European condominium over French North Africa was certainly a possibility. The open-door policy should be applied to North Africa, as it once was to China. The French should have few objections to such a policy, since their own interests would be best protected thereby, A Franco-German-Italian-Spanish condominium over Africa would at least be preferable to the loss of these territories to the Anglo-Saxon powers.

I mentioned that the traitorous attitude of the French generals in North Africa had come as a great disappointment here and had caused much bitter feeling. To this Scapini retorted that one could not have expected them to act in any other way. They, too, had no idea of how matters stood between their country and Germany. By insisting that French troops could not possibly fight on behalf of a country which was treating a million and a half of their comrades as prisoners of war, the British propaganda found it easy to attract deserters. The attitude adopted by the French generals, he asserted, had not been traitorous, but perfectly natural. All this was just another of the unhappy results of Germany's failure to reach a clear-cut understanding with France. He reminded me that in July-August 1941 France had sought an alliance with Germany, but had been repulsed. That, he said, had been the time when we ought to have initiated a joint defence of Africa. If France had been allowed to retain her fleet and a small army, these forces would have done their utmost to resist the landings in North Africa. The example set by a handful of French warships showed very clearly that the will to resist was there.

When I asked him whether he had submitted his views to the Führer or the Foreign Minister, Scapini replied that he had not Politically, he said, he was powerless; but he had discussed the whole issue with Marshal Pétain, who had agreed with him.

To my query regarding France's future Scapini replied: 'France has no future, except within the framework of the future of Europe. Some time or other France and Germany must come to terms. It will be late in coming, but not too late. We are all in the same boat together, and we can hope to survive only if we get together and stick together. If we don't, we shall all of us go under.'

Scapini's outlook is typical of those French patriots who would like to learn a lesson for the future from the defeat of their country, but whose task has been made immeasurably harder by German policy. Laval is credited with having said recently to the Führer: 'Make me your Foreign Minister for a year or two, and you'll live to see Europe materialise as a reality!' Abetz is one of the few who appreciate the political attitude adopted by the French. But he carries no weight here and has no option but to make way for people who are either *revanchistes* or idiots. As far as France is concerned, Hitler prefers not to commit himself. He will not rest until he has won the whole war and he overlooks the fact that a genuine reconciliation with France would be of more value to him than a whole series of victorious battles in Russia.

According to a Swedish journal, King Boris of Bulgaria recently said: 'My wife is for Italy, my Ministers for Germany, my people for Russia; I am the only neutral in the whole country.' In the version which I had previously heard, he is supposed to have finished: 'and I am for Britain.'

July 1943

Joys of existence in the Protectorate – Mussolini's downfall: consternation in our Foreign Ministry – Sweden abrogates the Transit Treaty with Germany

Wednesday, July 7, 1943

I have been away for three weeks, but find the overall situation unchanged. Sikorski's death seems to have been the result of an accident. He was regarded as the only Pole who could have brought about an understanding between the Polish emigrants and the Soviet Government.

Among the papers awaiting my attention I found a report on a controversy between the Foreign Ministry and the Ministry of Propaganda regarding the way in which our propaganda is handling the war in the air. To my astonishment it was stamped with an ordinary 'Secret' rubber-stamp. More surprising still is the fact that it has been printed by duplicator, which must mean that it has had a wide distribution. It has been a constant source of surprise to me that genuine State secrets are often circulated without any particular precautionary measure, while quite unimportant files are plastered with 'Top Secret' stamps.

The controversy arose because the Foreign Minister was of the opinion that our propaganda handling of the terror bombing was having a deleterious effect on the morale of the German people. In addition, he felt that, by publishing details of historic and cultural buildings damaged, we were giving the enemy valuable information regarding the accuracy or otherwise of his bombing. The Foreign Minister therefore insists that this practice should cease, but wishes at the same time to see our press reports on air raids angled in such a way as to increase the people's feelings of hatred towards Britain. The Foreign Minister's dictated comments are said to have been previously discussed with the Führer. The Minister for Propaganda and the head of the Press Section regard the Foreign Minister's comments as a criticism of their direction of the German press and have sent out a confidential circular to the newspapers, refuting Ribbentrop's arguments.

The German press has long been forbidden to publish detailed descriptions of terror raids. Photographs, too, have been released for publication only in exceptional cases, such as in that of Lübeck, and then only for reproduction in the local newspapers.

On the other hand the foreign press has been given a whole series of photographs of the destruction of cultural buildings. But since the sympathies of ninety per cent of neutrals lie with the enemy, these pictures are seldom reproduced. The public in foreign countries have no conception of the destruction caused by British strategic bombing, but they have a very clear recollection of the devastation wrought in Britain by the German air attacks.

Count Bossi, a Supreme Headquarters spokesman, has shown me some truly terrifying photographs taken during the recent attacks on Düsseldorf and Cologne. But I would not for a moment agree that publication of such pictures would diminish the war morale of our people. When the survivors have to carry on, surrounded by the concrete realities of these horrors, it is surely not too much to demand of those who have been spared such sufferings that they, too, should carry on, undismayed by the contemplation of these dreadful pictures.

As the war continues, the Foreign Ministry is attaching more and more importance to propaganda. In reality, of course, the war has now reached a stage when only military facts carry any weight. Among the mistakes made by the National Socialists is the assumption that propaganda is still, as it was before the assumption of power, a prerequisite to victory.

Friday, July 9, 1943

During the last three days there has been a sharp increase of activity on the eastern front, and the lips of our Supreme Headquarters representative have been sealed. Their communiqué states that heavy fighting broke out when German patrols ran into a strong advancing Russian force, and thus precipitated the launching of a major offensive. The Russians say exactly the opposite and publish fantastic figures of our losses. Both parties flatly contradict each other's version, and neither is prepared to admit that they were caught unawares in their preparations by the other side. Developments on the eastern front are being closely watched in Britain.

Friday, July 9, 1943

While I was on leave I read a book entitled *This Above All,* by Eric Knight, which was published in England about eighteen months ago and is considered there to be one of the best war books yet: it is a romance about a soldier from a slum family and the daughter of a famous London doctor, and 'What are we fighting for?' constitutes the main theme of the book. In Germany the book would have been banned as defeatist. But as the British do not know the meaning of the word 'defeatism', defeatist books of this nature do no harm, even though the hero is a deserter from the armed forces.

We spent Whitsun with the Arenbergs in Westphalia. In Hamm we were turned out of our sleeping-car because, as a result of a night raid on Dusseldorf, trains could not run via Dortmund. Dortmund has been burnt out, worse than Rotterdam, the station destroyed, the railway officials carrying on as best they can, housed in temporary shelters on the platforms. I managed to get hold of the only taxi available, invited two men on leave from the eastern front to join us and drove to Nordkirchen. The roof of the taxi was patched up with adhesive tape. During the last attack, while the owner was on his way home, an incendiary bomb had come through the roof and landed on the seat beside him. But the adventure does not seem to have bothered him. The people here display considerable stoicism. The two men on leave, who had in fact been granted leave because their homes had been destroyed, actually joked about it all. Most of the villages in the vicinity of Dortmund have been destroyed.

On the return journey on Whit Monday the train service was once again reduced to a state of complete confusion when the air raid warning was sounded about midnight. As my sleeping-car train was stuck where it was, I jumped into the first local train I could find, to get out of Dortmund as quickly as possible. We had only just moved off when the bombers arrived and were engaged. In Hamm we had to go into a shelter underneath the platform. The people here have got so used to these raids, that they seem to regard them as the most natural thing in the world, and always refer to the bomb-dropping as 'bowling' which somehow makes it sound less dangerous and less exciting. They advised me to catch such-and-such a train, because the British usually began to 'bowl' at such-and-such an hour, and then the trains could no longer leave the stations. Many of these people have been bombed out four or five times, but the industrial plants still continue to function, since they are obviously more difficult to hit than a residential quarter or, perhaps, are not being subjected to the same intensity of attack.

Nordkirchen, the Westphalian Versailles, a castle of gigantic proportions built by Cardinal Count Plettenberg, was inherited by the Arenbergs in 1907 from a Count Eszterhazy. After the First World War the Duke of Arenberg transformed the main building into a convalescent home for post office officials. The hereditary Prince and his wife live in a side wing which is beautifully decorated and furnished. There is an aviary housing exotic birds, in a garden stretching between the castle and the moat surrounding it. Their winter quarters are designed like a small living-room, the walls of which are hung with exquisite Chinese tapesteries. Through the park, which is screened from the main road by a spinney of trees, run several avenues of oaks, so wide that a four-in-hand can easily turn round in any one of them. The green-houses and stables are palatial.

On account of the danger from air raids, the art treasures, among them some beautiful Gobelins and a collection of Clemenswerther 'hunting' porcelain, have been stored away in the cellars. To please me, the Princess had unpacked a few pieces of faience and arranged them in the dining-room: these included two turkey-cocks and a pair of pheasants, for which the Berlin art dealer Lange had made an offer of thirty thousand marks. The hereditary Prince, who is a great lover of animals, also breeds wild horses. One afternoon, when we went for a drive in a shooting-brake drawn by two blood mares, we came across a small herd and were attacked by a wild stallion, which leapt over the brake-shafts with a complete disregard for the whip and which we eventually drove off only with great difficulty.

The father of the present Prince, who was a great admirer of Kaiser Wilhelm II, is said to have intended to pull down his palace in Brussels and re-erect it in Charlottenburg. After 1918 his pro-German sympathies cost him his possessions in Belgium. His eldest son, Engelbert (Enka), contracted a widely discussed marriage with a divorcee from Hungary, a Frau Wagner, who claims to be the natural daughter of one of the Dukes of Holstein, to be closely related to the British royal family, and who is shown in the *Almanack de Gotha* as 'Valerie zu Schleswig-Holstein', without mention of any title. With her ready intelligence, she has had no difficulty in acting as intermediary with the authorities, and helping her somewhat unworldly husband to preserve his very considerable estates throughout our difficult times.

Joslowitz – Saturday, July 10, 1943
On June 18 I went off on leave. I spent the first weekend in Ernstbrunn, where little has changed. The Reuss family are mourning the loss of their second son, who was killed at Stalingrad. The number of books in the library has grown to forty thousand volumes. When Alice Hoyos asked the owner of the castle whether he managed to read all these books, he confessed that the unpacking and cataloguing of the various consignments as they arrived was about as far as he could get. Nevertheless, collecting books is a noble hobby, and one not often indulged in by the nobility these days.

In Ernstbrunn I found a car for hire which got me to Joslowitz in three-quarters of an hour and thus saved me a whole day in the train. The taxi driver, a fat and well-fed man, is regaled with food and wine by the peasants wherever he puts in an appearance. For the twenty-mile journey he charged me forty marks. Where he gets his petrol, nobody knows. He referred to the *Reichsdeutsche* as '*Piefkes*' [a slang word for Germans living in Austria], little dreaming that his passenger was one of them! Then he told me a yarn about a man he knew who had been present when a furious mob had given Goebbels a thrashing! And he himself, he said, had seen a woman with a basket of cherries trampled to death by starving people at the East station in Vienna. All of which is nonsense, of course.

Joslowitz, an enormous castle built round a courtyard and situated in the midst of a range of vine-bearing hillocks above the village of the same name, was built for Kaiser Karl VI, who gave it to one of his mistresses. Later it came into the possession of the Counts Hompesch, who were all killed in the First World War, and they have been succeeded by the Spees. Although the yield from the vineyards has been very considerably increased under the supervision of an expert from the Rhineland, the income derived from them scarcely suffices for the upkeep of the extensive property. The Czech land reforms have robbed the owners of Joslowitz of their most valuable land, so that the castle has become a heavy financial burden to its owner.

The population – typical border-folk – is quasi-communist. In the village there are eighty bombed out refugees from Essen, who have caused much bitterness. They accuse the locals of eating like dukes and living like pigs, hang about all day long in the local tavern, or push elegant perambulators through the streets of the village, much to the wrath of the villagers. Maritschi Spee, whose husband is serving on the eastern front, is running the place in his absence; she has no easy task. The Labour Office in Znaim refuses to allot workers to the estate, so that much of the agricultural work remains undone. As soon as she manages somehow to get a few eastern female workers to live in, the labour office immediately removes them for other work.

In comparison with life in Austria, life in the Protectorate is a paradise. The authorities know this, and do their utmost to put a stop to individual crossings of the frontier. They do not want the Austrians to know how very much better off than themselves the Czechs are. The scale of rations is, admittedly, less generous than in the Reich, but the opportunities offered in the black market are very much greater. As the men are not liable to call-up for military service, the big estates do not lack for servants. Those of the aristocracy who have thrown in their lot with Germany are left unmolested on their estates. The population regards them as go-betweens between themselves and the German authorities, who in turn regard them as the backbone of Germanism. The future hangs like the sword of Damocles over them. If the war is lost, not one of them will preserve his possessions, and very few their heads.

Some of the aristocrats, among them some of pure German origin, have opted for Czech nationality and are being constantly harassed by the German authorities who in some cases go so far as to expropriate their estates. They, of course, are banking on a German defeat, and the Nazis are taking it out of them while they still have the chance. Whether, in the event of a German defeat, they will manage to retain their estates is, I think, very doubtful. Gratitude is not a virtue commonly found among the Czechs; servility is much more in their line. In none of the arms factories working for us have there been fewer cases of sabotage than in the Skoda works in Pilsen. As National Socialist 'hiwis' (volunteers), the Czechs are unsurpassed: they have but one ambition – survival.

Monday, July 12, 1943

An English journal, *The National Review,* in an article entitled 'The Anonymous War', complains of the tutelage to which the press is being subjected and which, with but few exceptions and in contrast to the First World War, is exercised to such a degree that any popularisation of leading personalities has been made quite impossible. The war, says the journal, is thus assuming an ever-increasingly 'anonymous' character in which the general public is becoming less and less personally involved emotionally. The article says:

> One of the most curious phenomena of this war is the way in which our propaganda is being handled. All press men are accustomed to the 'directives' which rain down on them by night and day and deal with matters both great and small.
>
> We have, for example, just received the following – marked 'Secret': 'On the orders of his doctor, Mr Churchill has gone over to smoking a pipe. This must not be reported, since it might create an unfavourable impression among the people, who are used to seeing him with his cigar.'
>
> Or again: a well-known Rumanian lady is shortly coming to England to bring her children to school here. Of this, too, no mention is to be made, since it might give rise to the idea that her country has become war-weary and that she has come to initiate peace proposals.
>
> These are the sort of things that descend on the unfortunate journalist from morn till eve. There must be hundreds of people, busily employed in distributing nonsense of this kind throughout the world.
>
> Any description of the war or the men waging it is not permitted, but sensational items of news about some tinpot politician are very much the order of the day. His daily activities are described hour by hour and in so mysterious a way that he eventually emerges as a really important person.
>
> The instructions issued regarding troops at the front are completely negative. We are not allowed to report that a famous Admiral has come home to see his family or that some great soldier is at present on leave. No – they must be allowed to move unnoticed in the shadow of our splendid, wise and wonderful politicians. If Admiral Cunningham or General Alexander

were to appear at the Dorchester Hotel tomorrow, who would recognise them? Precious few! In the last war the names of Lord Kitchener, Lord Haig, Admiral Jellicoe and Admiral Beatty were on everybody's lips; photos of them were displayed everywhere. But this war is an anonymous war. Only the People are great – and, of course, Mr Churchill.

But those who are responsible to the Prime Minister for the shaping of our propaganda should be made to realise that the people of this country, unbounded though their admiration for Mr Churchill may be, are of the opinion that wars are won by soldiers, sailors and airmen, and they would therefore very much like to hear more about these heroes. The only soldier who has emerged from the mists enshrouding the Army is General Montgomery – thanks to the fact that he has himself made quite sure we hear all about him.

The whole tendency of our war propaganda is aimed at ensuring that no individual shall be specially singled out for praise – unless, of course, he is so unimportant that no one will ever hear of him again. If some BBC commentator flies in a bomber on an air raid or goes to have a look at some coastal fortifications, the individual detailed to answer his questions is usually someone without sufficient knowledge to give a proper answer. Very seldom do we hear anything about the real leaders, the men who train the bomber pilots or the instructors who teach the gun-crews to serve their weapons.

The general impression given is that the greatest of them all, Tommy Atkins, goes to war with colours flying and performs his deeds of valour without any help from anyone – except, of course, the moral support accorded to him by the all-important politicians.

The Malta film affords an excellent example of what we mean. In it we are given a picture of a completely anonymous and leaderless war. Neither of the Governors, either the gallant Sir William Dobbie or that great soldier, Lord Gort, is even mentioned, let alone shown in the film. There are a few shots of aircraft taking off and guns firing, and that is all we see. No one must be praised for the resistance Malta put up – except the local civilian inhabitants of the lower social orders. The papers, we are proudly told, never fail to appear, and we are shown pictures of bombed-out newspaper offices; no one, however, mentions the fact that all this is thanks to the efficiency and heroism of Miss Strickland, whose initiative and gallantry are beyond all praise. Oh no – the newspapers just appear on their own, without any sort of endeavour or leadership. That is what we are expected to believe. And it affords a good example of the way our propaganda goes to work in this, the greatest of all wars, in which leadership is perhaps more important than ever before.

Well, well! The other side seem to be suffering from the same little troubles as ourselves!

Tuesday, July 13, 1943
Events on the eastern front have been overshadowed by those in Sicily. Our defence, which expected the main thrust to be made against Sardinia, has again been caught napping. Furthermore, we are still groping in the dark and do not know whether the attack on Sicily is an invasion or a feint which will be followed by the main blow somewhere else. Initially our chances of a successful defence were optimistically regarded as good. Today the picture is not so good. Our experiences in Africa are repeating themselves. Left to themselves, the Italians run away; shoulder to shoulder with the Germans, they stand and fight.

In Rome the consensus of opinion is that the war is lost. They say that the Duce is ill and that a caucus of Generals has been formed round Badoglio and Cavallero, which has made contact with a number of disgruntled fascists like Grandi. These people, it is rumoured, intend to place the Crown Prince on the throne and seek a peace by negotiation. All this seems to show that Italy is far weaker than people here are inclined to think. What I cannot understand is why the enemy has not attempted to make simultaneous landings in central Italy, the Gulf of Genoa and on the Adriatic coast. If he succeeded in establishing a number of fronts, our position in the peninsula would become untenable.

Our military leaders regard the situation in Italy with the same mixed feelings as they did that in Libya and Tunisia. We are resorting to half-measures. In order to free one solitary division for Italy, we have allowed the Bulgarians to march into Salonica and take up defensive positions in Thrace. From Athens Sissi Hurter reports that the Greeks are indignant about this and that the advent of the Bulgarians in Salonica will be answered with the raising of four local partisan-divisions.

As regards Sicily, I would add that every time something of importance occurs there is always an inordinate delay in the releasing of news. The nerve-centre of our war effort is Berlin. Yet despite this, the heads of our various departments are hardly ever there, but at some Headquarters, in the extreme east or the extreme south of the Reich, hundreds of kilometres from the capital. All the information reaching us here has to be sent either by teleprinter, in cipher or by telephone, with an inevitable loss of valuable time. The lines of communication become so congested, that very often hours elapse before reports can be sent on. Even then, they are still very far from being delivered to the Foreign Minister or the Führer. First they have to be set out in 'Führer-type' (double-spaced bold type) then sent to the various liaison staffs, who would then submit them to higher authority. In East Prussia, Raykowski, the liason officer of the Foreign Ministry Press Department, has to travel for half an hour by car, before he can submit some urgent report to the Minister. If everything were centred in Berlin, all these difficulties would disappear.

The custom, now adopted by our senior officials, of remaining far away from the capital for lengthy periods, is reminiscent of the Middle Ages, when a prince was wont to set up his court at his camp in the field. Today it gives rise to a crop of problems of a different nature. In Fuschl, the Foreign Minister's entourage complain of the soporific and ennervating climate of the Salzburg hills, which robs them of their power and will to act with energy. The continuous absence from Berlin of the Minister himself makes it more difficult for him to maintain his contacts with the accredited foreign diplomatic representatives. Even the Italian and Japanese Ambassadors hardly ever see the Foreign Minister.

I am reading Gallagher's *Retreat in the East,* which deals with the fall of Singapore. To defend the Malayan peninsula the British used old Rolls Royce armoured cars which had originally been used in Palestine in the First World War and were constantly breaking down. When that happened, the crews removed the guns, so that they could use them at least. During the first Japanese night air raid, the town's lights continued to burn brightly because no one could find the official who held the master-key for switching off the city's electricity system. The police thought that it was a practice alarm. When a two-storeyed house collapsed, a stoical English-woman was heard to remark: 'Well – if this is only a practice alarm, they're certainly carrying it out with real bombs!'

If, despite the experience gained from two years of war in Europe, the defences of Singapore, the strongest of Britain's fortresses, have been so lamentably neglected, one can easily imagine what the defences of Britain itself must have looked like in the summer of 1940.

Friday, July 23, 1943

Since Katyn, nothing has been of such great value to our propaganda as the stupid allied air raids on Rome. Cardinals and bishops all over the world are loudly expressing their revulsion. Only the German Princes of the Church are remaining silent.

Michi Lanza told me yesterday evening that the British had fixed the rate of exchange at four hundred lire to the pound – to the great joy of the Italians!

At the same dinner-party – at Ridomi's Lützowufer house – were Udo Laroche, Annemarie Boner's husband and Georg, Duke of Mecklenburg, a morganatic offshoot of the Russian branch of Strelitz, one of the most colourful figures in Berlin society. After his castle, Remplin, had been destroyed by fire, the Duke, who married the widow of Count Tolstoy, moved to Berlin, where he maintains a princely establishment in his villa in Grunewald. With typically Russian generosity the ducal pair, who have been blessed with a large family of highly intelligent children, entertained lavishly until quite late into the war. The Duke transformed the flower-garden of the villa into a kind of stockyard, whose winged population of chickens, ducks, geese and turkeys would have been a credit to any great country estate. Ambassadors, generals, princes (among them Pater Sachsen, the heir to the throne of Saxony, who was drowned in May, in the Havel, under very mysterious circumstaces) were frequent guests at luncheon, at which all the children, together with their English governesses and their French tutors, were always present. One of the most amusing members of the family circle was 'Gregory Darling', the youngest son, now a prodigy of ten years of age, who is an authority on jazz music and who never misses an art auction in Berlin, at which, unaccompanied by any grown-up, he bids, either on his father's behalf or on his own, for antique clocks and pieces of Chinese porcelain. At evening receptions a most venerable old Russian servant used to follow the Duchess wherever she went, carrying a silver tray, ready, at a sign from his mistress, to serve her a goblet of pink champagne. Deeply versed in Russian affairs from the time of his childhood, the Duke occasionally expresses his horror at the many mistakes we have made in the occupied territories. I need hardly say that the presence in Berlin of this expert, who could give them much good advice, is completely ignored by those who frame our 'Eastern policy'.

Monday, July 26, 1943

On our return at 10.00 a.m. from Buckow, where we had attended Freddy Horstmann's birthday party, we heard that Mussolini had resigned. Hans Flotow, who reached Berlin ten minutes before us, telephoned and gave us the news. My secretary apparently considered it of little importance since she did not bother to tell me about it. It is really astonishing how unpolitically minded the Germans are! When Marietti asked Frau Grunz, our charwoman whether she had heard of Mussolini's resignation, she replied: 'I heard something or other on the radio. We thought at first it was Churchill who had resigned, but it turned out to be only Mussolini.'

A state of complete confusion reigns at the Foreign Ministry. The one exception is Schmidt, who always remains calm in moments such as this. There are no instructions or any guidance from above, of course. The Führer, when approached, is said to have replied that 'it was just one of those things, and there was nothing we could do about it'.

At the moment a Council of War is being held at the Führer's headquarters, at which decisions of primary importance will have to be taken. Farinacci, the only prominent fascist who has succeeded in getting away, is expected at headquarters this evening.

The Duce is in custody, and the Italian people are only too eager to denigrate him. The 'new look of the nation', created during two decades of fascism, is already a thing of the past.

Here in Germany, too, it is not denied that a political earthquake has taken place. The two leaders, the two political systems were too closely united. The earthquake in Italy may well cause tremors in the foundations of the national socialist State. From the military point of view, the first essential is to withdraw our forces from the Italian mess. We cannot defend a country the inhabitants of which yearn for peace. It is quite possible that a state of affairs will arise between Germany and Italy similar to that which arose between Britain and France in 1940. If Italy surrenders, we shall be relieved of many of our responsibilities. We shall regain our liberty of action, shall be free to conclude peace with France at long last, to take Croatia under our protection and to bow the Italians out of the Balkans, where their presence has been a constant burden to us; and we shall also be able to halt our coal exports to Italy.

Badoglio's appointment has broken the back of the Axis. There will certainly be repercussions among the minor partners. The appointment of Szent Mikloszy as Deputy Foreign Minister of Hungary is the first symptom of this.

Our offensive in the East is making no progress. The heavy air raid on Hamburg the night before last and the raids on Rostock, Lübeck and fifteen other places in Holstein have brought the war in the air into the heart of Germany.

In the Soviet Union a 'Committee of Free Germany', composed of prisoners of war and German communists, has been formed. Its creation has caused more anger in London and Washington than here. Over there they fear that after the war Russia will pursue a policy of her own on the continent and use Germany as a battering-ram against Britain and America.

Tuesday, July 27, 1943
Lanza, whom I regard as the keenest intellect in the Italian Embassy here, is very worried that recent events in Italy may give the German authorities a false impression. The crisis, he maintains, has nothing to do with Italy's will to fight, but is the direct result of the fascist dictatorship. The régime and Mussolini himself have become so unpopular that they could no longer be tolerated. The people and the Army had quite simply refused to go on fighting for this Government and its system, a development which he had seen coming for a long time. The Italian people are quite different from the Germans. Even a totalitarian régime, he says, is not immune against upheavals, which, in this case as in every other, have been brought about by the dissatisfaction of the people, abetted by

influential circles. The King, he maintains, has acted in accordance with his duty as a sovereign, and has chosen a moment when the downfall of the régime could be brought about with comparatively little dislocation and without bloodshed.

Lanza does not believe that the Duce's downfall will be followed by a return to pre-fascist conditions. Fascism, he says, contained certain elements which have been a blessing for the Italian people. Changes will be introduced only gradually. The Fascist Militia, for example, has now been placed under the orders of the Army instead of being disbanded. It will be the aim of the new Government, he says, to draw a veil of oblivion over the past and quietly to eradicate the abuses perpetrated by the former régime.

The greatest mistake that Germany could make, says Lanza, would be to mistrust Badoglio. The Marshal will take no major decisions without first informing the German authorities of his intentions. His special emissary is expected to arrive at German Headquarters in the course of the next few days, though his despatch may be delayed until Guariglia, the new Foreign Minister and former Ambassador to Ankara, reaches Rome.

Alfieri, he thinks, is unlikely to return to Berlin as Ambassador. He had let it be known that he proposed to remain in Rome until Guariglia arrived there. Lanza fears lest Germany, from motives of loyalty, might be tempted to interfere in Italian current affairs and by so doing jeopardise Badoglio's position. Mussolini, he asserts, is finished, and any German attempt to intervene on his behalf or on behalf of fascism would merely create animosity against Germany, lead to a degeneration of Italian morale and confirm the contention of allied propaganda that Italy was fighting on behalf of Hitler.

Lanza hopes that a meeting between Hitler and Badoglio will take place as soon as possible. Germany must realise, he says, that the Italians had a right to expect absolute frankness from their allies. Badoglio was a man to whom any sort of illusory or propaganda-tinted approach to a situation was anathema. In the past the German and Italian points of view had been poles apart. The Germans had fixed their eyes solely on the eastern theatre, the Italians on the Mediterranean. Each was firmly convinced that only in their theatre could the war be brought to a decisive conclusion. If Germany were not in a position to defend Italy, then she could hardly expect the Italians to 'fight on to the very end'. Mussolini fell because the Italian people believed that he was sacrificing his country to no purpose and that his voice carried no weight in the German councils of war. If Germany and Italy were prepared objectively and soberly to face the military situation and, one way or the other, come to the requisite logical political conclusions, the worst might still be avoided.

This conversation with Lanza symbolises, to my mind, the fundamental attitude of all friendly-minded Italians. I felt that he was not merely passing on instructions received from Rome. On the contrary, he complained that the Embassy had been left without any instructions and that with the simultaneous absence of the Ambassador, the Military Attaché, General Marras, and his assistant, Colonel Count Cavallero, it found itself bereft of the means of contact with the German authorities. Lanza's opinions provide, I think, some valuable pointers regarding the future handling of the Italian question. They reflect the fears of so many Italians that we have misled them with regard to our war aims; and we must expect that this mistrust will continue in the future. Badoglio will certainly take great care to avoid giving the impression that he is allowing himself 'to be led up the garden path' by the Germans.

Wednesday, July 28, 1943

Many people find it hard to believe that the fascist era, which has lasted for twenty years and survived so many crises, can have been shattered by one single adverse vote. They seem unable to grasp the fact that fascism was destroyed by an act of parliament. For the majority vote cast in the Fascist Grand Council which compelled Mussolini to abdicate is just that. Mussolini seems to have completely lost his nerve. A letter from him to Badoglio has been published, in which he expresses his thanks for the military protection granted to him and assures the King of his continued loyalty. A miserable exit for so great a man.

Comments in the world press, even in those sections of it that are hostile to fascism, have been objectively phrased. Only the German press has been instructed to remain silent. Tomorrow is Mussolini's sixtieth birthday, but not a line about him will appear in the German papers. The man who has been presented to the

German people as the greatest statesman in the world after Hitler disappears from the German scene unheralded and unsung.

Badoglio's position is more than a little difficult. The Italian people expect him to give them peace. But how can he? If he negotiates with the British and is granted an armistice, then he will be compelled to place his country at the disposal of the allies as an advance base for future operations. If he fights on, Italy will still remain a theatre of war. Churchill's speech yesterday robs Badoglio of any chance he may have had of breaking off the fight. The British, obviously, feel themselves to be in a strong enough position to ignore the Marshal.

In a military sense, four courses are open to us. The first would be to throw our reserves into Italy and clear Sicily of the enemy. The second would be the creation of an Apennine front, the third a withdrawal to the Po, and the last resort would be to establish our front at the foot of the Alps.

Hamburg was heavily bombed the night before last and again last night. Twenty-four hours previously Hanover was attacked in broad daylight. This morning a hundred and twenty four-engined American bombers were flying on Berlin, but later turned away to Magdeburg, where their objective was the Fieseler-Storch works. In the air and at sea we are at the mercy of our enemies. On the eastern front we have made no progress. There seems no hope anywhere of achieving a decisive military success in our favour. The people are beginning to doubt the competence of our leadership. Goebbels' speeches no longer have the power to blind thinking men to the seriousness of the situation.

At the end of the last war, at the age of eleven I was so ashamed of our collapse that I regarded the death of my father on the field of battle as a merciful dispensation; otherwise I should have felt compelled to call him to account for our failure. In those days we schoolboys despised our elders who, in any discussion on the causes of our collapse, invariably avoided the issue by saying that there was nothing they could have done to prevent it.

Now I find myself in the same position. In full possession of my mental and physical powers, entrusted with a task far more important for the prosecution of the war than had been my father's as a captain at the front, I am condemned to the role of an impotent spectator, while we repeat the same mistakes that we made in the first war so that our people are being driven headlong to another catastrophe. How much happier one would have been as a soldier, relieved of all necessity to think for oneself! Those who have sought refuge from their share of political responsibility in the ranks of the armed forces are spared the nightmare of having to gaze into the abyss that yawns daily before my eyes.

With my official pass I could cross the frontier and emigrate any day I liked. Three or four times a year I have to go abroad on official duty. I have friends everywhere, who would give me and my family asylum, and I have contacts which would help me in the future. I don't think I should ever lack for money. But the very thought of decamping makes me feel sick. As long as the troops at the front continue to fight and the State, of which I am a servant, continues to exist, I shall continue to do my duty. Furthermore, I have lived abroad too long not to realise that the way of the political emigrant is stony indeed. The British, they say, agree with Napoleon, who declared that he loved treason, but despised the traitor. One might add that the traitor who abandons a bad cause is lower in the eyes of his fellow men than a man who betrays a good one, since his action has required less courage.

Whenever I am in Lisbon or Stockholm, I always have a guilty feeling when I think of all those to whom the respite of such excursions into the world of peace are denied. I almost miss the bombing.

Saturday, July 31, 1943
A report which I have drawn up for 'Diplo' reads:

On July 29, 1943, the Swedish Government abrogated the Transit Treaty with Germany regarding the passage through Sweden of members of the German armed forces and war material. This treaty was signed on July 8, 1940. The Swedish Government declared itself prepared to allow men proceeding on leave from Norway to travel through Sweden and vice versa. It further undertook to permit the transportation through Swedish territory, within the technical limitations imposed by the available means of communication, of all goods, including war material, from Germany and the German occupied territories to Denmark and Norway. As its reason for the abrogation of the treaty the Swedish Government has stated that the conditions under which the treaty had been signed have now ceased to exist. The Swedish Government at that time had acceded to the German request, it is stated, in the anticipation that Germany would create in Norway a military occupation government, which would put an absolute end to hostilities in Norway and ensure for the Norwegian people a reasonable measure of peaceful existence. This expectation has failed to materialise. The continuance in force of the treaty, the statement continued, placed a burden on Sweden's policy of neutrality towards Norway and constituted a strain on the friendly relations established between Germany and Sweden.

The Swedish Government's arguments do not hold good at law and are inaccurate in fact. The German-Swedish Treaty of July 8, 1940 bears the signature of the then Swedish Foreign Minister, von Gunther, and is a document that is equally binding on the Swedish Foreign Secretary and the Swedish Government. It contains no abrogation clause and it specifies no limitations as regards the period of its validity. It therefore remains valid for as long as Germany remains in occupation of Norway.

When the Swedish Foreign Minister hinted at the possibility of the abrogation of the treaty in his speech at Eskilstuna on May 7, 1943, the German Government invited his attention to the fallacies contained in his reading of the treaty. The Swedish Foreign Minister thereupon gave an assurance that the Swedish Government had no intention of curtailing the transit of men proceeding on leave, provided that no state of emergency arose which was militarily embarrassing to Sweden.

No such state of emergency has arisen. Apart from that, the text of the treaty contains no such restrictive reservation. Nor is there any mention in the treaty of specific preliminary conditions such as those invoked by the Swedish Government in its announcement of July 29.

The abrogation of this treaty is incompatible with Sweden's policy of neutrality. On May 7 in Eskilstuna Herr von Gunther, speaking of the policy of neutrality of his country, declared: 'In general terms it can be said that neutrality imposes an obligation to maintain an impartial attitude towards the belligerent nations and, above all, to prevent one's own country from becoming a theatre of war or a base for the conduct of military operations.'

91

Herr von Gunther stated that with the cessation of hostilities in Norway a situation had arisen, in which it was in Sweden's interest that she should review her own position and come to certain logical conclusions. In accordance therefore with the considerations examined (i.e. considerations of how to strengthen Sweden's position as a neutral power) the Swedish Government concluded two treaties: the first permitted German soldiers proceeding to and fro on leave to travel through Sweden, and the second placed at the disposal of the British Government six hundred thousand tons of Swedish shipping. 'It is obvious,' remarked Herr von Gunther, 'that this was of great practical importance to Britain.'

If the Swedish Government cancels the treaty with Germany, but leaves that with Britain in force, it will be guilty of a unilateral breach of its own neutrality.

This episode sheds a symptomatic light on the neutrals' assessment of our chances in this war. The Swedes are trying to make friends with the side which they consider is the more likely to win. Their attitude does not surprise me. I have never had any illusions about the political mentality of the Swedes. While the Swiss were the most hostile of all neutrals as long as Hitler was going from victory to victory, they became much more benevolent as soon as our fortunes began to wane; the Swedes have done exactly the opposite. As soon as Germany's waning powers became obvious, the Swedish obsequiousness of the early years of the war, resulting from our active policy in Denmark and Norway, was followed by a series of attempted stabs in our back. I am quite certain that as the fortunes of war turn further against us, we shall suffer plenty more of them.

August 1943

The exodus from Berlin continues – Rumours about 'secret weapons' which will win the war for us – German negotiations with Badoglio – More terror-attacks on Berlin

Tuesday, August 3, 1943

Our two divisions in Sicily have stabilised the situation for the time being. But, if Badoglio capitulates, shall we succeed in getting them away to join up with our forces north of the Apennines? Our occupation of northern Italy continues. In Milan and other big cities the atmosphere is tense. If we decide to defend northern Italy against its will, I presume we shall set up a rival fascist government there with, if possible, Mussolini at its head.

After we had decided to continue to support Mussolini and fascism, the press received instructions to make up for the absence of articles on Mussolini's birthday by giving great prominence to the birthday present sent to him by the Führer.

It now transpires that the Fascist Grand Council, in voting against Mussolini, did not appreciate the full implications of its action. The intention, apparently, was merely to curtail his powers somewhat. In fact, as a result of the vote, not only the Duce but the whole of the Fascist Council have been thrown overboard. The appointment of Badoglio came as a complete surprise to the fascists. Many had been quite sure that Grandi or some other Party man would be nominated as the Duce's successor.

As has so often happened before, reports from our Embassy in Rome have been beneath contempt. Doertenbach was the first man from the Embassy to be received finally by Badoglio.

Berlin is threatened with the same fate as Hamburg. On Saturday night leaflets were dropped on the city, calling upon all women and children to leave at once. The railway stations are being besieged by seething mobs. There is an air abroad as though the end of the world were imminent. The hot weather, with temperatures reaching 95 degrees Fahrenheit, has increased people's fears of incendiary bombs. Rumour has it that the attack will take place on

August 8, the second anniversary of the beginning of our air raids on London. People go to bed early, sleep uneasily, glance at the clock every time they wake up and are relieved when dawn at last comes and the danger, for the time being at least, is past.

Thursday, August 5, 1943

Today brought a typical example of how our Foreign Ministry works. I had drafted a 'political report' dealing with Turkey's silence with regard to the violation of her neutrality by British and American bombers, which have been flying over Turkish territory on their way to Ploesti. Braun von Stumm was unwilling to pass the memorandum and telephoned to Henke, the Under-Secretary of State and head of the Political Section, who replied that it was the first he had heard of the whole affair. Despite the fact that for two days now the press has been publishing reports of enemy bombers flying over Turkey, that eight of these aircraft have been compelled to make forced landings in Turkey and that our Embassy in Ankara has submitted detailed reports on the subject, the head of our Political Section remained blissfully unaware of the whole event.

Friday, August 6, 1943

The cancellation of the Transit Treaty by Sweden has made things difficult for our troops in Norway. The Commercial Section of the Foreign Ministry claims that eighty per cent of the traffic will unobtrusively still be able to get through as before. I have my doubts, since the Foreign Ministry has a way of throwing a cloak of secrecy over diplomatic defeats and lulling the outside world into a belief that it still holds all the trumps.

The question of how, from the publicity point of view, we ought to handle the British terror raids has again cropped up. Hepp, who returned from Sweden yesterday, says that people there have no idea of the havoc wrought in Hamburg. Not a soul in Sweden realises that there have been more than fifty thousand killed. Most Swedes presume that these attacks are reprisals for our previous raids on Coventry and are on much the same scale. Since we have kept silent about it, the neutral world is unaware that chemical warfare is now playing its part in the war in the air.

The exodus from Berlin continues. Although an assurance has been given that the authorities will not leave the city, lorries are drawn up before every Ministry, loading furniture and luggage. On every side one sees military transport vehicles, loaded for the most part with private effects. Objects of cultural or artistic value, on the other hand, cannot be removed from the city, because there is said to be neither the transport nor the petrol available. To move anything of this nature, prior permission has to be obtained from the Institute of Culture, and that takes a great deal of time.

The Swiss Legation has received advice from Berne to get out of Berlin before August 15.

Tuesday, August 10, 1943
In an article, 'The Battle of Berlin', the *Washington Post* describes the capital as an industrial centre, the second biggest inland harbour in Europe, the continent's greatest railway junction and the political centre of Europe. The article concluded with the sentence: 'Any dislocation of its life would cause disorder and confusion throughout the whole of the Nazi empire. The battle of Berlin may well prove to be the decisive battle of the war.'

Wednesday, August 11, 1943
A directive dated August 5 gives details of the alternative accommodation ear-marked for officials of the Foreign Ministry in the event of the destruction of their offices. From the detailed addresses quoted, it appears that the Foreign Ministry is at present occupying twenty-two buildings in seven different postal districts of the city. Before Hitler took over, it was housed in one block of buildings, 74-76 Wilhelmstrasse, At the time we maintained diplomatic relations with every State in the world. Today, in the fourth year of the war, our diplomatic relations are confined to seven neutral States, and to maintain them we have an establishment of several thousand officials and subordinates. And that, if you please, in a country which professes to think only in terms of Divisions! We all of us agree with Schmidt that the present crisis is a crisis of leadership and the Party, both of which have shown themselves incapable of rising to the gravity of the situation. During the Hamburg catastrophe, only the Army and the German Red Cross remained at their posts. The Civil Defence

Force failed so badly that the burning down of whole quarters of the city is being attributed to the cowardice shown by the wardens. In Berlin, too, there are no orders of any kind which would compel wardens, in the event of an alarm, to supervise movement of the people into the shelters and to post themselves on the roofs, as is invariably done in London. Nor are the 'Lords of the Party' required, at moments of crisis, to tour the threatened sectors of the city. Instead, most of them leave the town every evening, to sleep in peace and security outside. The trains arriving in Berlin are filled with women and children, none of whom have been warned that they should not return here.

I have been told to draft a note to neutral Governments, protesting against the methods employed by those in charge of enemy operations in the war in the air, and in particular against the use of phosphorus incendiaries. This task had in the first instance been allotted to the Legal Department, which took the view that there were no legal grounds on which complaints against the methods used in the Hamburg air raids could be based and submitted a correspondingly negative report. Fortunately, the Secretary of State did not agree. In any other country the Legal Department of the Foreign Ministry would spare no pains to formulate legal arguments in justification of a complaint of this nature. One cannot help wondering what is going on? The Legal Department took three whole days in which to produce its elaborate and useless memorandum. My draft was completed in three hours and was accepted, with minor modifications, by the conference of Directors.

On July 31 Lesko, the Director-General of Civil Air Defence, held a press conference in the Ministry of Propaganda on the subject of the Hamburg air attacks. In the extremely lively discussion that followed his statement, the journalists refused to be in the least intimidated by the presence of so high an official, and Lesko was compelled to make some very noteworthy admissions. To the question why the measures he had just announced were only now being put into operation, all he could say was: 'We all know, you and I and the whole of the German people know, that we had never anticipated attacks on this vast scale. You seem to have forgotten the events of the opening stages of the war, which created a situation in which it would have been quite impossible for us to foresee that one day attacks on this scale would later descend upon us.' To a journalist who wanted to know why the report on the Hamburg raids had not been circulated and made available to all civil defence workers, Lesko replied: 'Reports drawn up by the Air Civil Defence Association cannot be circulated until after they have been scrutinised by the Minister of Aviation and Commander-in-Chief of the Air Force and passed on to his Air District Commanders. These are military questions, upon which I am not empowered to issue any orders. Furthermore, reports of this nature must be treated as secret documents – they must, that is, be restricted in their circulation to a certain level in the administrative machine, below which items from it are passed on by word of mouth. One thing, however, I can tell you: In view of the severity of recent attacks, the Commander-in-Chief of the Air Force is considering the possibility of a swifter release of these reports to the nation as a whole.' (This is an extract from the official minutes.)

For some time now rumours have been circulating about secret weapons which are about to be used and which will change the whole aspect of the war in our favour. Nearly everybody knows somebody who was present when these weapons were being tested. Some people talk about a bomb which will be fired by rocket from an aircraft and contains an explosive force sufficient to wreck a whole city. Others declare that the new projectiles will be fired from specially constructed bases on the French coast. The people eagerly swallow these fairy-tales. Faith in the wonder-weapon is at present the one thing which stimulates their morale. The dressing-room attendant in the Rot-Weiss Tennis Club, for instance, told me that if it weren't for the wonder-weapon, we'd throw our hands in. In the spring of 1918 people were banking in much the same way on a long-range gun which was to bombard Paris.

Thursday, August 12, 1943

Lanza has given me his impressions of the talks between the German Foreign Minister and Guariglia, the new Italian Foreign Minister, at which he was present: The atmosphere was at first frosty. Guariglia's entourage had the impression that the gentlemen accompanying the German Minister showed no desire to engage them in friendly conversation. After the first session, however, the atmosphere improved and eventually became excellent.

In the whole of his ten years' experience he, Lanza, had never before heard such straightforward speaking. Guariglia had infused a new spirit into the Italian Foreign Ministry. First-class men had been detailed for this meeting with the German Minister, among them the new Italian chargé d'affaires, Count Ruggieri, who is regarded as one of the best brains in the Palazzo Chigi and will undoubtedly be a great asset to the Italian Embassy here.

Lanza assured me that the Italians now believe that the war need not be lost, provided we can hold out for another year. Since the assumption of power by Badoglio, the enemy had made so many psychological mistakes in its handling of the Italian people that the prospects of Italy's continuing to fight on have been greatly enhanced. Whether Badoglio would succeed in remaining in office was questionable. There was no doubt that the majority of the people desire peace. The events in Milan and other big Italian cities had opened the eyes of thinking Italians to the seriousness of the communist menace in Italy. Badoglio admittedly commanded great respect, but had he the political skill to master the internal situation? The King, on the other hand, was acting with great acumen. Fascism had been destroyed by the stupidity, the lack of imagination, the corruption and the general lack of human qualities of its supporters. Lanza said that the Germans would be making a great mistake if they tried to bolster up fascism. In view of the present temper of the Italian people, support for fascism would be senseless. He described the fascist broadcasts from Germany as a psychological error. Within three days of Mussolini's resignation the Italian Embassy here had been informed, he told me, of Germany's determination to restore the fascist régime. This was no trump card in German hands. On the contrary, it would split Italy asunder and merely hasten her collapse. Germany, he said, must associate herself with the political platform on which all Italian patriots had now taken their stand and where the point at issue was not one of personalities or political systems, but the question of the preservation of the Italian State and people and their place in Europe.

Lanza raised the question of the possibility that negotiations between Germany and Russia might be initiated. He felt that even the hint of such a possibility would greatly improve the political atmosphere. The Italians, he said, were now more convinced than ever that Germany could not defeat Russia and were wondering whether she herself did not realise it and would not be ready to draw the logical political conclusions.

The choice of a new Italian Ambassador for Berlin, he thought, presented his Government with an awkward problem. Had Alfieri not attended the meeting of the Fascist Grand Council, he would undoubtedly have retained the post. But he had obeyed the telegraphic summons to attend without taking steps to find out why the Council had been convened. Had he had any inkling, he would probably have remained where he was.

Lanza then mentioned the visit he had paid with General Marras to the Führer after Mussolini's downfall. Both Italians had been impressed by the Führer's calm reaction to the Italian nightmare, which seemed to have thrown his entourage, on the other hand, into a state of considerable panic.

Friday, August 13, 1943

Dined with Werner Blumenthal at his fourth-floor flat in the Lützowplatz. Blumenthal is a typical self-made man, of whom there are not many in Germany. As a former cadet-officer thrown on to the streets in 1918, he signed apprentice articles with the firm of Winter, which held the Berlin agency for the Opel cars. Within ten years he had risen to become co-director and partner in the firm. Shortly before the war, Winter and Blumenthal sold their business to General Motors, who had taken over the Opel concern. With the proceeds of the sale they bought aircraft and parachute factories. Blumenthal is the only German civilian who flies about Europe in his own private twin-engined aircraft. In his factory, aircraft are repaired in half the time taken by the Air Force workshops.

Just before midnight, as I was taking my leave, the sirens began to howl. We decided to make for the air raid shelter in the neighbouring Spanish Embassy. With some difficulty we found the entrance, groped our way from one pitch-black room to another, struck a light and eventually found ourselves confronted with one solitary man, lying on a camp bed and wearing a dressing-gown: he turned out to be the Ambassador himself!

The attack itself lasted only half an hour, but, as frequently happens, the flak units seized the opportunity to have a long practice shoot – a habit which disturbs the population and is the subject of numerous complaints.

Friday, August 13, 1943

Among Werner's guests was Burkhard Preussen, who as a prince of the royal blood must now leave the Army and is taking on a job with IG Farben. Recently he had been liaison officer with the Spanish Blue Division in the northern sector and told us that the Spanish soldiers had far better luck with the Russian girls than did the Germans. One of their gambits was to have women's clothes sent to them from Spain, which they then distributed among the local maidens. A few have married Russians, though these marriages are not officially recognised by Munoz Grande, the Spanish Divisional Commander. The Russians seldom dare to attack in the Spanish sector. They fear the Spaniards far more than the Germans. The valour and tenacity of the Blue Division have earned high praise at German headquarters.

Thursday, August 19, 1943
Yesterday's issue of the *Frankfurter Zeitung* confirmed that the newspaper would cease publication after August 31. The *'Frankfurter'* was the only German paper which was still being read abroad. The editorial staff is to be distributed among the German press organs. According to Schmidt, the Ministry of Propaganda is anxious to prohibit the three *Frankfurter* correspondents, Irene Seligo, Margret Boveri and Lily Abegg, from writing for the press in future. Schmidt is doing his best to save these three outstanding journalists for the Foreign Ministry. A Swiss paper, commenting on the closure of the *Frankfurter Zeitung*, calls to mind Bismarck's famous comment on another newspaper, when he said that the *Kölnische Zeitung* was worth an army corps to him. What sort of mentality must a government possess, which, in the fourth year of a war, liquidates an army corps!

Monday, August 23, 1943
Himmler has been appointed Minister of the Interior and Frick Protector of Bohemia and Moravia. This has not yet been announced in the press.

Several versions of the death of General Jeschonnek, the Chief of the Air Staff, are in circulation. One of these would have it that he died as the result of a serious illness; another asserts that he committed suicide in despair over the weakness of our anti-aircraft defence, which was not even able to prevent the attack on our experimental installations in Peenemünde.

Thursday, August 26, 1943

On the night of Monday, August 23, the alarm sounded at 11.40. It was followed by a long pause, which is always a sinister sign. The flak opened up half an hour after midnight, and things soon became so hot that we went down into the cellar. The firing continued till 1.45 a.m. and the 'all clear' was not given till 2.30. Once someone shouted: 'The house is on fire!' Armed with a regulation stirrup pump we rushed upstairs but could see no sign of conflagration. Later we found out that a flare had dropped in the courtyard and had illuminated the whole place.

We heard about the devastating results of the attack the next evening, when Freddy Horstmann asked me to drive him to Kerzendorf in Tino Soldati's car. He had come into town in the morning, but had been unable to take his usual route via Marienfelde and Tempelhof. For the return journey we therefore took another route. In the Kaiserallee we came upon the first signs of destruction. The Bulgarian Legation in the vicinity had been reduced to powder by an air-mine. In Steglitz, Friedenau, Lichterfelde and Marienfelde we came upon places through which it was impossible to pass by car. Craters filled with water, heaps of rubble, fire-hoses, pioneers, firemen and convoys of lorries blocked the streets, where thousands of those rendered homeless were searching the ruins, trying to rescue some of their possessions, or were squatting on the pavements and being fed from field-kitchens. Although eighteen hours had passed since the attack, fires were still burning everywhere.

The tramway lines had been destroyed. Burnt-out buses jammed the streets. Hundreds of trees had been shattered or bereft of their branches and foliage. Of one block of single-family houses all that remained was one solitary chimney. Notices everywhere gave warning of unexploded bombs. In the pale, dust-laden sky, the red, fiery ball of the evening sun glowed like the harbinger of the Day of Judgment. On the edge of the city herds of cattle wandered untended among the ruins. Then suddenly, beyond the town, destruction ceased. The first village, Grossbeeren, which is six kilometres from Berlin, remained unscathed. What a contrast between the torn and twisted profile of the giant metropolis and this countryside, dozing in the peaceful evening sunshine! The next morning we passed by the burnt-out works of Henschel and Siemens in Tempelhof. The attack had been plunged into the heart of Berlin, like a knife into a cake, and had sliced out a great triangle, the apex of which stretched as far as the Zoo railway station. There the last bomb fell in the Hardenbergstrasse, destroying the local military headquarters, blowing the roof off the High School of Music and smashing every window in the vicinity.

On the two following nights there were again alarms. Small formations of Mosquitoes dropped bombs, which caused no great damage, but which sorely tried the nerves of the population. In the areas which had been stricken twenty-four hours earlier thousands were still wandering about the streets, because no transport was available to take them away. On the faces of the poorest among them was written clearly the fear of another night, which, helpless and homeless, they would have to face. The official figures speak of 245 dead, two thousand injured and thirty-five thousand rendered homeless.

The question on everybody's mind is – was Monday's attack the beginning of the end, or was it merely a warning shot, designed to bring home to the Berliners the might of the Royal Air Force? The British state that seven hundred aircraft participated in the attack. Four hundred were definitely established by us, and of them sixty-one are claimed to have been shot down. The British put their losses at fifty-nine aircraft. On our side three hundred fighters engaged the enemy, some of them flying in from far afield. British reports state that the attack was directed by a pathfinder aircraft which cruised over the city and issued its orders to the seven waves of attacking bombers by radio-telephone. As at Hamburg, the British dropped metal strips to confuse our radar defence installation mechanisms.

No one dares try and prophesy what may happen in the next few days. The press and Army communiqués say very little about the attack. Opinions on how we are to angle our publicity with regard to these terror-attacks still vary. Yesterday, for example, the Ministry of Propaganda forbade the publication of the following Reuter report: 'Churchill's cook doesn't bother in the least about bombs.'

A few days ago, before an audience of German editors, Dietrich, the Press Chief, inveighed against the Italians, to whom he attributes ninety per cent of the blame for our military failures. *Sonderführer* Schrott, his representative in Paris, passed on his remarks to the French press. The Paris communiqué came to the ears of the Italians, who at once protested.

September 1943

The Horstmanns entertain regally while the bombs drop on Berlin: their country mansion is destroyed – 'Will they come tonight?' – Italy: 'unconditional surrender' – Mussolini liberated

Monday, September 6, 1943

We have just heard the dreadful news that Freddy Horstmann's house in Kerzendorf, thirty kilometres from Berlin, was badly damaged in last night's air raid. This small estate, with its miniature chateau built by Rnobelsdorff, is one of the most beautiful and elegant country seats in the vicinity of Berlin. Until fairly recently it was occupied by the Schwabach banking family, and then marriage connections brought the place into the possession of Freddy Horstmann, who transferred there the whole of his art collection. While Knobelsdorff was carrying out the work of restoration under Freddy's expert supervision, the Horstmanns installed themselves temporarily in the 'Cottage', a villa erected in the park about the turn of the century. Freddy believed that here his superb collection of furniture, pictures, books and Gobelins would be safe from air attack, and the catastrophe has been a bitter blow to him. The little chateau, which was still in process of redecoration, has been completely gutted, including all its hand-carved wood panelling, although it was hit by only two incendiary bombs. Unfortunately no one was there to combat the flames, and, in any case, there was no water. Not even the safe, in which the most valuable pieces of Dresden china were kept, was able to resist the fire. Ironically enough, a number of jars of preserves and pickles in the same room escaped undamaged. One incendiary fell between the stables and the cottage and caused the whole of the latter with the exception of the library wing to collapse. Freddy's bedroom was only partially damaged, but the two superb drawing-rooms filled with art treasures, and Gloria's and Lally's rooms above them were reduced to a great heap of rubble. Freddy and Lally, covered with dust and sitting, gazing at the ruins of their home, were a picture of misery. Nevertheless Freddy insisted on getting tea for us, which we drank, together with the Inspector, sitting some fifteen yards away from an unexploded bomb. Meanwhile we were told that, because of the 'dud', we should all have to vacate the estate, and Freddy does not know where he will be able to take anything that may perhaps be rescued from the ruins.

Freddy has not received the slightest assistance from the authorities. They have not even bothered to remove the unexploded bomb. So, with the help of two Serbian prisoners of war, I set to work myself. We cleared Freddy's partially damaged bedroom and then, despite the danger of further collapses, we groped about the ruins of Lally's room, looking for her jewels. Maria Dalen and Christa Tippelskirch came out from Berlin to lend a hand, and together we rescued Gloria's wardrobe almost completely undamaged. After five hours of searching in the debris we unearthed Helene Biron's jewels. All the cases had been burst open, and Christa Tippelskirch, working with a child's spade, saved jewel after jewel from the rubbish. Towards evening we came across a cupboard containing Gloria's and Marietti's jewellery and some first editions. It was difficult to get at the splintered cupboard, since part of the roof had collapsed on top of it; but we succeeded in salvaging the jewel-cases, and a Picasso belonging to Richard Kühlmann.

The next day I succeeded in getting a party of an officer and twenty men from the Potsdam Commandant, and they are to set about the task of clearing the place today. In the stables, where Freddy had stored the furniture from his Brussels and Lisbon legations, quite a lot of things seem to have survived the catastrophe. Cases containing Augsburg silverware and Dresden dinner services were balancing precariously in what was left of the first floor.

All the estates and villages in the Kerzendorf area were badly hit. Most of the crops have been burnt. The attack had obviously been directed against a munitions works, hidden in the Ludwigsfelde forest; but the attackers failed to find it, and it remained unscathed.

The Kerzendorf idyll is over: now the Horstmanns have nothing but their flat in the Steinplatz in Berlin, which they rented shortly before the outbreak of war, when their own house in the Tiergartenstrasse was requisitioned, and which they had furnished with exquisite taste. Originally envisaged as somewhere to spend the night when they wanted to go to a theatre in Berlin, this little *pied-à-terre* has now become the last genuine *salon* in Berlin. A whole book could be written about its owners.

Freddy Horstmann reminds me of one of those figures from the heroic period of American capitalism. His round head rests on powerful shoulders. Bushy, iron-grey eyebrows and a sea-dog's beard frame a face which radiates intelligence, energy and *joie de vivre*. All in all Freddy closely resembles one of those American millionaires who, when the *Titanic* sank, accompanied their fur- and jewellery-bedecked wives to a lifeboat and then, smoking a Havana, returned to the ship's ballroom to await their end, listening to the music of one of Strauss's waltzes.

Lally has been blessed with rare beauty. Beneath a snow-white forehead, encircled by raven locks, sparkle a pair of eager, vivid eyes, whose pupils contract by day, only to blaze like those of the denizens of the night forest as soon as the lights go on. The pallor of her face and the voluptuousness of her mouth are in strange contrast to features which at times seem almost negroid. Some ten years younger than her husband, with whom she fell in love at the age of sixteen, Lally might well be Freddy's daughter. And in one sense she is, for it is he who has moulded her, and at his side she leads an entirely unselfish existence that affords a delightful contrast to her own vivid interests.

Socially, the Horstmanns come from the upper middle class of the imperial era. Freddy comes from Frankfurt, where his father, the proprietor of the *Frankfurter Generalanzeiger,* left his children a considerable fortune. Lally is the daughter of the Berlin banker von Schwabach and his wife, a member of the patrician Hamburg family of Schroeder. Like the Mendelssohns, Oppenheims, Weinbergs, Friedländer-Fulds, Bleichröders, Goldschmidt-Rothschilds, Rathenaus, Guggenheims, Hahns, Salomonsohns, Fürstenbergs, Klemperers and Guttmanns, the Schwabachs were members of a circle of exclusive Jewish families, which, in the liberal atmosphere of the Empire, had achieved wealth and social position and lived in aristocratic style.

Affluence and inclination combined to lead Horstmann to the diplomatic service. As a young Attaché in Paris, where he learnt to play polo in the company of French dukes, he quickly became one of the *jeunesse dorée* of Europe. Towards the end of the first war he was attached to the staff of Richard von Kühlmann, who conducted the peace negotiations in Poland and Rumania and later became a Secretary of State. Horstmann reached the zenith of his diplomatic career as Minister in Brussels and then in Lisbon, where he became a host of European repute.

When the Horstmanns moved into their house in the Tiergartenstrasse in Berlin a few years before the war, the parties they gave very quickly became famous. Anyone who aspired to scale the social ladder did his utmost to become an accepted guest at the Horstmanns. Joachim von Ribbentrop was one of them. It proved to be a fateful encounter. As Foreign Minister, Ribbentrop had achieved his greatest ambition, and he offered Horstmann the post of Head of the Foreign Ministry Chancery, a post for which Freddy was ideally suited. Unofficially attached to this offer, however, was a condition which Freddy was not for a moment prepared to consider: he would be required, he was told, to divorce his half-Jewish wife. He preferred to send in his resignation and sacrifice a career to which he was utterly dedicated.

The impact made by his uncompromising refusal was all the greater, because those who envied him decried him as a mere social butterfly, describing his imperturbability as frivolity and his wisdom as cynicism. Apart from that, this was an era in which no very great value was attached to loyalty. Divorces as a means of advancement were very much the order of the day. [In the fifth year of the war the devotion of this happily-married couple was destined once again to be put to the test, when Ribbentrop informed Horstmann that he could no longer vouch for the safety of his wife, but was prepared to grant facilities to both of them to emigrate to Portugal. Horstmann advised his wife to accept the offer. He himself could not face the thought of emigration. But in the end Lally, too, refused to leave her husband.]

The Kerzendorf disaster has lent the Steinplatz *pied-à-terre* a character it was never intended to have. The residence consists of only three rooms facing the street plus a few back rooms. Horstmann, who has lorded it over so many palatial mansions, has now showed himself to be a master of the art of compression. The drawing-room also serves the Horstmanns as a bedroom. The whole interior is reminiscent of a Paris mansion, the walls being lined with wooden panelling, the windows, which are protected by steel rolling blinds, are framed by red damask curtains and pelmets, and the ceilings are painted with frescoes of clouds which give the whole place the classical atmosphere of the *Grande Epoque:* why, even the WC itself is encased in an authentic Louis Quinze arm-chair! A bronze bust of the *Roi Soleil* himself confronts the visitor in the entrance hall and makes it quite clear to him whose spirit reigns within these walls. Liveried menservants in blue tail-coats over red waistcoats conduct the newly-arrived guests to the threshold of the reception room where he is sure to be welcomed by the master of the house with a cry of 'What a great pleasure!'.

The solving of his personal problems is giving Freddy many a headache. His old servants have all been called up for service with the police, but come and work for their old master in their free time, whenever they can. Freddy is averse to having temporary servants in the house, having in the past caught one or two of them listening at the keyhole. Although he asks his guests not to indulge in political discussions, not all of them obey the rule. This applies particularly to foreign diplomats, who find in the war situation an inexhaustible topic of conversation, from which it is not easy to divert them. A confirmed cosmopolitan and at the same time a passionate patriot, deeply concerned though he is about his wife, Freddy is far too proud to bandy words with foreigners about conditions in Germany. But in private, with his friends, he sometimes opens his heart, and then, indeed, he finds it hard to restrain his tears.

Most of the diplomats appointed to Berlin come armed with a letter of introduction to the Horstmanns and are entertained by them even before they make their official calls and present their credentials to the Head of the State. Although there are a few other households in Berlin which entertain foreigners, the diplomats themselves are inclined to assess the social standing of their colleagues according to whether or not they are received by the Horstmanns. The members of the Foreign Ministry are advised to avoid attending receptions in the Steinplatz – though they might well learn there the lost art of how to receive one's guests. Quite a number of them, lacking in moral courage, follow this advice – an attitude which robs Horstmann of contact with his former colleagues and pains him deeply.

Horstmann likes to refer to his home as 'an evening beauty', because it is under artificial fight rather than in daylight that the full effect of its beauty is revealed. Before the war, his table decorations were veritable works of art. One hour before dinner was due to be served, for example, water-lilies would be gathered from the Buckow lake, brought to Berlin by car and then mingled on the table with water-lilies of Berlin porcelain. Another theme would be based on Dresden china parrots encircling a gilded cage filled with real humming-birds. For his Moorish dinners the decor would be provided by black Dresden figurines. In the years following the First World War, when so many princely collections came under the auctioneer's hammer, Horstmann amassed a great number of beautiful things. In this way he acquired superb vermeil, magnificent Augsburg silver and some pieces of the Dresden 'swan dinner service' which had been made for the Czar; Count Bruhl boasts of a duplicate set in his chateau at Pförten.

Malicious folk compare the soirees at the Horstmann establishment to a circus, but they are way off the mark in comparing the Horstmann formalities with the kind of organisation needed to launch a circus.

In this age of cocktail parties Horstmann still adheres to the reactionary idea that everyone present is under an obligation to make his contribution to the success of a social gathering, even if he does no more than arouse a measure of interest among some of the other guests. To be invited to the Horstmanns one must be either intelligent or wealthy, possess a handsome presence or be the bearer of a well-known name. Power and influence, regardless of the sphere in which they may be exercised, are welcome. To Horstmann, a gifted writer is as welcome as a dim-witted prince. Of women he demands verve and elegance rather than ancient lineage. But anyone fabulously rich is permitted to be stupid.

'Launching' new people gives the Horstmanns immense pleasure. Helga Nehring, the young daughter of a Grunewald lawyer, was introduced in this way into Berlin society which she now adorns with her classical beauty. Countess Gloria Fürstenberg, a Mexican by birth, owes her triumphant progress in Berlin society to the Horstmanns, who gave her so many brilliant opportunities of displaying her vivacious and witty personality.

The war and the air raids have caused Freddy to modify the timing and the style of his soirées. The crashing of the bombs and the thunder of the flak in the nearby Tiergarten leave him completely unmoved, or at the most elicit from him a sign to the servants to close the shutters more tightly in order to shield the ears of his guests from the din of the air battle.

Tuesday, September 7, 1943
Life is becoming ever-increasingly dominated by the war in the air. The behaviour of the Berliners has, on the whole, been marvellous. We get plenty of practice in dealing with incendiary bombs and the correct use of sandbags and stirrup-pumps. An incendiary which pierced the rafters of our house gave us some trouble because the bomb had stuck in an inaccessible place in the woodwork between the two storeys. The enemy aircraft have an unpleasant habit of dropping explosive bombs on areas already set on fire by incendiaries. The last attack caused its greatest havoc in Siemensstadt, along the northern circuit of the *S-Bahn* railway system, in the Müllerstrasse in north Berlin, in the Hohenzollernplatz, and in the Fehlbellinerplatz. Pieces of a shot-down bomber fell on the Komodie Theatre in the Kurfurstendamm and on the roof of the Strempels' house. In the Marchstrasse a metal fragment of the aircraft crashed through a furniture van filled with the Doernberg's household effects. Another lorry, laden with goods which Toni Soldati was sending to Switzerland, was burnt out in front of the Lehrte station. Bolko and Viktoria Richthofen's house in Schmargendorf was hit for the third time during the war and burnt to the ground this time.

Every evening the main topic of conversation is always: 'Will they come tonight?' Last night everybody was certain that there would be a raid, though no one seemed to know why. Hans Flotow gave a small dinner-party, attended by Missi Wassilschikoff, Lorimarie Schonburg, Aga Fürstenberg and Bernd Mumm among others. We talked about nothing but the air raids. The whole thing reminded me of a meeting of persecuted Christians in the Roman catacombs!

The Russians are advancing swiftly all along the eastern front. We are now forced to retreat across the Dnieper. Where it will all end no one dares to prophesy.

The audience granted to the Orthodox bishops by Stalin has caused considerable surprise here, since the powers which rule that country have closed minds as far as Church and religion are concerned.

We spent last weekend at Gramzow, Werner Blumenthal's hunting-lodge, now leased to the Portuguese Legation and an ideal place in which to enjoy an undisturbed sleep and a real rest. Unfortunately, his female cook fleeced us of coupons for six hundred grams of meat and five hundred grams of butter – the equivalent of of a whole month's rations!

Friday, September 10, 1943

In Italy the anticipated end has now come. Only the form of the capitulation has caused some surprise. I heard the news over the Deutschlandsender on Wednesday, September 8 at 11.15 p.m. At 1.00 a.m. Schmidt rang up and asked me to think over the question of what tone we should adopt in our propaganda announcements. The official slogan from above is that the King and Badoglio are both traitors.

It is interesting to note that although the armistice was signed on September 3, it did not come into force until the 8th. Between these dates not only was there quite a lot of fighting, as for instance in Calabria, but there were also air raids on Naples and Frascati, the latter directed against our Headquarters there. I wonder whether Badoglio knew about that beforehand? The capitulation is described as 'an unconditional surrender'. Why, then, did negotiations continue for three whole weeks?

Badoglio's proclamation, which is not to be published here, contains some logical arguments. Italy's sole wealth lies in her architecture, which would have been destroyed, had the war continued. If we condemn Italy's defection as a betrayal we should also bear in mind that for the past three years the Italians have been feeling that we have betrayed them. Again and again they have complained that we were not giving them authentic information regarding the situation on the eastern front and that we have consistently refused to consider the Mediterranean as the decisive theatre of war. They overlook the fact, of course, that Italy came into the war of her own free will, when she was certain that we should win and was anxious to be in on the division of the spoils.

From the military point of view, Italy has become just one more of our many enemies. The Supreme Headquarters spokesman who gives us a daily report on the military situation informs us that in northern Italy we have already taken seventy-five thousand prisoners and that our Air Force has sunk an Italian battleship and chased several other warships back into their harbours. A German-Italian Oran? In this war, nothing is impossible!

Politically, we can free ourselves from all the problems with which Italy had burdened us. We are now in a position to make peace with France, solve the Croat question and do our best to achieve a reconciliation with the southern Slavs, including the Serbs.

The 'national-fascist' Government, of which Farinacci, Pavolini and Preciosi are members, remains shrouded in mystery. Nobody knows where these gentlemen are living, nor what authority they may actually possess. They govern in the name of Mussolini, whose present whereabouts is unknown. As the stubborn resistance shown by the garrisons of Bolzano, Merano, Triento and Bologna has proved, feeling in northern Italy has turned against us. But Milan, Genoa and Turin were handed over without a fight, and Rome with all the Tiber bridges is in our hands.

The members of the Italian Embassy here have been placed under house arrest. They have been given the choice either of declaring their adherence to the fascist government or of returning to Italy. The majority will probably choose the latter. Only Torso, Giretti and Culturi, who have married German wives, have intimated that they would like to remain here.

On Tuesday evening we dined with Count Tovar, the Portuguese Minister, and Fräulein von Paleske, the daughter of Frau von Dirksen. After dinner Tovar took us to the Ufa-Palast cinema, to see a film, *Der unendliche Weg*, which deals with the life of Friedrich Liszt.

Tovar, a small man with an intelligent, aristocratic head, has sent his wife back to Portugal. Paintings of the Countess remind me of Velasquez' Infantas. The Portuguese Legation is housed in the Palais Deutsch on the Lutzowufer, a mansion recently rebuilt by the architect Breuhaus. The mirrors in the dining-room, the marble floors, the walls of the living-rooms lined with grey silk and the gilded furniture give the place an air of unreality. It becomes increasingly difficult to visualise the sort of life for which all this was intended.

Tovar told us that many years ago a rich lady in Lisbon adopted two poor children, in order to give them the chance to pursue their studies. One of them, he said, is Salazar, the present Prime Minister, and the other is now Cardinal Primas.

Saturday, September 11, 1943

The Führer's speech yesterday evening has outlined the official attitude concerning events in Italy. It was, perhaps, the toughest speech that Hitler has ever made, and it was certainly the shortest. It is always a difficult task for a statesman to explain a political misfortune. German policy can reasonably be reproached for not foreseeing that such a development might need to be faced up to. Italian national character has changed as little as has Italian national policy. With the experience of 1915 in mind, we had all the more reason to be on our guard. In Germany we were far too ready to believe what we wanted to believe, namely, that Mussolini and fascism had transformed the Italian people. Since Hassel's departure the reports received from our Quirinal Embassy have contributed their share to the strengthening of this wishful thinking on the part of our leaders. There is really little point in publishing a White Paper which shows us to be honourable idiots. We all know that now, anyway. What we ought to do is to rid ourselves of gullible information officers who, year in year out, gobble up every scrap of tendentious news dished up to them.

I heard the Führer's speech in the Hotel Adlon, where I was dining with Franzi Schmidt. Public apathy was symbolised by the fact that the speech was not relayed to the dining-room, as previously, and that in the small lounge where a loudspeaker was installed, not even a quarter of the hotel's guests bothered to listen. Most of the audience consisted of cooks, waiters and maids.

Perhaps political interest would be greater if our information service facilities were better and more extensive. A few days ago I received a letter from Dr Frick, the former Minister of the Interior and present *Reichsprotektor* of Bohemia and Moravia, in which he repeats his request to be placed on the list of recipients of *The German Political Report* for which I am responsible. About a fortnight ago Major Radtke, Frick's adjutant, had telephoned me, asking if this would be possible. Schmidt rejected the request at that time on the grounds that distribution of political information was made in accordance with instructions issued by the Führer and that no additions could be made without the sanction of higher authority. All I can do now is to send on Frick's letter to Ribbentrop, who – perhaps – will submit it to the Führer for his instructions.

Even for members of the Reich Cabinet restrictions have been imposed which one can only describe as grotesque. How can any Minister be expected to assess the political situation under such circumstances?

The Italian Embassy here has left Berlin *en route* for Munich. When the party will continue its journey is uncertain. Ridomi, taking his leave of Schmidt, presented him with a parting gift of a box of chocolates! What an exit at a moment like this!

Monday, September 13, 1943

Yesterday's sensation was Mussolini's liberation, which was announced about eleven o'clock by the *Deutschlandsender* in a special communiqué. But have we, I wonder, done him a real service? The fascist leader has, admittedly, escaped for the time being falling into the hands of the allies, and his liberation has prevented the allies from putting him on trial. But what of Mussolini's political future? Situations may arise in the life of a politician in which honourable captivity is preferable to a somewhat questionable form of freedom.

It was not until he was on the way to Hitler's Headquarters that Mussolini was told about the return of Dalmatia to the Croats and about the fighting that has broken out in northern Italy between the Germans and the Italians. A new policy statement regarding Greece was cancelled just in time. When he reaches German Headquarters, the Duce will hear that four hundred thousand Italian prisoners are in our hands and on their way to German labour camps. In these circumstances, what role can the unfortunate statesman possibly play? He cannot expect that, out of consideration for him, we shall be prepared to cancel a single one of these measures; after all, he probably commands the support of less than five per cent of the Italian people. Mussolini has nothing to offer us, either in a political or in a military sense. To quote an English phrase: Italy 'will have to take her place in the queue', not only with the allied nations, but with us as well.

On Sunday I attended the consecration of a memorial tablet to Bogislav and Hans-Melchior Studnitz in Buderose. The ceremony, with military honours, was short and impressive. The mansion in which my father and Bogislav were born passed, after the death of an uncle, into the possession of the town of Guben, which placed it at the disposal of the association of war poets. Since then the house and park have been falling into disrepair, and the destruction of this lovely eighteenth-century building has been completed by an Air Force detachment stationed in its vicinity.

On the evening train back from Guben I obtained a seat in a first-class carriage reserved for officials; the four elderly gentlemen who were already occupying it were engaged in such an animated discussion that they regarded my presence as an unwarrantable intrusion. They turned out to be senior railway officials, but none of them had the courage to ask whether I was entitled to travel in a compartment 'reserved for officials'. At the next station, when a lady modestly asked whether she might occupy the vacant seat, the four roared with one voice: 'This compartment is reserved for officials'. The lady mildly mentioned that she had a first-class ticket and that the railway, surely, was not justified in selling more first-class tickets than it had first-class places to offer, whereupon the most venerable of the four blandly exclaimed: 'My dear lady, don't you realise there's a war on?'

Wednesday, September 15, 1943
The liberated Duce is already involving us in political difficulties. Out of consideration for 'the new partnership', we are marking time not only as regards the Balkan problems, but also as regards our policy towards France.

Friday, September 24, 1943
I have been spending a few days with the Geyrs in Adolfinenhof (Jankovo). Since the spring, discrimination in the Warthegau against the Poles has been on the increase. All over the place one sees notices: 'Germans only' or 'Poles not admitted'. Even the schools remain closed to Poles, so that many Polish children have had no schooling for four years – a somewhat remarkable contribution to 'the colonisation of the East'. In Posen, Hohensalza and other places the air raid warning sounds every few days. These are mainly British or Russian aircraft dropping agents, arms and pamphlets.

In many ways the Wartheland gives the impression of being better cared for than the 'old' Reich. The cleanliness of railway stations and restaurants is very evident. In Thorn, in the station lavatory I actually heard the woman attendant tell a man to stand closer to the urinal!

The bombed-out refugees transferred from the Reich to the Wartheland are finding it hard to settle down. The East is too primitive for them. Many of them leave the smaller places because, they say, they cannot live without the cinema and electric light. This means that the trains are always overcrowded. Refugees from Cologne, Essen and Hamburg are all doing their utmost to return to their homes, because there they will receive additional ration cards, which they do not get in the East. These additional ration cards are issued in areas exposed to air attack with the object of strengthening the moral and physical resistance of the population. The Baltic refugees have settled down much more happily.

The return journey to Berlin was extremely uncomfortable. At Thorn station a crowd of children pushed their way on to the train and completely overran the only sleeper. When I finally succeded in finding the guard, there was not a berth to be had. Thanks to a twenty-mark tip, I was eventually allowed to board the train and was told that a berth might be available from Bromberg onwards. But another passenger, whom the conductor had left out of his calculations, put in an appearance, and my hopes for a berth faded. Nearly all the sleeping-berths were occupied by BDM-girls [the girls' section of the Hitler Youth Movement] and elderly women, travelling to Hamburg, where they would get supplementary ration cards. I spent the night on a tip-up seat in the corridor, next to a labour office clerk who was ill and over whom his mother fussed all night. To protect myself against the bitter cold I stuck my feet into a mailbag.

In the middle of the night a military patrol appeared, and I was asked whether I was entitled to travel in a sleeper? When I produced my official pass, the patrol commander slapped his thigh, giggled and said: 'Interesting, very interesting. I give up trying to keep order on this train'. He was accompanied by a Gestapo man, who spent the whole night drinking coffee with the sleeping-car conductor. At Bromberg and Schneidemuhl stations there were indescribable scenes, and hundreds of would-be passengers were left behind. One man with a falsetto voice tried to push his crippled mother into the sleeping-car after forcing her bath chair into the guard's van. The captain waved him back with the remark that pansies were not entitled to travel! One woman claimed a place because her home had been completely destroyed in an air raid. With a derisive laugh the captain retorted that the same thing had happened to him –

three years ago. And so it went on. Every now and then one of the compartments of the sleeper would open and a pyjama-clad figure would emerge, *en route* for the lavatory, to reach which he would have to clamber his way past me. As we approached Berlin – the attendant had woken everybody up two hours too soon – the train came to a halt, on account, it was said, of an air raid. At last, at eight o'clock, two hours late, we crawled into the station.

Monday, September 27, 1943

When I got back, I found a mountain of paper waiting for me in my office. When one is away for a few days and dependent for news solely on the German radio, one instinctively assumes that nothing much has been happening. It is only when one gets back that one hears that Churchill has made a speech, that Roosevelt has broadcast a message to the world and that a dozen more nightmarish situations have arisen. The military situation is deteriorating rapidly. On the eastern front our retreat has reached the line of the Dnieper. Fighting is in progress before Kiev. The evacuation of the Kuban bridgehead has begun. The Donetz basin is once more in enemy hands. The Japanese, too, are becoming uneasy about the situation in the East. Members of their Embassy have told Bassler that the worst thing about our retreat is the fact that we have been compelled to evacuate areas which we could have offered to the Russians as pawns of exchange in any peace negotiations.

In Italy we have evacuated Salerno. In these circumstances the drafting of official announcements becomes a bitter task.

Tuesday, September 28, 1943

This morning I had a visit from Hans Köster, the Transocean correspondent in Rome, who returned from Italy three days ago and compared the Italians to a boxer, lying slumped over the ropes and waiting for the count. The indifference of the people, he says, is absolute. When the armistice was announced there had been scenes of indescribable enthusiasm. Italian soldiers travelling by train at the time had fired all their ammunition into the air in sheer delight. Fascism, Köster asserts, is dead, and nothing on earth will resuscitate it. He had vainly sought to find anyone who still sported a fascist badge, so that he could report the fact to Berlin! We were treating the Italians pretty roughly, he said. At the moment everything that could be moved and was not an absolute and permanent fixture, was being confiscated and sent to Germany, including commodities such as textiles and leather goods. In the Venice hotels even the bed-linen had been confiscated. Anti-German feeling is increasing rapidly among the population. The food situation was also deteriorating, though it was still possible to get a good 'black' meal.

As regards conditions in our Embassy, Köster says that many of the women secretaries wanted to remain in Rome, because they would prefer internment by the British to being returned to bomb-shattered Germany.

Köster, the son of a German Minister to Belgrade and a mother who made a name for herself as a painter, is the kind of impassioned reporter who is rarely to be found in German journalism. On the outbreak of war he went first to The Hague, then to Stockholm and after that to Lisbon. We talked about the days when he and I had been together in London and about the circumstances under which, in the autumn of 1938, Carlos Pückler and I had been compelled to leave England, as a result of intervention by the Reich Press Chief. In our reports Pückler and I had hinted pretty plainly that Churchill would become Prime Minister, that Britain would participate in the war against Germany and that she would prove very hard to defeat!

Among the capers in which our policy towards Italy is at present indulging is the attempt to implicate the Crown Prince Umberto as an accomplice in Badoglio's and the King's 'treachery'. Although not a shred of evidence exists to implicate him, those at the top are insisting that proofs of his complicity be forthwith obtained. Now, after a fortnight of diligent searching, Rome has unearthed something or other. The information submitted, however, is of so paltry a nature, that Schmidt has refused to release it to the press. Umberto is accused, for instance, of having shot the fiancée of a *carabiniere*. The fact that Badoglio's daughter took cocktails with the Crown Prince is portrayed as the height of depravity. The only thing that might be held against him is the fact that he has never shown overmuch enthusiasm for fascism. On the other hand, he has equally never shown himself to be anti-fascist. I remember that on more than one occasion the Duce declared that his relations with the Crown Prince were excellent. And not very long ago Germany conferred a high Order on him.

Wednesday, September 29, 1943

Leo Fürstenberg told me that on September 4 the OKW invited the Economic Section of the Foreign Ministry to a conference to be held on September 8, for the purpose of clarifying the question of the withdrawal of German credit notes from France. He, as the relevant authority concerned, was informed of the invitation on September 28!

The *Deutsche Allgemeine Zeitung* of September 29 contains an article written by a war correspondent, entitled 'The Rome of the Traitors'. In it the author says that 'even now, in the third year of the war and despite the introduction of coupons, show-windows and shop-counters in Rome are never short of the things which contribute so much to the graciousness of life.' He then goes on to complain that at the main railway station in Rome taxis and porters are still to be had, and that 'midday strollers along the Via Veneto still enjoy excellent ice-cream sundaes and chocolate biscuits at Rosati's and preen themselves in their well-cut English style suits.' And he finishes by noting with surprise that a measure of aversion to Germany is becoming apparent in Rome. The *Völkische Beobachter*, the Third Reich's leading newspaper, casts reproaches at Alexandra Kollontay, the Soviet Ambassadress in Stockholm, because in her youth she was pretty, dressed well and was an advocate of free love. For these characteristics our *Völkische Beobachter* dubs her 'The Commissar of All the Prostitutes'! These two articles are typical of our complete lack of understanding of other peoples.

October 1943

Terror in the air: Hanover, Hagen, Kassel and Frankfurt bombed – Missions to Madrid, Lisbon, Paris – The French demand a Franco-German peace without annexations

Saturday, October 2, 1943

Hungary has chosen a curious way in which to signify her recognition of the Mussolini restoration. On September 30 the Hungarian press published an official communiqué, which stated that the German Minister in Budapest, von Jagow, had handed the Hungarian Foreign Minister, Ghyczhy, a message from the German Government, saying that the German Government had recognised Mussolini and asking the Hungarian Government to do likewise. The communiqué added that the German Minister was also presenting this request in the name of Mussolini, since the latter had no representative in Hungary to present it on his behalf. The Hungarian Foreign Minister, the communiqué continues, has replied as follows:

Heir Reichsaussenminister!
Allow me to convey to Your Excellency my particular thanks for the information that Benito Mussolini has formed a government. The existence of the government will be recognised by the Royal Hungarian Government.

As I am not at the moment in a position to establish direct contact with the Duce, I would request Your Excellency to be good enough to convey this to the Duce and at the same time to inform him that the Hungarian nation will never forget what he has done for it and remains eternally grateful to him.

I am,

Sir,

Your obedient servant,

Ghyczhy

Our Legation in Budapest states that it had no part in the framing of this communiqué and had not been informed of its contents.

The *Gazette de Lausanne* describes the attitude adopted by the Hungarian Government as 'a masterpiece of diplomatic adroitness'.

Tuesday, October 5, 1943

Today Urach returned from Italy. He says that the anarchy in Italy is a triviality in comparison with the anarchy that rages in German official circles. The struggle for precedence is being conducted more ferociously than ever. Every German department has sent its own representatives to Italy, where they are waging a furious war against each other. The German domination of the country is being exercised by enclaves, between which little or no liaison exists. It is not even possible to telephone from Rome to Milan. In the Ancona area guerilla bands of escaped British and American prisoners of war are operating. Astonishingly, the food situation has improved since the abolition of the rationing system. The people are obviously eating up their last reserves in anticipation of Anglo-American deliveries. Prices on the black market have fallen considerably. As Urach passed through Bolzano he saw a sight that is typical of the times. On one line stood a train bound for Germany with British prisoners of war under escort of fascist Italian Militia. On the line next to it stood another train filled with captured Italians of the Badoglio faction, under German guards; and between these two trains French prisoners of war were at work, repairing the track. The British prisoners were having great fun, showing their ample stocks of tinned food to the Badoglio Italians.

Today is the tenth anniversary of the coming into force of the German Press Law. To mark the occasion, Dietrich has issued the following statement:

> Today, German journalists will recall the passing, ten years ago, of the German Press Law. I cannot allow this anniversary to pass without expressing my conviction that the clear distinction drawn in this law between the journalistic and the economic functions of the German Press has proved to be a rich blessing, both for journalism and for the German people. Ten years ago today the German Press, which at the time did not enjoy the best of reputations, started along a path that has led to publicity successes of historic stature and to achievements that have earned for the profession of journalism the increasing esteem of

both our leaders and our people. The great moral test which the German Press has successfully passed during these years of war will ensure for journalism that place in the eyes of the nation, to which, in view of its heavy responsibilities as the political mentor of the people, it is entitled, since the introduction of this law, to lay claim. The last ten years have revealed a high degree of honest and vigorous devotion to duty, of responsible work in the field of publicity, of indefatigable endeavour to give moral and intellectual guidance, and the German Press can be proud of what it has already accomplished. By transforming our Press once more into a source of moral national strength, we have set our eyes both on the present and the future. By exhibiting to the German people in their hour of greatest trial an implacable fortitude, and by radiating fanatical determination, we shall bring to a successful conclusion the task which we began on October 4, 1933. We shall make not only newspapers, but history itself. We are acting not merely as the servants, but as the accredited representatives of our people and as the co-architects of their future. With these thoughts in mind, I wish to thank German journalism for having during these last ten years infused life into the letter of the law, and I am convinced that this devotion to duty on the part of the German Press will not be denied its due recognition, both now and in the future.

The terror in the air has started again. During the last week Hanover, Hagen, Kassel and Frankfurt have all been bombed. The enemy is becoming increasingly cunning in the methods he adopts. In the attack on Kassel the British aircraft first flew to Hanover and released hundreds of flares over the town, with the object of deceiving our defence forces into believing that Hanover was the main target of the attack. Then, without dropping a single bomb, they flew off to Kassel and rained down everything they had.

Madrid – Thursday, October 7, 1943
At 8.30 a.m. yesterday I left Tempelhof airport for Spain. At the airport I met Rütger Essen, who had brought the Baroness Beck-Frijs, the wife of the Swedish Minister in Lisbon, to catch the same plane. I thus found myself in pleasant company for the journey.

Apart from his post in Lisbon, her husband is also accredited to London, where he is the Swedish representative with the Norwegian Government-in-exile. At Barcelona, the Baroness had to break her journey because the plane was apparently fully booked on the Barcelona-Madrid sector and the airline in Berlin would only give her a reservation as far as Barcelona. My attempt to intervene with Lufthansa on her behalf failed. Later I found that only four passengers were making the onward flight; the remaining places were filled with air-freight, consisting for the most part of propaganda leaflets. A typical example of the ineptitude of our foreign propaganda. All the leaflets in the world would not make good the damage caused by the Baroness's resentment at the enforced interruption of her journey, which lasted for several days. For had she wished to catch the night train from Barcelona that same evening, she would have had to make her sleeping-berth reservation three weeks in advance, and to stand any chance of getting on the day train the next morning she would have been forced to queue all night long on the platform.

From Lyons onwards we were given a fighter escort. While at Lyons airport I could not help noticing the contrast between the warlike attitude of the German aircrew who were to provide our escort and the carefree demeanour of a French film unit shooting some scene or other on the edge of the runway. Before we took off from Lyons we were each given a 'lunch-box', the sole contents of which were one piece of stale corn bread, one worm-eaten apple, a few slices of beetroot and three lettuce leaves.

On landing at the Madrid Barajas airport I went and visited Lazar, whose house is full of the most beautiful antiques. I am staying at the Ritz, which is still, as it was before the Civil War, the happy hunting-ground of the wealthy, who shave at four o'clock in the afternoon, dine at eleven at night and spend the intervening hours chattering in the hotel lounges, bars and coffee houses.

Madrid – Friday, October 8, 1943

Yesterday the Lazars gave a dinner-party, to which they had invited the Mayaldes, the Montarcos, the Seefrieds, Betta Werthern and the Yebes'. Yebes is one of Romanones' sons and is Casilda Mayalde's uncle.

Today I visited the Prado with Casilda. We began with the El Grecos, passed on to the Velasquezes and ended with the Goyas. In the basement we glanced at the Duke of Alba's collection, which is being housed in the Prado until his palace, which was burnt down in the civil war, has been rebuilt.

Thanks to new bequests made to it, the Prado collection is now even richer in content than it was before the Civil War. In the Velasquez collection I was much impressed by the blond beauty of the Spanish Habsburgs. With the exception of Philip II they were all big men with fresh, frank faces. Even the portraits of the children radiate royal dignity. Goya's kings on the other hand – Carlos IV and Ferdinand VII – seem to be the personification of stupidity and degeneracy. That the Court should have tolerated these scurrilous portraits is proof of the liberalism of the epoch. Any painter who thus caricatured the great men of the present day would probably be given ample opportunity to ponder over his masterpieces – in a concentration camp.

I lunched with Gloria Fürstenberg in an Andalusian *taverna*. She is as beautiful and elegant as ever, but has grown thinner and has many troubles on her mind.

Madrid – Saturday, October 9, 1943
This evening I visited Dieckhoff. The Ambassador has acquired an insight which is all too rarely to be found among the politically so hopelessly inept Germans. In Madrid he is somewhat overshadowed by his predecessor, von Moltke, who in the three short months he was here acquired an almost legendary reputation, to which his famous name and imposing presence contributed more than a little. Because von Moltke had a large family, the Spaniards presumed he was a Catholic. In fact he is a member of the evangelical church, while Dieckhoff, who is a Catholic, is thought in Madrid to be a Protestant.

Madrid – Sunday, October 10, 1943
Had a drink with Agathe Ratibor, Hexe Podewils and the Duke of Tetuan, an old friend of Civil War days.

In the evening I dined in town with the Lazars and the Seefrieds. Later we met Gloria, Agathe and Federico in a night club which closed, however, at one o'clock. Gloria and Agathe are being boycotted by the German Embassy because they have exceeded the period for which they had been granted permission to be out of Germany. In addition Gloria had had the bad luck to be photographed by an English illustrated magazine while breakfasting in Madrid with the British film star, Leslie Howard. Shortly afterwards the aircraft in which Leslie Howard was returning to England was shot down over the Bay of Biscay by a German fighter.

One afternoon Gloria took me to a cocktail party at the X's. Since the end of the civil war the Xs have withdrawn to a sixteen-room flat on one floor of their vast palace. The couple, between whom there is a great difference in age, live together under one roof, but have so arranged things that each can follow an independent existence. The Marquésa, for instance, has a self-contained apartment which can be entered only through a secret door and which she can enter or leave unobserved. While I was there, three separate parties were in simultaneous progress on the same floor. As soon as a fresh guest was announced, the hostess gave orders for him to be shown into this or that room, according to his political opinions. The guests in one room had no idea who were the guests being entertained in the other two. From one of the rooms a door led into the host's bedroom, where he himself was in bed, suffering from lumbago but with a score of friends round him trying to cheer him up. When we went in, the patient was so exhausted by the sheer number of fellow noblemen pressing around him that we sent for a member of the Falangist Council to come and amuse him with jokes against the Franco régime. The aged Marqués had married his wife in order to be able to continue a relationship with her mother whom he had met while riding in the vicinity of his castle.

Lisbon – Monday, October 11, 1943

Early yesterday morning I went with Herr von Grote to the Escorial, where Dieckhoff had invited the Duchess of Durcal, Princess Isabel Metternich and ourselves to lunch in the summer-house of his predecessors, Stohrer and von Moltke.

After lunch we went to the 'Silla' of Philip II', a look-out point from which the King is said to have supervised the building of his monastery-castle. From it one has a clear view which stretches across the Sierra de Guadarrama and the Castilian plain as far as Madrid itself. But it was a view which we were unfortunately not allowed to enjoy in peace. When we got there we found fifteen cars from the Japanese Embassy, the occupants of which were swarming over the hillside, laden with picnic baskets, drinks and cameras. When they caught sight of Dieckhoff, the whole lot of them hastened up to us, to shake the hand of the German Ambassador.

Dieckhoff tells an amusing story about the Japanese Ambassador. An *aficionado* of bullfighting, this oriental diplomat is a regular attendant at all the arenas, where his box is surrounded by a claque of enthusiasts, who follow his lead whenever he gives a sign of approval or disapproval. If a bull of which the Ambassador shows disapproval enters the arena, the *toreros* refuse to start the contest, and this has led to complaints by the organisers to the doyen of the Diplomatic Corps.

Lisbon – Tuesday, October 12, 1943

There are trains three nights a week between Madrid and Lisbon. The 'Lusitania Express', a sleeping-car train, also runs three times a week and does the journey in fourteen hours. It is typical of travel facilities in Spain that both these express services run on the same days of the week. On the other four days one is dependent on an ordinary train, which takes twenty-seven hours. I left Madrid at nine o'clock in the evening and reached Lisbon at midnight the next day. We stopped for four hours at the frontier stations of Valencia de la Alcantara and Marvao, and we lost a further two and a half hours at Entroncamento, where we had to change.

The day I reached Lisbon manoeuvres were in progress. Once a week the town is blacked-out. By order of the police, strips of paper have to be gummed on all windows as a protection against the blast of exploding bombs, and the chromium parts of cars have to be camouflaged with blue paint. Gossip has it that all this sticking and painting has been engineered by an English firm, which has thus managed to sell its entire Portuguese warehouse stock to the local inhabitants. Others say that the Government is well aware that these measures are useless, but decided to introduce them in order to test the discipline of the nation. I am staying at the Avenida Palace Hotel, an ancient and extremely noisy building near the station.

Lisbon – Wednesday, October 13, 1943

The German Legation here has a staff of two hundred and forty, compared with the eight hundred in the Madrid Embassy, and are distributed in office buildings all over the city. Hüne occupies the mansion in which Freddy Horstmann spent the best years of his career. The Minister divides his visitors into two categories – those whom he suspects of being after his job, and those whom he does not suspect. In view of the very large number of those in Berlin who are pulling every string they can to get transferred to a neutral country abroad, I think his differentiation is a justifiable one.

Hüne exercises tight discipline over his subordinates, including the senior administration. He likes the Portuguese and they like him. The news broke today of the Azores agreement between Portugal and the Anglo-Saxon powers. Hüne is worried because Salazar, with whom he is on good terms, had given him no hint of what was afoot and Berlin first heard about it from Madrid, where Jordana broke the news to Dieckhoff.

Breakfasted with Odal Knigge. Among the guests were the son of the well-known industrial magnate Otto Wolf, and his young wife and Krehl the lawyer, who has been the administrator of the estates of both the last two Queens of Portugal.

I spent the evening with the Seligos, who have a delightful little house, which figures in Irene Seligo's *Delphina*.

Lisbon – Thursday, October 14, 1943

Lunch with the Hünes and Eggerth, the Consul-General, whom I had met in Jerusalem shortly before the outbreak of war. After lunch we discussed the Azores question at considerable length. In the afternoon Klein gave a tea-party in the Press Section, which was attended by local journalists and the Director of Propaganda. I dined with Ricardo Espiritu Santo, a friend of Freddy Horstmann and the owner of the foremost private bank in Portugal; the bank is housed in a fine old palace down by the harbour. Dinner, which was served on Chinese porcelain and with superb old Portuguese silver, was graced by the presence of the banker's four lovely daughters. After dinner we had a long discussion about political matters.

Madrid – Friday, October 15, 1943
Midday visited Major Fell, correspondent of the *Scherl-Verlag* in Lisbon. Then cocktails with Claus in the Palace Hotel. The bar was full of English people, mostly women and children, returning to England from America and waiting in Estoril for their air passages. The departure time of all flights is kept secret, and the passengers are only informed shortly before take-off. Dinner at the home of Klein, the Press Attaché. Later we went on to the Casino, which presented a forlorn aspect.

Flew back to Madrid at 11.00 a.m. At the airport Count Berold-ingen, the Lisbon head of Lufthansa, told me that he had received orders from Berlin to take over an Italian civil aircraft, which had been in Lisbon since Italy's defection, and send it to Berlin, with the crew as passengers. He has no idea how he can possibly carry out this order successfully.

The Duke of Maura was also a passenger on this flight, and further up the aircraft was a Swiss courier supervising the transportation of sacks of prisoners of war mail, which has priority over passengers.

Madrid – Saturday, October 16, 1943
Midday visited Lazar and then to the Mayaldes' home in the Calle Velasquez. Expedition to Toledo, to Pepe's *finca, El Castañar*. A strange feeling to be driving again, after so many years, along the Madrid-Toledo highway, through all those bitterly contested villages which I had known so well during the Spanish Civil War, when I had been a journalist reporting the news from the front. We passed through Torrejon de Valasco, Illescas and many other little places made famous by history. The landscape has not changed – melancholy stretches of open country, sun-baked yellow earth, clay-coloured peasants' huts, and cathedrals soaring above them into the implacable blue of the Castilian sky. In Toledo we went to see El Greco's *Burial of Count Orgaz* in the San Antonio church, and the El Grecos and Goyas in the cathedral. Pepe Mayalde is a well-known figure in Toledo. From alleyways and unexpected corners people came running to greet him, and beggars pressed forward to kiss the hem of his coat. When we reached the *finca* about six o'clock in the evening, we were asked with the customary Spanish formality whether we would take

tea, or dine, or partake of a cocktail, and whether we proposed to remain in Castanar or would prefer to dine in Toledo itself? Or, finally, whether it would not be better, after all, to give dinner a miss and go for a walk instead! In the end we drank tea and ate a dish of partridges. The *finca* embraces a whole range of hills, in which it is said that genuine bandits and wild pig still roam. The mansion, built forty years ago, overlooks a vista of gardens dotted with oak and olive trees. The Mayaldes' children sleep in a room as big as a ballroom, from the walls of which old masters watch over their slumbers. When the lord of the manor arrives, all his dependants come to greet him. They gather in a circle round his car and do not budge from the spot until he departs again. Many of them carry guns over their shoulders. This same patriarchal atmosphere is to be found throughout the countryside, where the relationship between master and man has lost none of its significance, though this did not prevent the peasants from murdering their squires when the Civil War gave them the chance!

Lunch at Tertsch's home with Victor Laserna and some Spanish journalists, who are highly indignant at the press censorship imposed upon them. The Spanish press labours under even greater difficulties than the German and Italian papers. Even non-political jokes are forbidden; no jokes allowed about men, because they are the breadwinners of the family, or about women, because as mothers they are entitled to our respect, or about children, because they are the greatest treasure the nation possesses. All the same, the Spaniards, in contrast to the Italians, enjoy a joke against themselves.

At Tertsch's I ran into Spitzi, who now has interests in Spanish industry. This adds yet another chapter to his variegated career, which led him via a post under Ribbentrop and the London Embassy to the Berlin Coca-Cola organisation and then a job as an official interpreter with the armed forces.

Meanwhile, Badoglio has declared war on us. A Third Secretary of the Italian Embassy, who had recently been transferred from Lisbon to Madrid, called on Dieckhoff, who at first refused to receive him, because he could see no reason for such a visit. The Italian, however, was so persistent, that in the end Dieckhoff agreed to receive him. The moment he entered the Ambassador's room, the Italian emissary drew a letter from his pocket and handed it to him. The first few lines revealed to Dieckhoff that this was a declaration of war. He refolded the letter, gave it back to the Italian and showed him the door, whence he was conducted to the street by Stille, Dieckhoff's major-domo, to ensure that he did not succeed in delivering the letter to any other member of the Embassy. The evening papers published a statement issued by the Italian Embassy, saying that Italy's declaration of war had been handed to the German Ambassador. Dieckhoff sent for Jordana, told him exactly what had happened and succeeded in having a *démenti* published in the Spanish press.

This episode had been preceded by an abortive attempt by Dieckhoff to enlist the support of the Italian Ambassador, Marchese Palucci, for Mussolini. Although Palucci had served Mussolini for many years as secretary, he had decided in favour of the King. But as the Reich's representative in Madrid was most anxious that the Italian Embassy there should remain on the side of the Axis, he hit upon another plan and had Berlin arrange for Mussolini to telephone Palucci. For this purpose the unsuspecting Italian was invited to the German Embassy, where his conversation with the Duce could take place undisturbed and could, at the same time, be monitored. The little plot failed, however, to achieve its purpose.

Paris – Tuesday, October 19, 1943

On Saturday I caught the night train from Madrid to Paris, breaking my journey at San Sebastian in order to spend a day revisiting the city in which I had spent so many weeks during the Civil War. When we crossed the frontier into France at Hendaye, my papers were inspected by a German Military Police officer, who tried to persuade me to join him in some illegal currency transaction. When I refused to play, this representative of German sovereignty tried to involve me in a racket he had organised involving the smuggling of perfume from France to Spain! Two thousand mounted troops were expected to arrive in Hendaye on the following day, to take over supervision of the frontier.

In Paris, Sieburg had got a room for me at the Ritz; half of the hotel is reserved for the Commander-in-Chief's guests of the rank of General and above, while the other half remains available for

French civilians. The dining-room was teeming with German generals, Foreign Ministry emissaries working with the archives commission and the usual crowd of war hangers-on whom one meets all over France. From the hotel lounge I watched German generals arriving in official limousines at the rate of about one a minute laden with packages apparently so precious that they could be entrusted neither to an orderly nor to a bellboy, since they insisted on carrying their goods personally to their rooms. The French staff of the hotel regards all this with an air of somewhat contemptuous benevolence.

The Embassy is in the charge of Schleier, a former cheese merchant. Schwendemann is head of the Press Section. He controls the whole of the French information complex, from the daily newspapers and periodicals down to the children's comics. The Press Section is installed in a building near the Embassy in the Rue de Lille, equipped with superb furniture appropriated from the Russian Embassy and the Quai d'Orsay. Who was responsible for this filching of other people's property on foreign territory I have been unable to find out.

Paris – Thursday, October 21, 1943

Parisian good taste is still triumphant, even in the fifth year of the war. Whether it be some luxury article or something of quite ordinary, everyday use, there is nothing here which is not beautiful to look at – a great contrast to our shops at home, in which one rarely sees anything that is not hideous. Many of the articles on show are made of substitute material. Shoes with wooden soles and ladies' handbags made of cloth are so beautifully finished, that no one bothers to buy the genuine article, which is still obtainable in the black market. The French have even created new fashions, based on the prevalent dearth of things. Felt is in very short supply, so the Parisian ladies go about tranquilly in turbans, which no woman in Berlin could wear without evoking cat-calls. Cars and horse-carriages are hard to come by, so the fashionable world has taken to the bicycle. One afternoon I went with Sophie Barcelot to one of Jean Piguet's fashion parades; these are held every afternoon and are so popular that it is very hard to get in. Suits, morning and afternoon dresses and evening gowns were being displayed. Charming young women come round, selling the costume jewellery, ear-rings and brooches that the mannequins had worn during the parade. Prices are very high. An evening dress costs twenty-five thousand francs, a tailor-made costume fifteen thousand and an afternoon gown nine thousand. Model hats sell at three thousand francs, and a decent handbag costs at least 2,500 francs – all, of course, plus purchase tax. People here live as though there had never been a war, and certainly not a war that France had lost!

The manicurist at the Ritz tells me that coffee is no longer obtainable in the black market, because the operators are hoarding it for the Americans. I have not yet come across any anti-German feeling, nor have I seen any sign of the murderous attacks on Germans about which one has heard so much. Even late at night in the Metro, sleepy *Blitzmädchen* [female wireless operators] and soldiers in German uniforms returning to their billets do not appear to be in any danger at all. Incidentally, there seem to be more German soldiers in Paris now than there were two years ago. For every one combed out by Unruh for service on the eastern front, two new ones pop up. The many *Blitzmädchen* in their dreadfully cut uniforms, devoid of lipstick and make-up and with their hair-style *a la* Scholz-Klinck incite pity rather than murderous intent. On the other hand, their presence has resulted in a reduction in the number of liaisons between our troops and French girls.

Tea with Helene Biron, who occupies a suite in the mansion of her uncle, the Marquis de Jeaucourt, in the rue de Varennes, Faubourg St Germain. There I met the Beaumonts, Kalle Arco, Elisabeth Ruspoli, Ruvier and Megre, two of Lally's friends, and Sophie Barcelot.

In the evening I took Helene to the Lido, which has deteriorated, and its pretty dancers now appear in very second-rate costumes, before a shabby decor. Going home, the cabby charged us three hundred and fifty francs for a ten-minute drive!

Dined with Erich Richter in a Basque restaurant, which has transformed itself into a club, in order to be able to serve black market meals. 'Red' Spanish waitresses serve a good dinner, which cost us two thousand five hundred francs for three of us. In Horcher's Maxim's, the dearest place in Paris at the moment, the clientele is almost exclusively German. At the Ritz, which is also under German management, one can get a meal for a hundred and thirty francs, which would cost a thousand at Maxim's.

Reelkirchen – Sunday, October 24, 1943

Supper Thursday evening with Klee and Tankmar Munchhausen at the Ritz and then went straight to the station to catch my train to Germany. We travelled via Aachen, Cologne, Duisburg, Essen, Dusseldorf and Dortmund, which resembled collectively one gigantic national cemetery. Hamm was the first undestroyed town through which we passed. Marietti was at Bielefeld to meet me and we took the Detmold-Meinberg tram. During the journey, the air raid warning sounded, and we had to complete our trip on foot. For an hour and a half hundreds of aircraft roared over our heads. Suddenly a blood-red conflagration lit up the sky over Kassel. An air battle was raging immediately overhead, and five bombers crashed to the ground in flames. We fled into a farmhouse, to avoid being hit by flying fragments. In the village of Tintrup near Reelkirchen incendiary bombs had set fire to a haystack, and one of the bombers dropped a bomb on the blazing bonfire, blowing the roof off a neighbouring farmhouse. And all this occurred in the immediate vicinity of Reelkirchen and the house to which Marietti and Georgine had been evacuated from Berlin. So much for the safety of the countryside!

Friday, October 29, 1943

I have had talks with the French Ambassador Scapini and the Italian chargé d'affaires, Rugieri.

Since I last saw Scapini two months ago, his political views have stiffened. Two months ago he regarded a peace between Germany and France as acceptable on condition that the French coastline remained occupied and defended by our forces, and that Alsace should be retained by Germany, while Lorraine would be returned to France.

Now Scapini demands a Franco-German peace without any annexations, which would, he claims, be intolerable to the French people and would poison the atmosphere between France and Germany.

One of the ideas that he developed was that we ought to deprive the allies of the slogans under which they were fighting this war. Germany, he said, could kill stone-dead the 'war of liberation' idea simply by restoring the *status quo ante* and thus leaving nothing waiting to be 'liberated'. The 'fight for democracy' slogan would then die a natural death. Scapini suggests that France should sue for peace and Germany should grant it. He reminded me that in the autumn of 1940 and again in August 1941 France had desired a settlement with Germany.

The Ambassador then turned to the question of the care of prisoners of war and complained about the impossibility of finding, in Germany, a 'responsible' person with whom he could deal on the question. The psychological mistakes made in the treatment of prisoners were, he asserted, indescribable. Recently, he said, a prisoner had been sentenced to three years' imprisonment, simply because, on being released by the man for whom he was working, as a gesture of farewell he gave the farmer's wife and her daughter a kiss on the cheek. Despite all this, he said, the French prisoners of war had no feelings of hatred for Germany. When the Russian successes began, he had noticed a rising of spirits in the camps, because the men hoped that they would now probably soon be set free. But now, when the Russian successes are turning out to be far greater than they had anticipated, the one question they all ask is whether Germany has taken the measures necessary to prevent the Russians from overrunning the whole of Europe. They were very far from being pleased about the Russian successes.

Rugieri, who speaks fluent German, described to me the state of the members of the Italian Embassy who are interned in Garmisch. When he visited them at the end of September, most of them, he said, had become human wrecks. Lanza, Ridomi and the other twenty-odd had, in their isolation, come to the same conclusion as had the forty-five million Italians in Italy and had not come down on the side of either Badoglio or Mussolini, because they had ceased to care what sort of government was in power. Exactly the same thing applied to Italy itself, where the people simply cursed like hell the moment they were approached by either side. Moral and intellectual anarchy reigned supreme. In Milan and the other cities enrolment lists for the Fascist Party have had to be withdrawn again, because not a soul wanted to join. Rugieri faces the terrible situation in which his country finds itself with admirable courage. Fundamentally, he does not know, any more than does his chief, Anfuso, in whom he can place his trust. He tells me that the only members of the Royal family still at the King's side are the Crown Prince and the Duke of Bergamo. Alfieri, he assumes, has fled to Switzerland, while Ciano, at Mussolini's request, has been transferred from Bavaria to a place in northern Italy, where he awaits whatever fate is in store for him.

November 1943

The Russians continue to advance in the Crimea: will Rumania be lost? – Berlin: 'one vast heap of rubble'

Thursday, November 4, 1943

The most important outcome of the Moscow conference is, I suppose, the fact that the Russians have succeeded in persuading their western allies to agree to launch their second front at a place outside the Russian sphere of influence – not, in other words, in the Balkans.

Hitherto the British and Americans have been counting on the conflict between Germany and Russia continuing for a long period and with fluctuating fortunes. Now, however, they must be worried lest the Russians should overrun not only Germany, but most of the rest of Europe as well. They have therefore no time to lose, if they wish to establish a foothold in the heart of the continent. Italy has now become merely a subsidiary front. We must expect an invasion of western Europe early in 1944.

From the fact that Austria was mentioned in the Moscow communiqué it can be assumed that that country will be the most easterly territory to be occupied by the western allies, while the twenty-year treaty of alliance between Moscow and the Benes régime means that Czechoslovakia will be incorporated in the Russian sphere of influence. Although the division of Europe into spheres of influence has been denied in the Moscow communiqué, it can be safely assumed that some sort of demarcation line – probably along the line of the Elbe – has been agreed upon. As far as we are concerned, the possible developments appear to be as follows:

1. We drive the Russians back and frighten the western powers off any idea of invading western Europe.
2. The Russians continue to advance, and the British and Americans land in western Europe.

(a) We may succeed in repulsing the invasion and throwing the western allies back into the sea. In that case, there may be a chance of concluding a separate peace with the Russians.

(b) The invasion succeeds. We shall then be caught between the pincers of the armies of the western powers and the Russians; and as we shall have to continue to fight in the south, we shall be faced with a war on three fronts.

Monday, November 15, 1943

Spent the weekend at Schloss Lichterfelde with Leo and Ebba Fürstenberg. After cycling for nearly four miles in glorious moonlight I arrived just as the air raid warning sounded. Ten minutes later two bombs fell in the immediate vicinity.

We have stored some of our effects in Lichterfelde, some in Reelkirchen and in Kerzendorf, and the rest have remained in Berlin. Widely separated though they are, all these places have either been hit by bombs or gravely endangered by near-misses. Only my mother's house in Potsdam has escaped unscathed so far.

The air raid alarms nowadays usually sound between 7.30 and 8.00 in the evening, lasting for an hour at the most. These early attacks are much more convenient, for it does mean that, once the all-clear has sounded, one can eat in peace and go to bed confident of being undisturbed for the rest of the night.

Last Thursday Werner Blumenthal gave a dinner-party for Colonel-General Loerzer and General Dahlmann and their wives. Both are members of Goering's immediate entourage and both are rather like him in the manner in which they move and speak. Loerzer has the same eyes as his chief and was wearing a pilot's wings set with brilliants.

The Russians have thrust forward in the direction of Zhitomir, with the obvious intention of cutting off our southern Army Group. We hardly dare ask what is the present position of our Army in the Crimea, a force consisting of eight Rumanian and three German divisions.

Wednesday, November 17, 1943

Fierce fighting is in progress in the Zhitomir sector where we are trying to compress the break-through achieved by General

Vatutin's armies. According to Russian reports the break-through has occurred on a twenty-mile front.

Marshal Antonescu has informed the Führer that his position in Rumania will become untenable if his troops in the Crimea are lost.

Wednesday, November 24, 1943

We have lived through an indescribable experience and survived what seemed like the end of the world. On the return journey from Puddiger in Pomerania, where we had spent a restful weekend with the Blumenthals, we reached Stettin at about 8.00 p.m., when suddenly the lights were all extinguished and someone shouted: 'Air raid!' The train drew out of the station and came to a halt on the open line a few miles further on. We could hear the rumble of gunfire, and to the south of us a faint glow lit up the night sky. After halting for an hour, the train moved on again. We reached Angermünde about 10.00 that same night, and then Eberswalde at 11.00, where we were told that a heavy attack had damaged the permanent way. The train crawled slowly forward, and at about 1.00 a.m. we reached Bernau, where we were told that we should have to leave the train and continue our journey by the *S-Bahn* suburban train service, because the Stettiner station in Berlin had been put out of action. Changing trains was a difficult business, since the local train could not accommodate all the passengers from the express. Apart from this, in addition to our luggage, we had two animals with us – a dachshund puppy for Gini and a Christmas Eve dinner in the shape of a turkey. In Buch we came upon the first evidence of havoc. At 2.15 a.m. our *S-Bahn* journey also came to an end. At Pankow-Schönhausen we were all told to alight, without the slightest idea of how we could go on. The air was filled with acrid smoke. We comforted ourselves with the illusion that the attack had been directed against the eastern section of the city and, gathering up our possessions, we made our way forward as best we could on foot, hoping to reach the city by way of the Schonhausener Allee. We left our luggage in an emergency dressing-station, to which a constant stream of injured was being delivered. The puppy and the turkey we took with us.

After an hour we gave up the attempt to reach the Alexanderplatz. The air was so polluted with the smell of burning and with the fumes of escaping gas, the darkness was so impenetrable and the torrents of rain so fierce, that our strength began to fail us. Our progress was further barred by uprooted trees, broken telegraph poles, torn high-tension cables, craters, and mounds of rubble and broken glass. All the time the wind kept on tearing window-frames, slates and gutters from the destroyed buildings and hurling them into the street. At 4.00 a.m. we saw a light come on. We went into an inn, where newspaper-women had gathered to collect the newspapers for the morning delivery. From them we heard that it was not only the eastern sector of the city that had been attacked, but that the central and western sectors had also been severely damaged. The bearing of these delivery-women evoked our admiration. Every one of them had been bombed out or suffered other severe losses during this night, but not one of them made any fuss about it. They had all arrived at the usual hour, calm, collected and courageous, to see that people got their morning papers as usual. At about 5.00 a.m. one of the women showed us the way to the underground station in the Rosenthalerplatz.

The road leading to it consisted of nothing but a row of smouldering shops and offices. Through the flickering flames, the smoke and the showers of sparks we made our hazardous way to the underground station. Hundreds of people had taken refuge on the subterranean platforms, with such of their possessions as they had been able to salvage. Wounded, bandaged and their faces smothered in dust they hunched apathetically on their bedding or whatever else they had been able to bring with them. The underground train took us to the terminus in the Alexanderplatz, whence we emerged into the burning hell that was Berlin. Thus broke the grim morning of November 23.

All around the destroyed station in the Alexanderplatz the great warehouses were burning fiercely. Further towards the city stood the Schlüters Royal Palace, the former residence of the Hohenzollerns, in the middle of a tornado of fire and smoke. From one wing gigantic tongues of flame shot skywards. We crossed the Spree into the burning banking quarter. The Zeughaus, the university, the Hedwigskirche and the National Library had all been reduced to ashes. From the Unter den Linden dense clouds of smoke obliterated the view into the Friedrichsstrasse and the Wilhelmstrasse. In the Pariser Platz the headquarters of IG Farben was burning. The

Hotel Adlon opposite seemed to have escaped damage. The French Embassy, the Friedländers' mansion, the Schautenkasino and the corner houses built by Schinkel which flank the Brandenburg Gate displayed the beautiful profile of their architecture for the last time against a background of flickering flame.

On the other side of the Gate the Tiergarten looked like some forest battle-scene from the First World War. Between whole battalions of fallen trees stood the jagged stumps of oak and beech trees, bereft of the crowning glory of their foliage. The Charlotten-burger Chaussee was strewn with torn camouflage-nets and the twisted wreckage of burnt-out cars and lorries, between which a mass of dazed and wandering people were stumbling along; the Siegessaule still towered over the Grosser Stern like the Sword of the Day of Judgment. Around the mighty memorial the bronze busts of Moltke and the paladins of the 1870 war gazed down on the troubled mirror of an artificial lake, created during the night by the bursting of the water mains.

Then we reached the Handelallee and our own home. Here, too, the park had been ploughed up by the bombs, the Kaiser Friedrich church had been reduced to ruins by a direct hit and the four-storeyed buildings to burnt-out shells. Our own house, No. 12, had escaped damage in the attack itself, but had succumbed to the flames consuming its neighbours. Of the thirty-three houses in the street only three had survived the night. And our own house was the last to catch fire. We gazed up at the windows of the second floor, behind which there was a ghastly, flickering glare. Like a six-armed torch, our Empire chandelier, the only thing inside the room which was still recognisable, swayed to and fro and then plunged like a shooting-star through the burnt ceiling of the first floor into the cellars below.

In the dim light of the dawning day we found, at the corner of the Tiergarten, some linen and a few clothes which our cook, Klara, had been able to rescue from the raging inferno. Everything else was irretrievably lost – our supplies of food, which we had built up over the years, three hundred bottles of wine, our furniture, everything. Klara had made superhuman efforts. She had no one to help her, for everyone was too busy with his own problems. The failure of the electric current and the water supply had very greatly impeded the work of rescue. Before the house caught fire, the blast from a bomb that exploded next door had wrought havoc, tearing the pictures from the walls, creating chaos in the library and smashing our mirrors and chandeliers. Had we been here, we could have saved many things. As it was, we had at least been spared the hours in the ramshackle air raid shelter, in which our neighbours had been calling upon God, sure that their last hour had come. The following morning, the survivors were possessed of an almost bacchantic frenzy. Surrounded by the still burning ruins they danced together, embraced one another and indulged in quite indescribable orgiastic scenes.

What the first attack spared was destroyed by the second during the following night. Those who lived through both say that the latter was the worse, since an even higher proportion of explosive bombs was dropped. The burning town made a clearly visible target for the attackers. When we left Berlin with the Italian Ambassador, Anfuso, two hours before the second attack, the streets were still lit up as bright as day by the glare of the still-raging conflagrations.

Between the Charlottenburg and the Alexanderplatz stations practically everything has been destroyed. Only in the Kantstrasse, the Rankestrasse and along the Kurfürstendamm can one find a few blocks of houses still standing, like islands in a sea of ruins. The Gedachtniskirche is surrounded by ruins, the Zoo has been burnt out, the Aquarium and the Eden Hotel have been demolished, the old western sector, from the Budapester Strasse as far as the Potsdam bridge, has been wiped out, the Tiergartenstrasse and the northern edge of the Tiergarten have ceased to exist. In the Zoo most of the animals were killed, either by the bombs, by fire or by the November storm. Fantastic rumours are circulating. Crocodiles and giant snakes are supposed to be lurking in the hedgerows of the Landwehr canal. An escaped tiger made its way into the ruins of the Café Josty, gobbled up a piece of *Bienenstich* pastry it found there – and promptly died. Some wag, who drew uncomplimentary conclusions regarding the quality of Josty's cake-making, was sued for libel by the *Konditorei's* owner. The Court ordered a post-mortem of the dead animal which found, much to the satisfaction of the confectioner, that the tiger's death had been caused by glass splinters found in its stomach. So much for the gossip!

Of the hotels, only the Esplanade, the Adlon and part of the

Kaiserhof remain standing. Nearly all the Ministries and banks, the old Reichs Chancellery, the Wilhehn I mansion, the Charlotten-burg palace and the whole of the Lützowplatz quarter lie in ruins. With few exceptions, the embassies and legations have been reduced to smouldering ashes. The Italian and Japanese Embassies have suffered heavily. The rafters of Ribbentrop's mansion and the upper storeys of No. 74 Wilhelmstrasse have been burnt out. All plans for assembly areas and evacuation procedures have been completely nullified by the magnitude of the catastrophe.

The streets are crammed with thousands of lorries, and an army of soldiers, prisoners of war and convicts is at work, fire-fighting, salvaging furniture and conveying people to a place of safety. The behaviour of the population has been beyond all praise.

Practically all our friends have lost everything, including the Doernbergs, the Lutis, the Oyarzabals, Tino Soldati, Sieburg, Fries, the Spretis, Achim Stein and the Laroches. Only one, in compensation, perhaps, for the Kerzendorf catastrophe, has come off scot-free – Freddy Horstmann. The roof and top floor of his house in the Steinplatz caught fire, but the flames were put out by a naval party which was guarding one of Doenitz's offices nearby. Freddy's furniture had just been carried out into the street, when the house lift gave way and came crashing down on to the roof of the vestibule of his flat, which, in some miraculous way, stood fast. Freddy, who has dozens of places in which he could seek refuge, refuses to budge. The next morning order in his flat was completely restored, even to the re-laying of the carpets, just as though nothing had happened. During the first attack the whole family had been in the flat, since it was Lally's birthday. For the second raid the old gentleman had remained at home alone, in order to look after his possessions. Freddy, who has a weak heart and is voluntarily facing all these hazards, has never been more admired by his friends than he is in these grim days. Richard Kühlmann's house in the Tiergarten and Eberhard Oppenheim's flat in the Graf-Spee Strasse have vanished. A beam fell on Paul Schmidt's head, while he was helping to put out the fire in the Foreign Press Club. Helmut Fries' servants still remain buried beneath the débris. The husband of the cook of another of our friends was also buried in the ruins of the collapsed house. After twenty-four hours he was dug out, still alive. In his rucksack were half a dozen shirts, stolen from his master and a few pieces of jewellery which had found their way there in 'some mysterious fashion'. As our friend did not wish to lose a good cook, he refrained from prosecuting the man. The art dealers, with the exception of Grosse in the Esplanade Hotel, have lost everything. Main line trains are running only from the Schlesischer station, from Potsdam and from Bernau. The Stettin station has been completely destroyed, and the Potsdam station is out of action. The *S-Bahn* is running a restricted service between Pankow and the Potsdamer Platz.

For the moment we are staying with my mother in Potsdam. Today we rescued our bicycles, which we had to push home because the broken glass in the streets would have punctured the tyres. Such few odds and ends as I have managed to rescue I have placed in the Foreign Ministry for safety, because people are stealing everything which is not under strict guard.

Worse than the loss of our things is the pain of no longer having a home of our own, a place in which we can do as we please and to which we can invite the people we want to see. And worst of all is the virtual impossibility of rebuilding one's own personal world. My Directoire bookcase, a Regency chest-of-drawers and the early nineteenth-century Russian chandelier are things which cannot be replaced. Only a week before the catastrophe I had been rash enough to buy a Louis XVI long-case clock. But we had all been doing much the same sort of thing, with Freddy leading the van. And now we have gone down, with colours flying, filled with the satisfaction of having to the very end lived as we would have wished to live and of having made no concessions to the barbarous spirit of the times. But now it is all over. Now we shall be dependent on other people, shall have to live for years as guests or 'lodgers'; now we are nomads who wander, not because the spirit takes us, but because we are homeless.

Tuesday, November 30, 1943

A third major attack hit Berlin on the night of Friday, 26-Saturday, November 27, directed primarily against Spandau, Siemensstadt and Tegel. No alarms the past three nights.

The British press has been exultant. Air Marshal Harris has stated that twelve thousand tons of bombs have already been dropped on Berlin, or two thousand tons more than on Hamburg.

To 'hamburgise' Berlin, he says, a total of sixty thousand tons will be required. So I suppose we have another forty-eight thousand tons coming to us!

The behaviour of the population has been exemplary. Although a few gruesome scenes have occurred, there has been no panic anywhere. The evacuation and care of those bombed out is now proceeding in a better-organised manner and the train services have been restored with surprising swiftness. Soldiers and prisoners of war are engaged on clearing-up operations. By the third day after the catastrophe the main streets have already been cleared of rubble, and we no longer go in fear of those irritating punctures. Notices on the walls give the addresses of assembly areas and food offices. Red placards in German, French, Russian and Polish issue warnings to would-be plunderers.

Many streets still remain closed. From the upper storeys of the Ministries and public buildings rubbish and rubble is being thrown down into the road below. The Foreign Ministry is busy shifting the contents of the first three floors of the burnt-out No. 74 to the Wilhelmstrasse. But no one has given a thought to the mending of the central heating.

The Foreign Ministry cannot be said to be mastering its own particular catastrophe with any great success. Although plans for alternative accommodation were prepared months ago, although directive after directive and memorandum after memorandum have been circulated on the subject, and although a senior official (Keppler) was detailed to prepare plans for evacuation and any other measures that might be necessary, nothing has gone right. While some sections have directed their personnel to report at once for duty, the Personnel Section itself has given all those whose homes have been bombed out leave until December 9. Discussions on whether the Ministry should be moved to Krummhubel went on for five whole days. Now at last an advance party of three hundred is setting out for the Riesengebirge to prepare accommodation in Krummhubel. How they think the everyday work is to be carried on, God alone knows. The files which we need urgently and the provincial archives are being transferred from the Press Section to Krummhubel. The confusion has been compounded by the fact that Schmidt is still suffering from concussion. The catastrophe would have been an excellent opportunity to reduce the personnel of the Foreign Ministry radically. These last few days have shown only too clearly just how great a redundancy exists in the Department. The war still goes on, and not a soul notices the fact that the Foreign Ministry is *hors de combat*. Every bureaucracy which hampers the war effort should now be liquidated. It is typical that the Supreme Headquarters Representative whose job it is to brief us on the military situation either fails to put in an appearance at all, or comes hours late, with the excuse that the official car pool had no vehicle available! It does not seem to have struck him that he could walk from the Bendlerstrasse to the Wilhelmstrasse in about ten minutes. This is just typical of the sort of thing that goes on. The German is not good at coping with unforeseen situations.

Berlin has become one vast heap of rubble. One of the very few oases is the Hotel Adlon, where one can still get a meal of sorts at lunchtime and where one comes across many acquaintances. I was there yesterday and met Scapini, Dorothea Sieburg, Carl Clemm, Ulrich Dortenbach, Konstantin Oesterreich, Alfred Chapeaurouge, Helga Nehring, Hasso Etzdorf, Aga Fürstenberg, and Edgar Uxküll; and today I met Hans Henckel, Wendla Langen, Klaus Kieckebusch and Anka Fries. All bear their losses with dignity. The catastrophe has been so general, that no one cares to make a fuss about what he himself has suffered.

It is only on the various forms of public transport that people seem to get out of hand, and here it is generally a case of free-for-all and the devil take the hindmost.

Erni Studnitz, who lived in a beautifully furnished flat in the Landgrafenstrasse, died in a horrible way. Against his will, he had been carried on a stretcher down into the air raid shelter. When the heat from the burning house above it became intolerable, the people rushed out, but they forgot to take him with them. Kries is to be buried today. Estimates of the numbers killed vary greatly, and the number of those rendered homeless is said to be between four hundred thousand and half a million.

December 1943

'Total war' produces its own brand of humour

Monday, December 6, 1943
In the Adlon today I met Wittgenstein, the holder of a Knights' Cross with Oak Leaves, who was staying with us during the attack on the night of Thursday 18-Friday, November 19, and who is in a night-fighter division in Holstein. He looks pale and haggard, and, like most young pilots, is suffering severely from nervous strain; he has to take strong sleeping pills to get any sleep at all, and even then he wakes up every half-hour. Wittgenstein says that because we are approaching full moon we shall probably be free of any major attack for the next ten days. The attack on Leipzig, carried out by five hundred aircraft, is regarded as the heaviest single raid of the war.

The Foreign Minister is still in Berlin. The foreign diplomats who have taken refuge in the country would have had the opportunity, for the first time in the war, of meeting the Minister at his official headquarters. And, of course, they are not there to seize it! The terror raids have aroused a certain amount of anti-German feeling among some of the diplomats, who seem to hold us responsible for the discomforts they have suffered.

Living without a house of one's own is becoming more depressing every day. I feel like a snail which no longer has a shell in which to take shelter.

Half our long-distance and teleprinter communications with the outside world are still out of action. The evacuation of the Foreign Ministry to Krummhubel is a blunder of the first magnitude, since there are no good rail connections, only one telephone line and no air raid shelters at all. The proper course would have been to prepare in good time alternative accommodation for the Foreign Ministry in the immediate vicinity of Berlin, as was done for the War Office. Had it been distributed over a number of villages and estates, the Foreign Ministry could never have been affected as it was by such a catastrophe as that of November 23. In Krummhubel, on the other hand, an identical disaster might hit them any day.

Walking through the destroyed streets of Berlin, one's thoughts turn automatically to the problem of reconstruction. Will a more beautiful Berlin arise from the ruins – and if so, when? When the war ends, the need to clear the city swiftly and provide room for the building of dwelling-houses and office-buildings will overshadow every other consideration. As a result, jerry-built housing will probably spring up like mushrooms in the field. Houses with more than three rooms will hardly be considered, and the rooms will certainly not be high and spacious. The new dwelling houses will probably be like beehives, in which the people will live as though inside honeycombs.

The planned and half-completed special air raid shelters for diplomats, situated in the Tiergarten district amid the ruins of embassies and legations, is, to me, a most provocative sight! Thousands are at work there for the sake of a privileged few, whereas no progress, of course, has been made in the provision of shelters for the mass of the population.

Tuesday, December 7, 1943
The bombings have produced a particular brand of wry humour. Children are offered the following 'prayer' to recite at night:

Wearily I go to bed
Bombs still falling round my head
O flak, now let thy watchful eyes
Guard us till the sun doth rise
O Father God, avert Thy gaze
From the havoc that the Tommies raise
With Thy help we'll not despair
And soon the damage will repair
Friends and neighbours, each must roam
Parted from his blazing home
Great and small must share the woe
Of ruins and no place to go
Shut little mouth, sink little head
Pray for final Victory instead

Tuesday, December 7, 1943

Help the farmer, God, we plead
In his present hour of need
Restore to him his portly frame
Let Goering once more be his name!

A 'grace' starts off as follows:

Good day, Herr Ley, come on and be our guest
Bring half our promised rations – we'll forgive you the rest
But no jacket potatoes, please, with salted herring
No, let's have what *you* eat when you dine with Hermann Goering
But hush, our feast must never come to little Goebbels' ears
Or else he'll kick our arses till we're all in tears ...

and ends up:

No butter with our eats
Our pants have no seats
Not even paper in the loo
Yet, Führer – we follow you!

Another piece of doggerel deals with the 'total war':

Life is really so delicious
One should use poetic terms
Race to shelters, endless queuing
For a cabbage full of worms

Tramcar filled to bursting point
With shoving, sweating, howling brutes
Nothing in our butter-dishes
No coal coming down our chutes

Ruins looming everywhere
Uprooted trees and blocked-up drains
Fire-bomb canisters, time-fused mines
Which the Good Lord upon us rains

Houses without doors, roofs, windows
The rain will wash us all away
Men as thin and pale as ghosts
Rations smaller every day

Tired out from a hard day's work
As evening comes back home you trot
While the storm-clouds unleash on you
Wetness, darkness, dread – the lot!

Good old mum has set the table
And now sets down a steaming dish
– Long queuing at the local shop
Had finally produced one fish

Down you sit with watering mouth
Belly rumbling without end
And gobble up with horrid greed
– Führer, to thee our thanks we send

On a slightly bomb-struck sofa
You stretch at ease and start to puff
At a cabbage-leaf whose rich aroma
Fills the house – what curious stuff!

Peace – then through the night air screams
The siren's love-song, peace to mock
'This bloody war will drive me barmy
Must they *always* arrive at six o'clock?'

Mum has got the stirrup-pump
Clutches bed-rolls wrapped in sacking
'Son, let's beat it to the shelter
Come on Herbie, let's get cracking'

Trunks are dragged into the street
People scurry, brolly under arm
Children whimper, doors bang shut
Christ! there goes the full alarm

The shelter's entrance-way is jammed
With a struggling throng, all swearing blind
After a long and tiring search
At last! a place for your behind

Babbling gossip from a corner
Herr Baldrian's voice can now be heard
Privy Councillor Ahrens chips in next
And we listen agog to every word

'Six-minute warning', he declaims
'Enemy aircraft proceeding inland
Another even stronger wave
Due now over Heligoland'

'Just a few, well maybe eighty
Well, a hundred at the most
Flying southwards and quadratic
Straight towards us from the coast'

Flak's dull boom can now be heard
And the shelter starts to shake
Thud – we're sitting in the dark
Exploding shells keep us awake

The din continues quite a while
Till at last the all-clear shrills
Then we trudge home, slowly, calmly
Veterans of such nightly thrills

Windows, doors are still intact
Thank God, the enemy departs
And our luck is in again
In we go, courage in our hearts

Feeling gloomy, dearest friends?
Why, our victory is sure!
Over the slogan 'Stick it out'
Just write the headline 'Total war'

The régime is making rather pathetic attempts to counteract such expressions of feeling. Their latest effort is a six-pfenning postcard bearing the message: 'The Führer's whole life is Struggle, Toil and

Care; we must all take part of this load off his shoulders, to the best of our abilities.'

I understand that as long as Goebbels, whose Ministry, in contrast to the Foreign Ministry, is still intact, stays in Berlin, the Foreign Minister intends to remain here, too. For the last two weeks, we have been working in unheated and only partially-lit offices. On top of that, we are required to act as air raid wardens.

Wednesday, December 8, 1943

Laux, who has just returned from Italy, showed me a photograph which he had taken of Ciano in prison – a real journalistic scoop. Ciano is seen seated in a cell, through the window of which the chimney of a stove sticks out. In the left foreground is a table, on which are an opened bottle of mineral water and some papers. Ciano, with a newspaper in his hand, is in civilian clothes, and his appearance seems to have changed completely. His hair is hanging down over his eyes, although the photo shows clearly that he is shaven. He looks older than before.

The night before last I was hauled out of bed by a telephone message, asking me to write a diplomatic comment on the allies' Teheran conference. I worked on this until 2.00 a.m., with the sole result that my completed 'Diplo' has still not been passed for publication, which means that it will be quite useless to the press when they eventually do get it. Under such circumstances, how on earth can one be expected to prepare up-to-date directives!

Air raid warden duty in the Ministry now begins at 6.00 p.m. and ends at 8.00 a.m. When I had the second watch, I discovered that most of the top-storey rooms no longer existed and that the special watch-post under the roof with its telephonic connection with the command post in the cellar had been blasted away. On the roof, the water in the fire-buckets was frozen, and I had to use a hammer to break the ice. There were no sandbags available, and the direct communication system was out of action, because the Ministry is no longer linked up with the central alarm stations. Since the sound of the sirens does not reach the cellars, we never hear the alarm when it sounds. To keep watch in a house that is already almost a complete ruin really does seem rather superfluous.

The water supply at my hairdresser's, Becker, in the Neue 150 Wilhelmstrasse is not functioning, so that a shampoo entails the old-fashioned procedure of having a kettle of water poured over one's head.

Friday, December 17, 1943
Yesterday I succeeded in persuading a removal firm to take my possessions from Potsdam to Neu-Westend, in exchange for a coupon for five litres of petrol. My cook Klara travelled in the van, perched on a sofa. In Neu-Westend I am staying with Hermann Abs, and arrived just in time for dinner. No sooner had we sat down at table than the radio reported strong enemy air formations approaching Berlin. We clambered down into a roofed-in split trench which Abs had constructed in co-operation with his neighbours. The family of the neighbour, a Herr Schmitz, had already installed itself in the shelter, in wickerwork chairs, including a daughter who has been suffering for six years from sleeping-sickness. Just as the third radio report, sent out from the command post of the First Antiaircraft Division, came to an end, the air was filled with the detonations of heavy bombs. During the next twenty minutes we counted twenty explosions in the immediate vicinity, which caused our deeply-dug trench to rock. The Schmitz family began to pray aloud, which helped us all to keep calm. When the noise had subsided a little we clambered back to the surface, to find the whole neighbourhood ablaze. Two yards from Abs's house an incendiary bomb was blazing fiercely in the grass. I had escaped by a hairsbreadth from being bombed out for the second time.

Monday, December 20, 1943
With Lily Schnitzler in Frankfurt-on-Main. The station, the west end and most of the centre of the city have escaped unscathed, the old town has been battered and the eastern area of the city severely damaged. In the evening Professor Rousselle came to see us. He is a former Chairman of the China Institute in Frankfurt, but was unseated as the result of some Party intrigue. One of his translations from Lao-tse has been published by the Insel Verlag.

More and more, exclusive clubs are making exaggerated efforts to show that the loss of their premises through bombing attacks is nothing less than a death-blow. The Berlin 'Red-White' tennis club, for instance, circularises its members as follows: 'We regret to inform our members that our beloved 'Red-White' Club, was on

Thursday December 16, 1943, entirely destroyed by enemy action. On our premises, only a few of the important locations which are so essential to the satisfactory running of the Club could be saved from destruction. The Club management is, however, in a position to move shortly to alternative premises where space has courteously been offered to us by a fraternal association, and where we intend to resume our activities and do our utmost to work towards the restoration of our former facilities. We shall keep our members informed of the Club's future plans. Most important of all, the Club's address remains unaltered ...

Since the club-house, the office premises, the enclosed area of the grandstand and both cloakrooms have been consumed by fire, we urgently request our members to renew their outstanding subscriptions, making use of the enclosed postcard, so that we may set in process the restoration of those facilities no longer available through damage or destruction by enemy action ...

We would be most grateful if members would co-operate in sending us the addresses of those fellow-members who are at present serving in the forces, since our file of service members has been destroyed. And we ask all our members to inform us of any change of address. Heil Hitler!'

January 1944

Tuesday, January 11, 1944

Behind us lies a year full of defeats and disasters. Stalingrad, the downfall of fascism, the defection of Italy, retreat in the East, the sinking of the *Scharnhorst* and ever-increasing destruction in all the great cities of Germany. 1943 has seen the end of our superiority on land, demonstrated our inferiority in the air and proved the fatuity of our idea that the U-boat campaign would bring Britain to her knees. Hatred of us in the occupied territories has increased, the sympathy of friendly nations has cooled, while the attitude of the neutrals has become more hostile.

Officers returning from the eastern front admit that the Russian High Command is now extremely efficient. Fortunately this is not true of the intermediate and lower strata of command. The excellence of the Russian strategy is not supported by any comparable tactical dexterity. With us, the reverse is the case. Subordinate commanders, up to and including divisional commanders, are regarded as being efficient, but the higher command seems to have lost that adroitness which was so evident during the first years of the war. No overall plan for the waging of a defensive war is forthcoming. All the measures introduced during the last few months have been in the nature of patchwork repairs, devoid of any fundamental guiding principle. Since Stalingrad, the *élan* of the High Command has deteriorated more sharply than has the morale of the troops, which continues to be described as good by those returning on leave.

The greatest evil is the duality of control being exercised at Supreme Headquarters. In practice there are two General Staffs, one of which, under Zeitzler, is concerned with the eastern front, and the other, under Jodl, with all the other theatres of war. And neither gives any consideration to the requirements of the other. It is astonishing that our Führer-directed régime should have produced in every sphere of activity a duality of command, which renders impossible the exercise of authority and gives rise to a general absence of any sense of responsibility in the conduct of our affairs.

Once again, in 1943, we have repeated our classical mistake of underestimating the Russians. The summer offensive against Kharkov affords a good example. Even today opinions regarding the strength of the Russians vary. There is much speculation, for I instance, as to whether or not the Russians have a special army trained for winter warfare. Some sources maintain that there are sixty to eighty such divisions, which have not yet been engaged, while others declare that this is a phantom army or, alternatively, the enemy's last reserve.

Hitler is said to have asserted that, come what may, the war will be decided on the eastern front and that whether the last battle is fought in Russia, in Poland or in Germany is a matter of no consequence. One might add, however, that the nearer the front comes to the frontiers of the Reich, the less favourable our military chances become.

The laurels which our armies have won in Russia have quickly wilted in the hands of the political authorities installed to administer the occupied territories. We have made no friends among the peoples of the Soviet Union. The most bitterly disillusioned of all are the Ukrainians. Even in the Baltic States we have not succeeded in establishing friendly relations with the local populations. Inhumanity, incompetence and corruption have robbed us of any chance of winning the affection and esteem of the occupied territories.

Our administrators have done absolutely nothing to reconcile the defeated nations with their fate. They have shown themselves to be as lacking in background and education as in their ethical standards. The negative side of the German character has manifested itself all too clearly in the occupied territories in the East. So we lost the East politically, even before military necessity forced our gradual withdrawal.

Our personal future is just as gloomy. Since the air attacks of last November, life has taken on a new pattern. Before that, we preferred to eat at home or with friends, but now we have to frequent the restaurants. We used to go to bed about midnight after an evening spent with friends; now we spend the evening in solitude wherever we happen to have found accommodation and retire at nine o'clock. Even our office hours have been changed. Because of the constant danger of evening air attack, and because none of us now has a home of his own to which to return in the afternoon, set hours have been abolished, and we work right through the day. During the early months of last year we still paid attention to our wardrobe, but now we hoard the clothes we have managed to save, making the maximum use of each garment and keeping our best things in reserve.

Thursday, January 13, 1944
The execution of Ciano by shooting has left people here unmoved. The former Italian Foreign Minister was never a particularly popular figure. Only those who knew Ciano personally have shown any emotion. The justification for his condemnation seems dubious, since the trial showed clearly that Marshal Cavallero, who committed suicide, was the real culprit. The charge of high treason against Ciano cannot be regarded as having been proven. He and the other fascists were delivered into the hands of the executioner because at the meeting of the Fascist Grand Council they had voted in favour of a motion against the Duce. All this has little to do with justice. A Swiss newspaper remarks that it would have been understandable had Ciano been condemned on charges of corruption and the other misfeasances which were characteristic of his life. Mussolini must have found himself in a terrible dilemma. Rumour has it that he and his daughter were planning to rescue Ciano, but had been unable to put their plan into execution. As the Head of State of the new Fascist Republic, the Duce could not have exercised his right of pardon without extending it to all the other accused; and that would have made nonsense of the whole political object of the trial. The mental conflict which Mussolini endured must have taken further toll of his spiritual and physical resources.

Friday, January 14, 1944
At Speer's suggestion, we are to launch 'a propaganda campaign for the maintenance of secrecy' – a somewhat contradictory term. The Germans' capacity for chatter is unlimited. There can be no other country where an enemy can obtain top secrets so easily. Even in

the trains strangers swop State secrets which are kept under lock and key in the Ministries. In this connection, I have heard that there exists a 'German Propaganda Group' which will be responsible for the carrying out of this measure.

A radio reports says that unsuccessful attempts have been made on the lives of both Abetz and Laval. Abetz has now been back at his post for seven weeks. His return coincided with a change in the most important personnel of both the Embassy in Paris and the Consulate General in Vichy. Schleier, the envoy who became chargé d'affaires of the Paris Embassy during Abetz's absence (he rose within the *Auslandsorganisation* of the Nazi Party) is now back in Berlin, awaiting a new post.

Krug von Nidda, who has been doing a fine job in Vichy, rashly promised to obtain an answer from the German Government to a query of Pétain's within forty-eight hours: he has been replaced by Renthe-Fink, Best's predecessor in Copenhagen. Hemmen, who for many years was the leader of the Wiesbaden armistice commission, has been appointed First Secretary in the Paris Embassy. Oscar Schlitter, who has been consul in Eugano for three months, has had to hand over to Konstantin Neurath, since Rommel has no further use for the latter's services.

Wednesday, January 19, 1944

Pravda asserts that Anglo-German peace negotiations are being conducted in Spain between Ribbentrop and an influential British group. London and Washington are both highly indignant and are making strenuous endeavours to clear themselves of the Russian accusation. If our own people had any comprehension whatsoever of the war of nerves, their logical course would have been to refuse to deny or to confirm the statement. In this way they would perhaps have increased the confusion in the allied camp and might even have roused suspicions in the minds of the Russian inventors of this newspaper story. It would be hard to imagine a more favourable opportunity of bedevilling relations between England, Russia and America. Instead we have issued an indignant denial! The Foreign Ministry seeks to justify the attitude we have adopted by saying that we must not give the Hungarians, the Finns and the rest of our somewhat untrustworthy junior partners any excuse for being able to say: 'Aha! If the Germans are conducting unilateral negotiations, so can we!' But, surely, there was nothing to prevent us from informing our allies of our real motives.

Here is yet another example of the clumsiness of our news policies. According to the United Press, 'strong concentration of German forces in the vicinity of the Pyrenees frontier' points to the possibility of a German onslaught on Spain. Instead of remaining completely silent, the Foreign Ministry has instructed Dieckhoff to assure Franco and Jordana that there is not a word of truth in the rumour. In addition, the German Ambassador has been further directed to request the Madrid Government to send a Spanish officer to southern France, to satisfy himself of the falsity of the UP report – which is exactly the object the enemy had in view, when he launched the rumour. What he wanted to find out was whether there was still any possibility that Germany was toying with the idea of an occupation of the Iberian peninsula. Had we allowed the American report to go unchallenged while refusing to name an invasion point, the Spaniards, whose attitude towards us during the past weeks has been lukewarm if not unfriendly, would again have felt uncertain.

Similarly, the allies would have had to take a possible German flanking movement into account, in formulating their invasion plans. Such aspects, however, are never visualised by anyone here.

Monday, January 31, 1944

Another heavy air raid last night preceded by a false alarm during the day. When the sirens sounded at 8.00 p.m. I was with the Traubs in Zehlendorf, where I had gone to meet Ernst Ludwig Grolman. When the party broke up about midnight, we found that communications between Nikolassee and Grunewald had been interrupted. The next morning, going via Zehlendorf-West, we reached Steglitz, where we got a lift on a three-wheeled delivery van as far as the Anhalter station. Steglitz and Schoneberg again suffered severe damage. There is no communication with Neu-Westend, so I have no idea whether my room in Abs's house is still intact.

Grolman was staying at the Continental Hotel during last night's air attack. He was sitting in the hotel's air-raid shelter, dressed in pyjamas, a sheepskin coat and red slippers, when there was a cry of 'Fire!' Grolman rushed up to help put it out. On the fourth floor, where some incendiary bombs had fallen, he found a crowd of French, Italian and Russian waiters, all of them yelling for water in their own languages and none of them understanding a word the others were shouting. Then they had started to throw sand on the rafters, which were burning fiercely. Grolman succeeded in getting them to abandon this futile endeavour and began organising them into groups. Fire-engines summoned from Dresden, arrived at last. A Saxon fireman directed a two-foot long stream of water against the fire which was at least fifty feet away from him. When Grolman roared: 'Go up closer, you idiot!', the man turned and directed his jet straight in Grolman's face, saying: 'Thank you, *Herr Kollege!*' A lieutenant, who was sitting in the foyer, doing nothing, then chipped in and said: 'If I had a company of troops, I could save the whole works. This is a lot of damn nonsense!' Instead of helping to extinguish the fire in the roof, the officer ordered the hotel servants to carry the luggage piled up in the hall into the street, despite the fact that the luggage was in no danger at all, and that it was raining outside. Grolman, whose room was destroyed by fire at 8.00 p.m., was rewarded for his help in putting out the fire by being presented, next morning, with a bill for the night's lodging!

Hans Flotow, who was with Vicky Schack in Grunewald when the alarm sounded, waited for the all-clear and then went home on foot from Halensee all along the burning Kurfurstendamm. Firemen were still at work extinguishing the flames, intermingled with courting couples, an old gentleman with a little dog, girls in slacks wearing steel helmets, people with portable radios and men selling newspapers. A female voice was screaming for water. When Flotow turned round, a young girl asked him if he would like to take her home: she would give him a good time. When he reached home at last, he found that the neighbouring Magdeburgerstrasse was in flames. Hurrying across, he discovered Frau von Gersdorff in her burning kitchen, calmly making sandwiches for the firemen. In another room of the Gersdorff house lay the corpse of a man who had died several days before, covered with a tartan rug, a crucifix laid on the chest: the body could not be removed to the mortuary because of the incessant alarms. Hans went to bed at 7.00 a.m., slept for an hour, then got up, played some dance music on his gramophone to keep himself awake, shaved and then drove to his factory on the Hallesches Tor, where a fresh conflagration awaited him.

Owing to the dislocation of the underground and other forms of public transport, lots of people could not get into the city, and the only friends I met in the Adlon Hotel were Soldati, Valeanu, Leo Fürstenberg and Oskar Schlitter. The hotel had been hit by only one incendiary, and that had been quickly extinguished. The Press Section now has a room of its own in the Adlon's deep cellars, complete with radio communication facilities.

After spending three days at the Foreign Minister's Field Headquarters in East Prussia, I returned to Berlin on January 30. The object of my visit had been to discuss the 'Diplo'. I caught the special Government train which leaves Berlin at 7.00 p.m. My destination was not shown on my ticket, because every aspect of a journey to Headquarters is kept secret. The train was under military supervision, with soldiers acting as guards and officers as controllers and conductors. For security reasons, the train is routed each time over a different track. The sleeping-cars are crammed with officers. When we arrived, the passengers split up, some going to the Führer's headquarters and others to the headquarters of the *Reichsführer* SS, the Foreign Minister or the Commander-in-Chief of the Army.

All these headquarters are surrounded with barbed wire, and a host of sentries is kept busy, inspecting identity cards. The password is changed every day. While I was there, the passwords used were *Krefeld, Slowakei* and *Wasserkuppe*. Each headquarters has its own code name, like *Wolfsschanze*. Visitors are accommodated in one of the sleeping-cars which are drawn up in the vicinity of each headquarters.

The Foreign Minister's Field Headquarters are on the shores of a lake, and the Minister himself has taken up residence in the nearby Schloss Steinort, which belongs to the Lehndorffs. The various headquarters are half an hour or more by car from each other, and this involves a great waste of time. The first night I slept in the office, and the second I spent in the special train. Only a single adjutant is staying with the Foreign Minister. Ribbentrop's associates at Field Headquarters are Ambassador Gauss, Minister Altenburg, Counsellor Hilger, First Secretary Sonnleithner and Secretaries Raykowski (Press), Timmler (Radio) and Steeg (Information). Dr Limpert is Chief Adjutant and the Air Force Adjutant is Captain Ötting. Also on the field staff are Dr Megerle, Herr von Schmieden and Legation Secretaries Tafel and Kutscher. The armed forces representative is Colonel von Geldern and medical command of the Field Headquarters is held by Dr Conrad. The chief secretary is Fräulein Blank. While I was there, visitors included Privy Councillor Hesse and Ministers Windecker and Ettel. Office personnel, chauffeurs, a barber, a warrant officer in charge of sanitation, telephonists, cooks, waiters and a personal valet for the Foreign Minister complete the establishment.

The other field headquarters are organised on much the same lines. They remind me of what the imperial camps of the seventeenth and eighteenth centuries must have looked like, when princes and their courts followed in the wake of their armies, while the residents were banished from their own property.

The Foreign Minister himself occupies one wing of Schloss Steinort and the Lehndorff family is housed in the other. The Schloss, an ancient mansion containing beautiful family portraits and guarded by mighty baroque gates, has been appropriately 'adapted', with the result that the furniture and fittings provided by the Foreign Ministry strike a somewhat incongruous note in their present surroundings. The 'hall of knights' has been embellished with clumsy, orange-coloured Empire furniture from the Polish Embassy in Berlin and with a beautiful glittering Louis XVI chandelier. The Minister's office contains a writing desk, and two leather armchairs for visitors. A portrait in oils of Frederick the Great hangs above a modern sofa.

At the office, I had breakfast with Altenburg and then visited Megerle, who is in bed with a cardiac complaint.

Provision has even been made for a court jester. Y. sustains the role with more aplomb than ever. Within the course of a few minutes he claimed that the famous night-fighter pilot Wittgenstein was a cousin of his, and that all the Schinkel buildings had been built by his grandfather and that Schinkel had merely put his name to them. He even claims to have personally organised the Kapp-Putsch. He has lately taken to attributing his oriental appearance to the Doges of Venice, from whom he claims to be descended!

I had a long and futile talk about the German diplomatic correspondence service with Gauss, a sensible but ageing and tired old man, who has now acquired the habit of agreeing with everything that is said to him.

After dinner, consisting of a tough stew and an obscure pudding –

synthetic honey and flower-petal coffee are two further specialities of the Field Headquarters – Kutscher took me to a nearby military cemetery. Driving back through the thick forest we suddenly came across a General in full panoply and looking for all the world like a rutting deer, hurrying across a clearing; when he saw us, he nodded graciously and then took to his heels!

In the evening we dined off roast hare at a restaurant frequented by officers from Supreme Headquarters. Later there was a sing-song in Herwarth's room, attended by some of the secretaries and lady typists, who brought alcoholic drinks and gramophone records with them.

Next day, at 1.00 p.m., we went with Schmidt and Strempel to see the Foreign Minister. We had to hang about in the reception room until about 3.30, when Schmidt alone was admitted to the presence and invited to have lunch, while the rest of us ate with the councillors and adjutants. At 5.00, just as I was about to go for a walk in the pouring rain with Altenburg, I was sent for by the Minister. The graciously conciliatory conversation that followed concerned a note on Spain which I had drafted. We also discussed the south-east front, England and the anticipated invasion.

In the matter which I had really come to discuss – the removal of the 'Diplo' from the Minister's control – I made no progress whatever. The Foreign Minister was unwilling to surrender his right to make such amendments as he deemed desirable, and I was quite unable to convince him that a 'Diplo' represented an official expression of opinion with which the Foreign Ministry could identify itself, if it wished.

Like at a royal court, one has to hang around these field headquarters aimlessly for hours. We availed ourselves of the opportunity of talking to the Minister's entourage and with Ambassador Hewel, his liaison man with the Führer. As regards the breaking-off of relations with the Argentine, Ribbentrop said that the Ministry of Defence had made a complete mess of things for us by falling nicely into the trap set for them by the British. It seems that they had collected all the relevant material and, in conjunction with the United States, had presented it in a form which left Buenos Aires no option but to break off diplomatic relations with us. Last Tuesday, when I rang up Luti, the Argentinian chargé d'affaires, he had known nothing about it. He and his wife Crucita are both very pro-German.

How suddenly the diplomatic break occurred is shown, for instance, by the fact that only one week ago the Argentinian Consul General, who had been home on two years' leave, returned to his post in Germany with his wife, children and servants.

On the return journey from East Prussia I spent a long time pondering over the case of Ribbentrop. How is one to classify him? Is he really one of the Party leaders, or is he rather one of the *ancien régime* who has come to terms with the dictatorship? Is he a business man simply doing good business with the Third Reich? Or is he an adventurer? If so, what adventure is this unhappy and repressed man seeking?

Of good yeoman stock, adopted by a titled aunt and rendered financially independent by his marriage to Anneliese Henkell, Ribbentrop belongs to a class to which war and inflation could not do much harm. The owner of a fine house in Dahlem filled with good furniture and a collection of modern paintings, he led an elegant existence at the side of a cultured wife. What caused him to throw in his lot with Hitler? Certainly not any feeling of personal discontent, nor the urge to better his position. His own ambition, or that of his wife?

There is no doubt that Ribbentrop was personally greatly attracted by Hitler. In Berlin in the late nineteen-twenties the Ribbentrops were regarded as an enlightened couple. They cultivated Hitler in the same way as they would have cultivated some new modern painter. To Hitler, on the other hand, Ribbentrop seemed to be the personification of a type which he had hitherto not met in Germany. He saw in him a man of the world, with a panache, which the Nazis did not possess, a personality who, with his connections, might come in very useful.

Today they both realise that they have misjudged each other. But the relationship which emerged from their tragic misunderstanding of each other has nevertheless endured. Whatever one may think of Ribbentrop's capabilities – his vision, his sense of the relevant, his reactions – one must say this for him: he understands the working of Hitler's mind as does no other man. In their exchanges of political views Hitler feels that his Foreign Minister grasps his point instantly and fully. In conversation Ribbentrop has the gift of putting crisply into words ideas which are only just beginning to take shape in Hitler's mind. That, at least, is the impression gained by Hewel, Schmidt, Likus and others who are in a position to form an opinion of the relations between the Führer and his Foreign Minister.

Ribbentrop's greatest handicap as Foreign Minister stems from the fact that as an egocentric he has failed to make himself familiar with the mentalities of other nations. His ideas on events in the field of foreign politics are fantastic. It may well be, too, that, in his position, he feels he must over-emphasise his possession of the one attribute he lacks – self-confidence. It is this lack of self-confidence alone that can account for the discrepancy between the pipe-dreams in which he indulges and the day-to-day realities with which he has to cope.

Ribbentrop's chief characteristic is his arrogance – a mixture of disdainful haughtiness and taciturnity that makes it difficult to establish contact with him. Apart from Steengracht and Doernberg, the Minister has no friends among his colleagues. As far as the senior officials are concerned, he remains an outsider whom they refuse to accept. The Nazis distrust him as a man with a 'handle' to his name, whose closeness to Hitler strikes them as unnatural. As a net result it has proved impossible to build up any feeling of confidence between Ribbentrop and his colleagues. They all obey him. of course, including those of the old school, who will obey anyone who speaks sharply to them. They put up with the great Bismarck and bowed to his violent son, Herbert; and they confidently expect to survive Ribbentrop. The Nazis back him, because he wears the same uniform. And so the Minister finds himself surrounded by much bowing and scraping.

One of the few exceptions is Schmidt. Ribbentrop's temperamental outbursts do not impress him in the least. On the telephone he allows the Minister to indulge in a lengthy monologue, hands the receiver to someone else, goes over to his cigar-cabinet, selects a cigar, lights it, takes over the receiver again and blandly enquires: Are you still there, *Herr Reichsminister?* I can hardly hear you.' Most of the others stand to attention at their desks when Ribbentrop rings them up.

Sieburg once said that dealing with Ribbentrop was like wrestling with a cobra. He may be right. What irritates me, though, is the slowness with which Ribbentrop takes in the contents of any paper I submit to him. He reads it like a child, from top to bottom and then again from bottom to top, and takes longer doing so than it took me to draft the thing. Perhaps he acts in this manner out of deference to his dignity. Even when he has finished, he never comes to a decision, but ends up by saying: 'I must discuss all this once again with Gauss!'

The above is typical of Ribbentrop's way of conducting business, which fluctuates between over-hasty, regretted and finally retracted decisions and a complete inability to come to any decision at all. His decisions, like his hesitations, are accompanied by a constant fear of how the Führer will react. As for his mulish obstinacy, I cannot make up my mind whether it is due to his lack of intelligence, his helplessness or to a fear of being thought unable to make up his own mind. It could, of course, be nothing more than a pose. One must remember that the Nazis regard mulishness as a positive virtue, synonymous with strength of will and one of the 'virtues of a leader'. To Ribbentrop's credit it must also be said that he is not one of the revolutionaries of the *Kampfzeit*, the period of the struggle for power, nor is he a 'strongarm man', like so many of the ruffians who have now risen to high office. He therefore finds it difficult to assert himself in the company in which he finds himself and which has entrusted him with one of the highest posts in the State. The strength of Schmidt's position in relation to Ribbentrop lies in the fact that he invariably adheres to his own opinion and would not for a moment dream of giving way to the Foreign Minister, simply because the latter is his chief. Nor is it to Ribbentrop's discredit that he allows exceptional latitude to a subordinate of this calibre – one, incidentally, whom he himself discovered.

The war and everything to do with it is altogether too much for Ribbentrop. Far from being the 'man of iron' he pretends to be his prematurely aged features betray how much he suffers. The Foreign Minister has put all he possesses on one card – Hitler. A single frown from Führer Headquarters, and his whole world tumbles about his ears. His greatest agony occurs when he has been unable for some considerable time to obtain an audience with Hitler. Over him, as over all the other 'paladins,' hangs the Damoclean sword of disfavour. But his skin is thinner than that of the others.

February 1944

Tuesday, February 1, 1944

In Neu-Westend I found my bed covered with a film of dust and fine rubble, which the blast of a bomb that fell in the Wurttemberger Platz had blown into the room. Thanks to the present phase of the moon, we hope from tomorrow to have ten days or so of peace. For five days before and for three days after the full moon there are usually no air raids. The moon, which once was greatly feared, is now our best friend. The tactics of the war in the air have completely changed. Previously, raids were confined to clear, moonlit nights; now the bombers prefer bad weather which is a greater handicap to the defence than to the attackers.

With eighty-three victories in the air to his credit, Wittgenstein has finally been killed. His aircraft crashed just over fifty yards from Schloss Gross Wudicke, to which the Swiss Legation has moved to avoid the air raids. The radio operator and rear-gunner dropped by parachute, but the Prince, who had obviously been wounded, had been unable to get free of the cockpit.

Saturday, February 5, 1944

On the morning of February 1, I handed to Raykowski my suggestion that a 'Diplo' on the Russian constitutional reforms should be published, together with a request that he would obtain the Foreign Minister's approval. By the evening of Wednesday, February 2, the Minister had still not made up his mind. That same night the Führer issued a decree, directing the press to deal with these reforms. At eleven o'clock on the morning of February 3 the Foreign Minister telephoned to me and directed me to draft a 'Diplo' on the subject. My draft was approved by him on the night of February 3, but not released, and then on the evening of February 4, rejected once again. On the morning of February 5, came the text of a new draft, drawn up by Dr Megerle and approved by the Foreign Minister. This was released to the press at midday; but it does not contain one single point of view which the press could not easily have put forward on its own account five days ago.

The following comment from *Suisse* is worthy of note:

If the Germans launched their campaign against the Soviet Union on June 22, 1941, with the object of overthrowing bolshevism, then at least they should have taken steps to get the non-Russian peoples on their side; it would probably have been easy to detach them from Moscow with a promise of independence in the event of a German victory. Instead of this, Germany immediately disclosed her plan, which was to assume sovereignty over these eastern territories herself and to plunder them to her own advantage. As a result, the point of issue for these non-Russian peoples was no longer one of liberation from Russian domination, but one merely of a change of foreign masters.

Russian propaganda has taken advantage of this blunder on the part of German politicians, and now the German armed forces are regarded by all the peoples of the Soviet Union not as potential liberators, but as conquerors who must be repulsed at all costs. The power of the Moscow Government over all these peoples has not been shattered, but has, on the contrary, been strengthened. Its authority is now so great that, without fear of any splitting up of its power, it now feels that it can concede to the various member-republics a considerable measure of autonomy. That this autonomy will be apparent rather than real is immaterial. The measure is nevertheless well calculated to help the Moscow Government to the attainment of its dual goal: promoting the accession of new republics to the Soviet Union and increasing its political influence in world affairs.

Vienna – Tuesday, February 15, 1944

For five days I have been in Vienna, living in a fairyland. There is an atmosphere about the place such as I have not encountered anywhere for years. Nobody talks about the war. Visitors from Bohemia-Moravia and Hungary fill the great hotels and vie with each other in issuing and accepting invitations. Hungarian

noblemen from the *Puszta* flock into the city in cars driven by
wood-gas. With them they bring not only the food for their
dinner-parties, but also fodder, in order to be able to drive about
Vienna in a cab, which they hire for a hundred marks a day. The
whole town looks more elegant, while the *Reichsdeutsch* element,
which up to six months ago had been predominant, is now in
a far more precarious position. The conquest of Vienna by the
Prussians has ended in the same way as the conquest of China
by the Japanese: the conquerors are being assimilated. Their one
ambition now is to be taken for local inhabitants. The Viennese
are quite sure that they will not be bombed. The art dealers are
furious with the German Governor, because he has ordered them
to remove their treasures to the safety of the countryside. The
Party has issued a statement to the effect that only a fool or a
traitor would believe that Vienna will be spared – a warning that
has not had the slightest effect on the population. The city is ablaze
with light until 11.00 p.m. In comparison with the old days, the
shops seem a little empty, but in comparison with Berlin, they are
abundantly full. The antique dealers are earning vast fortunes. In
the Siebensterngasse I saw a picture, *Moses in the Bulrushes,* by
Poussin, which two years ago was valued at ten thousand marks
and which is now priced at double that figure. The theatres are sold
out. Politically, one follows one's own bent. Karl Anton Rohan,
for instance, gave a talk in the Allianz Building on 'The Future of
Europe', a self-willed interpretation of the times, and afterwards
we all spent the evening drinking beer in a private club decorated
to look like a wine restaurant. Even in this fourth year of war, the
Spanish Riding School gives two performances a week, at which
one is constantly encountering one's acquaintances.

Last Saturday I went to the wedding of Arthur Strachwitz and
Sissi Liechtenstein. It was celebrated in the Liechtenstein's Palace
in the Bankgasse. Among those present were a dozen or more
Liechtenstein princesses, in mink coats and Viennese imitation-
Parisian hats. Mariza Liechtenstein was well to the fore: she is a
most high-spirited young Hungarian, who often spends a week
in Berlin to take part in the last convulsions of society life in the
capital. That same evening the Archduchess, the bride's grand-
mother, passed away.

Berlin – Thursday, February 17, 1944
Tonight, according to their own statement, the British dropped 3,300 tons of bombs on Berlin. Hermann Abs's house in Neu-Westend, Mecklenburgallee 13, where I am now living, was hit by twenty-five incendiaries. There were eight separate fires, but we managed to extinguish them all.

When I arrived about midnight, I found the electric light in the upper storey out of action, a bombed-out refugee in my bed, the room grimy with the smoke from incendiaries and the floor covered with pools of water. There is a stench of charred wood, and an icy draught whistles through the damaged roof. Abs's bedroom has been completely burnt out. It is a miracle that the house is still standing. The refugees to whom Abs has given shelter have rewarded him handsomely for his hospitality. But for their efforts the whole villa would have been destroyed, like those of the Karstadt-Schmitzes and Mackebens next door. Every room that is still habitable has been filled with refugees, who are stumbling over each other.

There is now hardly a single undamaged house in West Berlin. In many parts of town, air-mines came hurtling down by the dozen. The Bismarckstrasse is just one heap of ruins, and the underground and overhead railways have been severely hit. This morning I thumbed my way into the city and had to change cars five times in the process. The cars which refuse to give one a lift are invariably 'official cars', which hurtle past half-empty. Delivery vans, green-grocers and coalmen are much more helpful. From Knie I was taken as far as the Brandenburg Gate in a car, the hood of which had been ripped off by the blast of an exploding bomb.

Friday, February 18, 1944
Visited the Dippes in Wilkendorf, where I found the Oyarzabals and the Karajans. Before dinner I went for a long walk through the woods with Karajan, who is full of bitter complaints against Furtwängler. The latter, he says, is doing all he can to injure his career. He has closed the doors of the Philharmonic to Karajan and refuses to allow him to conduct in Vienna. Furtwängler's jealousy has been aroused by a newspaper article entitled 'The Miracle named Karajan'.

Saturday, February 19, 1944

Spent the night with Leo Fürstenberg in Lichterfelde. As usual, there was no connection between Eberswalde and Lichterfelde. Laden with pictures, candlesticks and assorted parcels, I managed to get hold of an 'iron steed' in Eberswalde and biked the four miles through the icy night and dark woods to Lichterfelde. What will one not accomplish, in order to take a few of one's worldly possessions to some place where they will be safe from the bombs!

Monday, February 21, 1944

With Helga Nehring and a married couple named de Notaristefani to spend the weekend in Munchenhofe, where the Strempels have leased a hunting-moor with attached shooting-box. Hidden deep in the forest, this hermitage, like the neighbouring little summer-house belonging to Tino Soldati where I am to sleep, offers a wonderful haven from the air raids. The journey from Berlin was extremely trying and, indeed, was only possible thanks to the help of Bobeff, the 'refugee' Bulgarian Press Attaché, who has a car driven by wood-gas. The Countess de Notaristefani is the daughter of a Bohemian industrialist; her husband is an Italian cavalry officer who succeeded, after Badoglio's defection, in fleeing to his wife's home. In the evening Aga Fürstenberg, Max Schaumburg and Pepe Career turned up for bridge. Late in the night, when I went back to my quarters five minutes' walk away and in darkness stumbled into the room prepared for me, I trod on something soft, which I took to be a rug beside my bed, until a furious growl told me that I had trodden on the Hungarian sheepdog belonging to the artist Scholz, who had leased the place from Tino Soldati. I spent an uneasy night side by side with this extremely ferocious beast, which refused absolutely to budge from my bedroom, until Tino's Spanish servant Enrique arrived in the morning and freed me from my precarious situation.

Tuesday, February 29, 1944

I have just spent two days with Gerda Blumenthal in Puddiger in Pomerania, where I met Herr Schimmelpfennig, an elderly dendrologist from Kassel, whose collar seems to be about six sizes too big for him. He looks half-starved and is obviously one of that unfortunate section of the German people which has to exist on its rations alone.

Another guest was a Fräulein Müller, who is *Reichsminister* Speer's housekeeper and whose tongue never stopped wagging, telling us all about her experiences in finding villas for the high Party and State officials. Breakfasted with Luis Luti in the Hotel Adlon, where the Argentinian chargé d'affaires and his wife have been allotted an unheated single room. Crucita Luti served us a homely picnic of potato salad and cold meat, on plastic plates. With it we had water to drink and a thermos of coffee – an astonishing meal, when one thinks that Luti is the diplomatic representative of the greatest State in South America and the Hotel Adlon is the foremost hotel in the German Reich! Luti is very disturbed about events in the Argentine, about which he is still partly in the dark. He and his wife are living in Grünheide and only spend the day in town. The members of his Embassy are scattered all over the place, but are apparently content with things as they are and have refused to move into the country house which the Foreign Ministry had placed at their disposal. The sons of the Argentinian diplomats are all students at Berlin University.

March 1944

Peace contacts between Finland and Russia – The Turkish question: rivalry between Ribbentrop and Papen – Americans over Berlin – Crisis in Hungary – The Russians reach the Dniester

Wednesday, March 1, 1944

Political interest is centred chiefly on the rumours of peace with Finland. Yesterday evening *Pravda* carried a report of exploratory contacts between the Finns and the Russians in Stockholm. The Finns, obviously, have initiated these talks without having previously consulted us. A week ago, the German Minister to Finland told the Finnish Government that the conclusion of a separate peace would be regarded by us as a betrayal.

Although the world press has been giving considerable prominence to the Finnish crisis for the past three weeks, we have still not made known our own attitude. Even today we have been forbidden to make any comment – and we have thus been deprived of any chance we may have had of influencing future developments.

As regards the Turkish question, too, it seems to me that some immediate statement of the German Government's attitude is highly desirable. Papen is insisting that we should furnish the Turks with arguments to discourage their entry into the war on the side of Britain. As always, clarity and courage are the salient features of his despatches. No other Ambassador would have the temerity to use such blunt language. Papen's reports, couched in such very different terms from those of the other heads of missions, annoy Ribbentrop all the more, because of the obvious importance that Hitler attaches to them. Although it would be false to assert that Hitler follows the advice Papen gives him, he nevertheless certainly pays great attention to what the latter has to say. On most occasions on which he visits Germany, Papen is ordered to report to Führer Headquarters even before he calls on Ribbentrop; and the Foreign Minister, who sees a possible rival in every shadow, is extremely irritated by these meetings. In many respects the relationship between Papen and Hitler is reminscent of that between Talleyrand and Napoleon – with the difference, admittedly, that many Germans hate Papen, because he adopts the same attitude that caused them so greatly to admire Talleyrand.

Thursday, March 9, 1944

On Saturday, March 4, American aircraft appeared for the first time in the vicinity of Berlin. The American communiqué speaks of 'an offensive sweep' over the German capital. On Monday, March 6, came the first American daylight raid, carried out against the south-eastern and south-western suburbs and Konigswusterhausen. After a break on the Tuesday, a heavier attack was made on Wednesday against the outskirts of the city. The sirens usually go off at about 1.00 p.m. for these American attacks. In contrast to the British night raids, which usually last about forty-five minutes, the American daylight raids go on for two or three hours. Whereas the British prefer to attack on dark nights and in bad weather, the Americans like daylight and a clear sky. Both Monday and Wednesday were beautiful days, without a cloud in the sky. The British drop their bombs quickly and at random – 'carpet-bombing' is their speciality – while the Americans prefer to take their time and make two or three trial runs over the target before releasing their bombs. It is now 12.40, and the alarm has just sounded.

We have just spent two hours in the shelters. The main target was the eastern sector of the city.

A sojourn in the Adlon air raid shelter is the very reverse of pleasant; the air is foul and the place overcrowded. As these attacks occur round about midday and the hotel restaurants remain closed after the all-clear, most of us have to return unfed to our offices.

Sunday, March 12, 1944

Highlight of the past week has been the sequence of events in Hungary. Kallay's successor is not Imredy, but Sztojay, the present Hungarian Minister to Berlin, an old gentleman who gives one the impression of being completely worn out. First as military attaché and then as Minister he has been in Berlin for sixteen years, is a Lieutenant-Field-Marshal in the Imperial Hungarian Army, a Croat and an intimate friend of Horthy. We are, I think, justified in expecting that he will serve us well. But whether he will be able to master the internal situation in Hungary is another question. The powers given to Veesenmeyer, our new Minister in Hungary and an expert in the forming of satellite governments, are greater than those accorded to Best in Denmark or Abetz in France. He has, for instance, been placed on an equal footing with the military commander-in-chief. Jagow, his predecessor, who was not really up to the job, returns to the Foreign Ministry. In connection with Jagow's relief, it should be added that he had never hankered for a diplomatic career and had regarded his appointment as Minister to Budapest as a punishment.

To win over Hungary into taking an active part in the war will be a hard task, even though the Russians are at her gates. The 'land hunger' of the population remains unsated. The aristocracy, which produced so many able statesmen at the time of the Imperial monarchy, is no longer politically active. After 1918 scions of the great families showed clearly that they regarded the Hungarian political stage as altogether too unimportant to merit their active attention. Men like Bethlen, Teleki, Czaky as well as the Archduke Albrecht, who was so expert at manoeuvring behind the scenes, were the exceptions which proved the rule. There thus remained at the disposal of the State only the gentry, the landed middle class which was as politically zealous as it was unskilled in the art of statecraft. After Hitler had conquered Europe, the Hungarians were always at the head of the queue when territory was distributed, at the expense of the Czechs, the southern Slavs and the Rumanians. Under Kallay they laboured under the naive illusion that, even if Germany were defeated, they would still be allowed to retain the territory Hitler had bequeathed them. The occupation of Hungary by German troops will add fuel to the fire of resentment felt against all Germans.

A New York paper writes that Hitler is now celebrating his final victories, in which he must content himself with conquering his allies, having failed to subdue his enemies.

Monday, March 13, 1944
To the State Opera to hear Karajan's concert. The bombed-out interior, which is said to have been restored in accordance with Knobelsdorff's original design, is much more like a Sarotti bon-

bonniere. The colours are too sugary, the gilt-work of inferior contemporary quality, the purity of the rococo decoration has been spoilt by modern additions, the great chandelier in the auditorium is an eyesore and the whole stage lighting system too glaring. A good example of the difficulties of authentic period restoration.

Thursday, March 16, 1944

The Russians are now seventy-five miles from the borders of Slovakia and ninety-five miles from the Hungarian frontier. In the Ukraine we are fighting for the last square mile. Kherson has fallen, and the battle is now approaching Nikolaiev. The Russians have crossed the Bug. To the north, where fighting in the Narva bridgehead continues, the picture is a little brighter.

The daily 'confidential' report which we receive from Supreme Headquarters becomes daily more meaningless. If one ignored the constantly changing place-names, one might well believe that we were still holding our own at Stalingrad. It is always the same old story: the breaches have been closed, counter-attacks have driven the enemy back, enemy attacks have been caught in the concentrated fire of all weapons and repulsed, and so on. In advancing in one year from Stalingrad to Tarnopol, the Russians have covered a distance equal to that from Tarnopol to Paris.

All we hear from the top people is that Führer Headquarters is full of optimism, that we have 'nerves of iron' and a fistful of trump cards, that the military situation on the eastern front presents no problem and that thirty divisions will be ample to enable us to resume the offensive. And that the latter will take place, if you please, as soon as we have repulsed the invasion in the west!

The air raids on Berlin have diminished somewhat in intensity. But Brunswick, Stuttgart and Leipzig, on the other hand, have suffered very severely. Over Brunswick the Americans appeared for the first time with strong fighter escort. The official line is that we have no intention of reacting to every American trick and that the time may well come when we shall refrain from putting any fighter aircraft into the air at all! Nobody is going to tell us when and how we are to use our fighters. English commentators say that the war in the air will be concluded in sixty days. That means the end of May, and this should coincide with the anticipated date of the invasion.

In Italy the military situation is stationary. The Russians, who have recognised the new Italy, are courting Badoglio as zealously as they have been courting de Gaulle, banking on their conviction that the Anglo-Saxons will in due course subject both of them to some humiliation.

Sunday, March 19, 1944

The Russians have reached the Dniester. Their latest communiqué talks of 36,800 Germans dead on the field of battle and 13,859 German prisoners. Although events on the eastern front follow one another with dramatic speed, the same old optimism prevails here. And yet we are already fighting with our backs to the Carpathian mountains!

On Friday evening I set out to spend the weekend with the Putlitzes in Gross Langerwisch, but on Saturday afternoon a telephone message from Schmidt recalled me to Berlin, where I arrived just after an air raid warning had sounded. The reason for my recall is the crisis in Hungary. For twelve hours nobody knew whether the negotiations with Horthy would be brought to a satisfactory conclusion, and only the next twenty-four hours will show whether the reshuffle in Hungary, described by us as 'an intensification of German-Hungarian military co-operation', has been completed without a hitch.

April 1944

Krummhübel, the Foreign Ministry's evacuation centre, for Slovak State visit – I and the poet, Tido Gaspar, visit Gerhart Hauptmann – The Russians at Sebastopol: Manstein and Kleist relieved of their commands – British diplomatic pressure on Turkey

Monday, April 17, 1944

I have been spending Easter in Reelkirchen (Lippe). A journey to the west is now quite an adventure. The day after my arrival, the Bielefeld-Lemgo train on which I had travelled on Good Friday, was subjected to a low-flying attack. Twenty people were killed. When I returned on the Tuesday after Easter, every gun in the neighbourhood seemed to be firing from 9.00 a.m. onwards. While I was waiting for my train in Bielefeld, the alarm sounded twice. In the evening I reached Berlin to the sound of the sirens. The Zoo station was packed with hundreds of people, who spend the night, sitting on their suitcases, ready to move swiftly into the Tiergarten shelters if the alarm should sound. It all reminds me of scenes in the stowage section of an emigrant ship.

The other day I travelled to Krummhübel to greet the Slovak Minister of Propaganda and Press Chief, Tido Gaspar. I travelled for eight and a half hours in a wood-burning gas-driven bus along the *autobahn* as far as Bunzlau, and then via Hirschberg to Krummhübel. Every thirty miles or so we had to stop, discharge the gas, cut off the fuel supply and clean out the engine. On a long journey the fumes from the wood-gas become very unpleasant inside the bus. The driver is allowed by regulation one litre of first-quality milk a day; but, of course, he never gets it. Those travelling with me were Kaesbach (Transocean), Petweidic (Transconti), Schindel, plus Rudolf, one of the servants at the Foreign Press Club. Schmidt is following in a Volkswagen.

Krummhübel is a pretty place, the pensions and hotels are primitive, and the local inhabitants do not take kindly to strangers – not, at least, when they come from the Foreign Ministry, which they regard as their evil spirit. As the Ministry has requisitioned all available accommodation, but does not use it, the people earn no money during the season. On the other hand, the Ministry places at the disposal of foreign diplomats houses which the owners are permitted to let to foreigners, provided they undertake to hand them back to the Foreign Ministry within three days on demand.

The Riesengebirge is a typical 'Strength-through-Joy' area, pre-eminently suited to the demands of the less exacting type of tourist. The Ministry has evacuated five hundred people to Krummhübel. The place stretches from the foot of the valley to the snowcapped summit. Transport between the widely scattered rest-homes is provided by one motor vehicle and twenty-two two-horsed carriages. The cabbies, who look like Chinamen, come from Azerbaijan, don't speak a word of German and don't know the first thing about a horse. As it is difficult to make them understand anything, a German police sergeant-major sometimes take charge, driving a three-horse carriage and directing the activities of his Azerbaijanis with such words of command as 'Start up' and 'Stop'.

The best thing in the place is a small wooden chalet which is reasonably comfortable and has been prepared for Schmidt's use. Among the more senior officials living in Krummhübel are State Secretary Keppler and Consul General Wüster, who is also Station Commandant, and a number of elderly Consuls General and Counsellors. Schulenburg, who, with his staff, has also been transferred to Krummhübel, lives under such primitive conditions that he has to go to Missi Wassiltschikoff's once a week to have a bath. As all the servants in the place are Czechs and all the workmen in the sawmills are Serbs and Badoglio-faction Italians, Krummhübel has become a spy's paradise. Air raid shelters are non-existent, but I hear that an old silver mine is in process of adaptation for the purpose. Telephonic communication with Berlin has been improved. But as an emergency headquarters, Krummhübel is quite unsuitable, for not only is it readily visible from the air and therefore extremely vulnerable, but the rapid Russian advance has also rendered it geographically unsafe.

The Slovak State visit is being conducted with the usual round of drinking parties and banquets. Tido Gaspar, who began his career as a Paymaster in the Imperial Austrian Navy and has preserved his Tegethoff-style beard, is Slovakia's greatest poet and a most entertaining person, and has been rewarded by Slovakia with his present post as press spokesman.

We paid a visit to Gerhart Hauptmann, whom I have occasionally heard referred to as 'the lord of Agnetendorf' and whom I expected to find living in a typically Tolstoyan country-house. Actually, he lives in a forty-year-old 'big businessman's villa', of the type to be seen by the dozen in the Grunewald district of Berlin. It is beautifully situated, though tall pine-trees spoil the view of the facing mountains. The garden teems with pieces of sculpture, some genuine and some bogus, and Italian earthenware urns. And one wanders through leafy bowers of interlaced birch-trees.

In spite of his eighty-four years, Hauptmann is alert in mind and body, charming and devoid of any pose. His appearance is as Goethe-esque as Tido Gaspar's is Tegethoffian! Curiously enough both these poets wear the same kind of clothes, homespun tweed with a small check pattern. Gaspar sports a flowing cape, while Hauptmann favours a high-buttoned jacket from the top of which protrudes an unknotted checkered cravat. Hauptmann's friend and collaborator, Dr Behl, also affects the Goethe style. The poet's second wife, a wiry old lady with snow-white hair, intervenes constantly in the conversation of the two Olympians. She treats Hauptmann as though he were some exotic being.

The great poet's rooms are filled with mementos arranged with the precision of a museum. But he has some fine modern paintings, among them a portrait of the actor Moissi, painted by Leo Konig and a new portrait of Hauptmann himself by Padua. Frau Hauptmann told us that negotiations were in hand with Konig for another portrait of Hauptmann entitled, to use her own coy phrase, *The Master in his Old Age*. The poet's manservant, whom Frau Hauptmann addresses as 'Herr Stief', served us with real coffee. Hauptmann showed us his collection of Greek coins, dilated on literary problems, expressed admiration for Turgenev and remarked about translations that they were like women – either faithful or beautiful!

Wednesday, April 19, 1944
The British Government has cut off the diplomatic corps in London so completely from the rest of the world that everybody is betting on an early invasion. This has engendered a considerable amount of nervousness in Berlin. As a matter of fact, in view of

the unexpected rapidity of the Russian advance, the sooner the invasion comes the better. If it is delayed much longer, we shall have no space left in the East in which to take evasive action, and shall be exposed to the temptation of repeating the mistake made by the second Moltke, who, in the decisive phase of the Battle of the Marne in the first war, withdrew several army corps from France and launched them against the Russians.

The military situation in south Russia keeps on producing all sorts of puzzling surprises. Manstein and Kleist were no sooner decorated with the Knight's Cross with Swords than they were both relieved of their commands! Now that the Russians have reached the gates of Sebastopol, the position of our armies in the Crimea seems to be hopeless. On the Carpathian front and to the north and east the situation remains unchanged for the time being. The Russians are obviously marking time while bringing up reinforcements.

The pressure being exercised by the British on neutrals, and the peace articles in the Spanish press are our two major political preoccupations at the moment. The views expressed in the *Arriba* leading article seem to have been inspired not by Franco alone, but also by Sir Samuel Hoare, the British Ambassador to Madrid.

Exchange-Telegraph made a successful scoop out of the fact that two British naval officers have succeeded in escaping from a German prisoner of war camp in full uniform and reaching England thus garbed! The agency explained that there were so many foreigners wandering around Germany in ragged uniforms of every variety that they were never detected, even though they had meals in restaurants and openly took refuge in air raid shelters during their cross-country flight.

Monday, April 24, 1944

Today someone sent us a copy of the following printed memorandum, written by the Mayor of Schoneberg district:

With reference to your communication of 19.4.1944, I regret that I am unable to accede to your request for the issue of coupons for a new frying-pan. The satisfaction of the requirements of the armed forces and the devotion of the whole of German industry to the needs of total warfare demand, today more than ever, that the individual modify his way of life and restrict his demands to the absolute minimum. I trust that you, too, Sir, will appreciate this and will in future refrain from submitting even justifiable demands. No appeal against this decision can at present be considered.

Tuesday, April 25, 1944

Three important events have taken place during the last few days: the stopping of chromium deliveries by Turkey, the rejection of the Russian peace terms by Finland, and the Duce's visit to the Führer.

The stopping of the chromium deliveries came as a complete surprise to the Economic Section of the Foreign Ministry. Only one day previous to Menemencioglu's announcement, Clodius' representative issued a directive which included the statement that all was well. Turkey, he said, was receiving such valuable deliveries of manufactured goods from us, that there was no reason to fear any cessation of chromium deliveries.

The Turks told Papen that, in the face of a British ultimatum, they had had to choose between a cessation of chromium deliveries and the abrogation of their treaty of alliance with Britain. The guiding principle of Turkish policy is: 'everything short of war'. The Turks hope that they will escape becoming involved in the war if they accede to the British demands on the chromium question. Since Britain has made similar demands to other States (Spain, Portugal and Sweden) Turkey's subservience creates a precedent which may well be followed by others. We have reacted with a sharp Note. The advisability of withdrawing Papen is being discussed.

The Russo-Finnish exchange of Notes is remarkable for the mildness of the Russian contribution. The Finns have adopted exactly the right attitude, correctly appreciating the Russian mentality, which delights in protracted argument and negotiation.

The Duce's visit, despite Italian complaints about the South Tyrol, seems to have produced positive results. In the South Tyrol, some of those who elected to migrate under the terms of the Italo-German agreement have now returned to their former homes and have joined forces with those who remained to demand that the South Tyrol be returned to the Reich. Wüster reports that the South

Tyroleans do not wish to remain Italian subjects at any price. If Berlin forces them to do so, he says, then they threaten to rise in armed revolt. Gauleiters Rainer and Hofer are paying due heed to these aspirations, but the German Embassy in the Salo Republic is maintaining a reserved attitude.

May 1944

'No invasion, so far'

Monday, May 8, 1944
On Saturday, April 29, Sunday, May 7, and again today, despite bad weather, there have been heavy daylight raids, directed primarily against the city centre and the governmental area. The Foreign Ministry branch at Karlsbad 8 has been destroyed. One bomb hit the shelter in front of the Kaiserhof Hotel. The area between the Tiergarten station and the Grosser Stern was subjected to carpet-bombing. Moabit, too, has suffered severely. The Americans are now using explosive bombs with containers which have deeper penetration action into the ground.

Thursday, May 11, 1944
The barbaric cold of the last few weeks has now given way to spring. Green shoots are springing up between the ruins, the heavily-hit Tiergarten has a new air of freshness. Nature is covering man's misdeeds with a mantle of green. The bomb-shattered trees are beginning to burgeon anew.

At a Press conference at the Propaganda Ministry it was announced that members of an English SS-formation, which has recently been established, would soon be appearing on the Berlin streets, wearing royal British insignia!

Wednesday, May 17, 1944
Yesterday there was another invasion alarm. 'Reliable sources' reported that the enemy had landed at six places. It turned out, however, to be nothing more than landings by night scouting parties, which usually land from six to ten men.

The military authorities do not expect any major landings before the weekend, when moon and tide offer favourable conditions which will not recur for another four weeks.

The prospect of the invasion is still being faced with confidence. Everyone is hoping that when the invasion has been repulsed there will be a turn in the tide of war in our favour.

Regarding the evacuation of Sebastopol and the Crimea nothing is known beyond what has been stated in the OKW communiqué.

Tonight again, some thirty aircraft flew a sortie over the city. They come in so swiftly that one scarcely has time to reach a shelter before being surrounded by flares and exploding bombs.

Tuesday, May 23, 1944

No invasion, so far. The next 'critical date' is said to be June 20. On the other hand the air offensive has been stepped up. In Berlin the sirens go off every day. Last Sunday in the Brandenburg-Mecklenburg area, trains, cattle in the meadows, haystacks and pedestrians were for the first time attacked by low-flying aircraft. On the journey from Eberswalde to Berlin we passed blazing freight-cars full of potatoes at the Bernau marshalling-yards. The military value of these attacks is practically nil, and the inconvenience and irritation caused to the general public is so much the greater.

The enemy Ministry of Information reports that National Socialist 'political commissars' are to be posted to all units of the Armed Forces.

June 1944

The invasion is launched – Our 'secret weapons' come into action: prompt retaliation by the enemy – The enemy's 'vast material superiority' versus 'the iron will of the German soldier'

Tuesday, June 6, 1944

Contrary to all prophecy, the invasion was launched last night. At 7.00 a.m. the Duty Officer passed on to me the first reports, received from German sources. The first allied communiqués came later. Speeches by Churchill, the King and the heads of Governments-in-exile and Eisenhower's proclamation leave us in no doubt that D-Day has dawned.

This morning both sides assert that they are pleased at the results of the initial operations. The majority of the first wave of invading troops is said to have been destroyed. But the invasion fleet, enveloped in a smoke-screen and protected by the guns of the Navy, is at anchor off the coast. At the moment it is not possible to say whether this is an exploratory probe or the main attack. The restrictions to be imposed on travel in the event of invasion have not yet been put into operation. But the postal authorities have stopped all telephone calls. While the State Railways have shown themselves equal to all demands made on them, the postal service seizes every excuse to curtail its activities. When a railway station is destroyed, twenty-four or forty-eight hours suffice to put it in working order again; but the patching-up of a telephone connection takes weeks, despite the fact that tens of thousands of connections are no longer required, since the houses of the subscribers no longer exist.

Wednesday, June 7, 1944

On this second day, the situation on the invasion front looks less rosy. During the night the enemy, who enjoys a quite fantastic superiority in the air, succeeded in landing very considerable forces and gaining a firm foothold; the Atlantic Wall is said to have been breached to a depth of twenty-two miles on a twelve mile front. As happened at Anzio and Nettuno, there is a grave danger that the bridgehead will be extended.

From Italy, too, comes bad news. Alexander has not stopped at Rome, but is hard on our heels in pursuit.

Tuesday, June 20, 1944

It is now two weeks since the invasion began, but we have still not yet succeeded in throwing the enemy back into the sea. The Cotentin peninsula has been cut off by the Americans, and our land contact with Cherbourg has been broken. The great port is threatened with the same fate as that which overtook Singapore, Sebastopol and other naval bases, which were captured from inland, with hardly a shot having been fired at them from the sea.

It is estimated that the enemy has landed twenty-five divisions, or one-third of the total forces earmarked for the invasion.

In the meanwhile the Secret 'V1' and 'V2' Weapons have come into action. Although they are causing some measure of confusion, I do not believe they will have any decisive effect on the invasion operations, let alone on the outcome of the war. But they are proving to be a morale-booster at home. In Berlin in particular, their introduction is being discussed with great excitement.

In view of the invasion, the fall of Rome has evoked but little interest. Yesterday we evacuated Perugia.

A notice is being circulated round the Foreign Ministry by the house administration stating that there are three vacant floors in a requisitioned building in Dahlem which are waiting for occupants. The various sections will be only too delighted to occupy these rooms. I am afraid that our bureaucrats will not need a second invitation. What a lovely opportunity to set up more wholly superfluous new offices! In this fifth year of war, officialdom is quite content to leave premises unoccupied for months on end in sections of the city in which forty per cent of the living accommodation has been destroyed.

Wednesday, June 21, 1944

The fear expressed by many Berliners that retaliation for the use of the Secret Weapon would not be long in coming have been swiftly justified. This morning we were hit by a heavy attack. The enemy formations came over in two waves. The first came in over the North Sea into Mecklenburg, turned south near Stettin, followed the course of the upper reaches of the Oder and attacked Berlin from the east. The second appeared in the Brandenburg-Schwerin area, set course for the Spreewald and approached Berlin from the south-east. The alarm went at 9.00 a.m., and it was 11.15 before the all-clear was sounded. The dense clouds of smoke from burning buildings have made it so dark, that we have had to turn on the electric light, and cars in the streets have their headlights on. The Chancellery has again been severely damaged. The Foreign Ministry received three direct hits. My own office was undamaged, although one bomb landed within a dozen yards of it. It protrudes from the surrounding wreckage like a cigar box. The window-panes are shivered once again and the floor is buried in rubble, glass splinters and brick-dust. One large mirror came crashing to the ground, but did not break. The worst hit were the offices of the Press Section.

Tuesday, June 27, 1944

Today the Foreign Minister returned from a short visit to Finland. A joint communiqué states that the Finnish Government has asked for the help of German arms and that Germany has agreed to come to Finland's aid. The reshuffle of the Finnish Government has obviously been postponed. The results of the Foreign Minister's visit are regarded as a diplomatic success. How long they will continue to be so regarded will depend on what happens in the military field.

The new Russian offensive has been marked with considerable initial success. Vitebsk has been surrounded. On the western front, the fall of Cherbourg is imminent. Against the vast material superiority of the enemy all we have is 'the iron will of the German soldier'. Cherbourg will furnish the allies with the high-seas port which is essential to the prosecution of their future operations. They can now make a start with the transportation of their heavy material.

July and August 1944

The military situation deteriorates – Repercussions of the July 20 plot: 'indescribable general confusion': the Wehrmacht dissatisfied with our political and military leadership – Mission to Switzerland: news of the 'liberation' of Paris – Rumania's defection

Wednesday, July 5, 1944

The military situation is visibly deteriorating. One hardly dares to read the Army's communiqués. No details are available regarding the nature of the catastrophe that has overtaken our northern Army Group. Busch is to be replaced by Model and Rundstedt by Kluge. As if a change in the high command could achieve any useful result under the present circumstances!

The battle for Vilna and Dünaburg has begun. The first phases of the battle for Warsaw are in progress. How, in these circumstances, can we go to the help of the Finns? How can Finland be defended, if the Russians cut off the Baltic?

In Italy one city after another is being surrendered to the enemy – partly out of respect for cultural and historical values, or so the OKW communiqué would have us believe!

Saturday, July 15, 1944

The British and Americans have launched a new major offensive on the western front. Because yesterday was France's national day, many people expected that a second landing would be made in celebration. And because no such landing took place, the confirmed optimists now say that the Normandy operations are obviously tying down greater forces than the enemy anticipated.

The absolute prohibition on all travel in East Prussia and the partial prohibition on journeys in the remainder of the Reich are significant pointers to the difficulty we are experiencing in sending supplies and reinforcements to the eastern front. The present situation is that our north-south lines of communication have been cut by the Russians, and only those running east-west remain open to us. In East Prussia the first preparatory measures for the evacuation of the civilian population are in hand. If the Russians approach any nearer to the German frontier, Draconian measures will have to be introduced if we are to avoid a repetition of what happened in France in the summer of 1940, when the streams of refugees temporarily so impeded the military movements of the French forces that the defence of the country became extremely difficult.

The question naturally arises whether there is any political way out of a military situation which has become impossible. As far as the West is concerned I see no way out, and my opinion is confirmed by that of the Irish chargé d'affaires here. With regard to the other side, I very much doubt whether Hitler could ever bring himself to negotiate with the Russians. It must not be forgotten that co-operation with Britain was the cornerstone of his political conception, coupled with a determination to destroy bolshevism and acquire new *lebensraum* at the expense of Russia. In my opinion he still adheres to this goal today. The military situation, which so urgently calls for some sort of understanding with the Russians, obviously does not disconcert him. But there is a further question which one must ask oneself: to what extent do the Russians now think that any negotiations with us would be worthwhile? As long as the military situation remains unstabilised, the Russians will, I think, show little enthusiasm for negotiation.

Friday, July 21, 1944
Yesterday afternoon, sitting in the foyer of the Hotel Elefant in Weimar after having attended Peter Puckler's wedding to a Fräulein Brand, we heard on the radio a special announcement stating that an attempt had been made on the Führer's life. We had all come together in Weimar on the evening of July 19 for an eve-of-wedding dinner party. During the evening Peter Yorck, who shared with me the duties of best man, was again and again called to the telephone and eventually declared that unforeseen events compelled him to return immediately to Berlin. The wedding party was thus reduced to thirteen, and the Pücklers' gardener, who had brought venison and a mass of flowers from Branitz with him, was co-opted to make up the numbers for the wedding breakfast on July 20. As the special announcement had been extremely terse, we had no idea of the extent of the treason involved, and it never entered our heads to think that Peter Yorck might have been implicated in it. It was

only this morning in Berlin that I gathered a general impression of what had happened. The general confusion is indescribable. Every hour items of news – often contradictory – come seeping through. Everyone, with the exception of Goebbels, seems to have lost his head.

Monday, August 7, 1944

From the publicity point of view, the handling of July 20 by the authorities has been just about as inept as it could possibly be. Legatus is quite right, when he writes in the *Basler Nachrichten* 'It is not the attempt itself, but the nature of the proclamations issued to the people and the armed forces in connection with it, that have done such severe damage to the prestige of the Third Reich. This will come as no surprise to the observer of internal political affairs in Germany. He must have noted the same symptons as appeared both on June 30, 1934 and after the *Burgerbraukeller* plot, after the outbreak of war and, indeed, also after the disappearance of Rudolf Hess. In all these moments of crisis, the normally so self-confident régime lost its head and displayed a measure of uncertainty which surprised even its opponents and led to the drawing of conclusions that were as noteworthy as they were unflattering to the Third Reich.

Tuesday, August 8, 1944

There can no longer be any doubt that the July 20 plot and attempted *putsch* was the result of a deeply-rooted dissatisfaction in the Wehrmacht with our political and military leadership. The official explanation that it was the work of a small clique of reactionary officers is contradicted by the facts of the case. The conspirators are for the most part officers who owe their careers to National Socialism; and that applies equally to Stauffenberg, who is already a Colonel at the age of thirty-seven.

Public reaction to the plot is less violent than one would have expected, although July 20 brought home to the masses the crisis in our national leadership, it has not reduced their readiness to follow that leadership. Since no one has a comprehensive view of the situation that has arisen or can see any way out, and since everyone fears that any display of disloyalty might well contribute to a deterioration of the situation, the régime can continue to rely on the further support of the people. The situation today differs from that in 1918 in many respects. For today, despite the burden of the air attacks, the morale of the nation is unimpaired.

Berne – Wednesday, August 30, 1944

I have been in Switzerland since August 21. The Swiss press is completely fascinated by the spectacle of the avalanche of events, hurtling downwards with ever-increasing momentum. In Geneva the expulsion of our troops from southern France has left a lasting impression. Police battalions and customs officials, most of them unarmed and many of them wounded, are arriving there from the Haute Savoie and asking to be interned. The German Consulate is having a rough time. Negotiations with the appropriate Swiss authorities are proving by no means easy to conduct. In the pubs the 'liberation' of Paris is being noisily celebrated. Cars, decorated with tricolours and packed with French *maquisards,* are parading through the streets. But I have not been subjected to any inconvenience because I am a German. I was still in Geneva when the news of Rumania's defection came through.

In Switzerland the question of who is going to win the war is now regarded as having been answered, and attention is now concentrated on the potential aspects of the post-war order. The collapse of Germany, regarded as inevitable, is regarded with considerable uneasiness by the Swiss. They fear that the war will now come still closer to their frontiers. The call-up of men to the colours still continues apace, and the trains are crammed with mobilised soldiers. There is a feeling that, if north, west and east Germany are lost, the German Government, with the support of a few SS divisions, might withdraw and establish itself in a stronghold in the Alpine regions on the Swiss frontiers.

Recent events have had the same demoralising effect on the German colony in Switzerland as we have observed in the German colonies in other countries. Recalled members of the diplomatic and consular services are refusing to return to Germany. One of them has suddenly discovered that he is an epileptic and has gone into a Swiss nursing-home. Very soon, side by side with the 1933 emigrants we shall have the emigrants of 1944. Very little is seen or heard of the Italians who fled to Switzerland after

Mussolini's downfall. Alfieri, Marcellino and Cyprienne del Drago have discreetly gone to ground somewhere or other. The Crown Princess of Italy is busy organising gift-parcels for Italian prisoners of war, adorned with the cornflower-blue wrapper of the House of Savoy. In Geneva the Italian colony ducked underground at once on the collapse of fascism and is only now very cautiously poking its nose above the surface. Politically, these Italians are split into neo-fascists, Badoglio-Bonomi adherents, monarchists and communists. Neither the old Italy nor the new is having a bad press in Switzerland. The Swiss press continues, as before, to assert that it was Mussolini who prevented us from overrunning Switzerland.

With me on the train from Berne to Zurich were twenty Canadian, New Zealand and Australian Air Force pilots. On the same train on the return journey I ran into a drunken Polish football team, which had just won some cup or other in Zurich. The great Polish stronghold here is the town of Freiburg, where there are said to be no less than seventeen thousand Poles, many of them students. The latest wave of emigrants to arrive in Switzerland consists of Rumanians. The Carol-emigration has now been followed by the Antonescu-emigration. Herr von Janner of the Federal Political Department tells me that since the spring Marshal Antonescu has been trying to save members of the Rumanian intelligentsia from falling into Russian hands and has been trying to get all his friends into Switzerland. The Rumanian Legation in Berne has come down on the side of King Michael; the Rumanian Legation in Berlin has reaffirmed its staunch support of Germany! In Geneva I met Sveto Radeff, who had previously been attached to the Bulgarian Legation in Berlin. He told me that the people in Geneva simply could not understand how Germany, which had had so many trumps in its hand, could have got into the situation in which it now finds itself.

In Basle I looked up Juan Barcenas, a Spanish diplomat who was a friend of mine in Vienna. A British colleague had hinted, he said, that the British would have to fight the Russians at the latest by 1965. Barcenas thinks that the allies are planning a purely military administration of Germany and that the inauguration of any kind of democratic German government is not at present being contemplated. This explains the cool attitude adopted by the British towards the events of July 20.

September 1944

Berlin – Saturday, September 2, 1944

On the return journey we were surrounded in the blacked-out station in Karlsruhe by a terrific, ear-splitting din. Two thousand Hitler Youths, aged from ten to sixteen, were waiting, spade in hand, to go off to Alsace, where they are to dig trenches.

I find it difficult to make head or tail of the articles that are at present being handed out to the Press. An article entitled 'The Secret of the Final Struggle', by an SS war correspondent in the *Börsenzeitung* of August 29, has evoked considerable comment. In it the writer asserts:

1. Churchill had known all about the Secret Weapons, well in advance.
2. He had been unable to prevent the construction of them.
3. He had failed to beat us in the making of them.
4. He had evolved no defence against them.
5. He knew, that a time would come, when the war would enter its third phase, in which, exactly as he himself had done in 1942, Germany would begin the war afresh and that this time Germany would be on top.

Just as he knew all about the V1, he will soon make the acquaintance of some more "horrible things". And there is something else, even more terrifying, that he knows: he knows exactly when he can expect them.

It is for this reason that he wrote: '1919=1943' and decreed that the end – our end, that is, from sheer exhaustion – must be encompassed in 1943. Well – 1943 has come and gone. Even we ourselves have no conception of what this has meant to Churchill and Roosevelt. Now there was only one course open to them: at this last moment to make a desperate joint attempt to end 'their' phase of the war in 'their' way; and this is what is now happening.

If any further proof is needed of the way in which his mind was working, then Churchill himself has furnished it, when in a recent interview he said: 'We must end the war by the autumn, otherwise ...' and then the old fire-raiser stopped.

'By the autumn'. At least we know why we must now make our last, great effort. To do so is not beyond our power. In this war, never once have we given up at the critical moment. And whatever the last price may be, we are prepared to pay it, with every means and with all the strength at our disposal. Victory now really is very near.

The excitement over July 20 has now died down somewhat. But the cases before the People's Court go on, and the wave of arrests continues. The most contradictory rumours are circulating about the fate of some of the arrested men. No one knows who has been hanged and who still lives. Quite a number of people have been arrested simply because their names, often without their knowledge, were on some government list or other.

Not a word has been published about Field-Marshal von Kluge's death. Some say that he committed suicide and give involvement in the July plot and the defeats in France as the reason.

There are to be two further departures from the diplomatic corps here. This week Federico Diez returns to Madrid. As a friend of the new Foreign Minister Lecqueria, he has been recalled to take up a post in the Ministry. Among the Swiss, Tino Soldati, whose recall has been demanded by the Security Services, is also to leave us. Soldati has been under surveillance for years without anything against him coming to light. The origin of the suspicions against him lies in a remark he is said to have made to a Hungarian diplomat while on leave in Berne, which the latter repeated to the German authorities. It was his bad luck to have been a friend of many people who have been arrested or are under suspicion. It is our good fortune that he is a man possessed of outstanding intelligence, which will help him to rise superior to the persecution mania of the German Security Services and to retain his objectivity concerning recent events.

The 'total' war is now entering upon its last phase. All cultural institutions are to be disbanded, the Charlottenburg Opera is to be closed and its members have been 'called-up' to work at the Siemens factory. The ticket collectors have disappeared from the underground. It has taken five years of war to rid us of these people, who disappeared from the New York subway system twenty years ago. But the laborious process of selling and clipping tickets continues.

Wednesday, September 6, 1944
Brauchitsch has published an article in the *Völkische Beobachter*, condemning the July 20 conspirators.

Herr von Killinger, our Minister in Bucharest, has committed suicide; he shot his female secretary and then himself. Obviously because they were about to be handed over to the Russians. There is still no contact with our Bucharest Legation, and nothing is known regarding the fate of the other members of the staff. Of Clodius, Rantzau and Adelmann there is no trace. Only Langenhan, who was not a member of the Legation staff, has got away.

I lunched with the Spanish Ambassador. Should the Russians occupy Berlin, Vidal plans to move to Sigmaringen. The Swedish Legation, on the other hand, proposes to stay where it is.

Russia has declared war on Bulgaria. I trust we shall not be stupid enough to stand by the new Bulgarian Government against Russia. Now that we have in any case lost the Balkans, we should do nothing which might prevent the Russians from advancing to the Turkish frontier. The sooner the Russians reach the Mediterranean and thus impinge upon the British sphere of influence, the better. For this reason we ought to evacuate Greece. In the situation in which we find ourselves, the only thing that can still help us is bickering among our enemies. Incidentally, Bulgaria has been manoeuvring behind our back and has severed all her treaty obligations with the Axis.

The Rumanians are doing their utmost to justify their defection. The day before yesterday Popescul told me that my article, 'The Third World War' in *Berlin-Rome-Tokio*, had helped the Rumanians to come to their decision, since the article is supposed to have suggested that we ought to negotiate with the Russians. In fact, the article did not contain a word on the subject. It attracted considerable attention in England and was sharply attacked by Lindley Frazer on the radio. These repercussions prove that even to this day our publicity can still be effective, provided that we are prepared to call a spade a spade. I wrote:

> For a long time enemy publicists have been discussing the question of a Third World War. It is a curious fact that, the longer the present war lasts, the stronger rather than the weaker does interest in the subject become. It is being approached from a variety of angles. Most observers start by examining the possibilities when this war has ended and peace has been restored. All assume that it will end in a complete victory for the allied powers, Great Britain, the United States, the Soviet Union and Chungking China, and with the unconditional surrender of Germany and Japan. Then, however, the observers part company. One side maintains that absolute peace can be assured and a third war avoided only if the defeated nations – that is, Germany and Japan – are kept in perpetual subjugation; and with this purely negative object in view they demand that the active co-operation of the powers at present allied against Germany and Japan be continued in the post-war years to come. The other school of thought, heavily in the minority, takes exactly the opposite view. Its advocates assert that the danger of a third war will arise only if the conditions imposed upon the defeated nations are too. severe. They wish, therefore, to see a post-war world in which Germany and Japan also will be permitted not only to live, but to live on terms of relative parity with the victors.
>
> If the future peace is not in a position to reconcile the interests of all the belligerent powers, victors and vanquished alike, then it will not be a lasting peace. And in that case the Second World War will have been fought in vain, as was the First World War before it. The seeds of a Third World War will have been sown, which will germinate as soon as war-weariness has been overcome and a new generation, untouched by war, has taken over from the generation which waged the present conflict.
>
> The Soviet Union will emerge as the greatest land power, and the United States as the greatest maritime power. Great Britain,

even including its Empire, will be unable to compete, either on land or at sea, with either of these two, let alone with both of them in unison. The same will apply to China. There will, then, emerge only two Great Powers, in the true sense of the phrase – Russia and America. For the other two – Great Britain and China – the only course that will be open to them will be to attach themselves either to the United States or to Russia and to pursue a policy that will ensure their survival as second-class powers. Apart altogether from Germany and Japan, both of whom, if the victors of tomorrow have their way, are to be reduced to a state of technical impotence, it is naive to assume that the rest of the world will be content to live more or less permanently under the sovereignty of the four principal powers. The idea of a world police force has always proved to be Utopian, and Utopian it will remain. No alliance in the past, formed with this object in view, has endured.

A Russo-American world police force, with a sprinkling of British and Chinese added to it, will fail, not only in the face of the opposition of those over whom it professes to stand guard, but also because of the impossibility of organising such a force. The Russian world policeman and his Chinese colleague will build up friendships and enmities which will be entirely different from those developed by the American world policeman and his British assistant.

The creation of zones of interest dominated by these Great Powers will be equally impossible. Zones of interest in this sphere are, equally, zones of power. It is absurd to imagine that a Europe which opposed domination by Napoleon and which has refused to accept German leadership, will be content to acknowledge perpetual allegiance to Moscow. Any Russian attempt to dominate Europe is far more likely to throw into the arms of the defeated Germany the very nations which previously had refused to accept the sovereignty of a victorious Germany. On the other hand what possible function could be fulfilled by an Anglo-West European zone of interest, in which the German nucleus had been politically sterilised? The moment that Germany is declared to be a political no-man's-land, a common European frontier will at once spring into being between the Anglo-Western and the Russian zones of interest. It is a mistake to believe that the traditional animosities which constantly break out between Great Britain and Russia in the Far East, on the frontiers of India and even in China – in fact in the wide open spaces of the world – will not manifest themselves in the restricted areas of central and western Europe. It can, indeed, be asserted with far more certainty that an Anglo-Russian understanding, burdened as it would be with common European problems, would constitute a far greater danger to world peace than was ever constituted by the Russo-German understanding, which was confronted merely with the problems of Eastern Europe.

And, since the United States will presumably emerge as a very strong power, the intensity with which Russian and American power potential will clash will be far more violent than that engendered by an overlapping of Anglo-West European and Russian power potential.

That is the sort of world in which the enemies of Germany and Japan will find themselves. It is difficult to see what attraction a world of this nature can have for them. On the other hand, the dangers of war which are inherent in it are plain for all to see. It would be a world which would with deadly certainty conjure up a Third World War – even if one assumes that vanquished Germany and Japan would not be able to rise to their feet again.

During the last few days a number of members of Laval's government have been seen in the Wilhelmstrasse and the Hotel Adlon, among them the three Big Ds – Doriot, Déat and Darnand. They all look very dejected.

Yesterday's *Morgenpost* published an editorial proclaiming that war within the confines of the Reich had now become a citizens' war.

The Americans are at Saarbrücken and the British have crossed the German frontier near Aachen. I very much doubt our ability to wage a partisan war. We are not good at improvisation, and a partisan movement which cannot be kept adequately supplied and equipped stands no chance of success.

The Swiss Legation has advised its nationals to leave Germany by September 15, after which date, it says, no guarantee of transport facilities can be given.

Saturday, September 16, 1944
People now have to have a special permit to travel anywhere by train. To go from Horn-Bad Meinberg in Lippe to Berlin and

Vienna, Marietti had to obtain special permission from the authorities in Blomberg (Lippe). As the reason for her journey, she was advised to say that she had business to conduct in connection with property rights.

Monday, September 18, 1944

Toggenburg has been forced to resign his post as representative of the *Hamburger Fremdenblatt* and other German newspapers in Stockholm, because his wife is an American. Thus one of our best foreign correspondents and an expert on British affairs falls victim to those who persecute aristocrats and members of 'families with foreign connections'. The Ministry of Propaganda refuse even to allow him to bring his family back from Sweden. For similar reasons I have been instructed to dismiss Dr Ambroz, a representative in Agram of the *Europäische Korrispondenzen,* the foreign news service run by the Foreign Ministry. I have not the slightest intention of complying with this ridiculous demand.

I spent the weekend with Tovar, the Portuguese Minister, in Hohenfinow, where, in order to escape the air raid hazards, he has rented the country house belonging to Herr von Bethmann. Count Tovar has recently returned from three months' leave in Portugal. On the return journey he had the misfortune to land at Stuttgart-Echterdingen airport just as the town was being attacked by American bombers. According to Tovar, Salazar is extremely pessimistic and of the opinion that nothing can prevent the worst from happening. He told me that two years ago, at Salazar's instigation, he put forward a tentative suggestion that Portugal should act as mediator in peace negotiations, but had been rebuffed by Berlin. Such a chance, he says, will not occur again, even if we were now prepared to accept it. Like Vidal, Tovar is very uneasy as to the fate of his Legation if the Russians take Berlin. Since Portugal, like Spain, maintains no relations with Russia, he is anxious to make sure of securing a place of refuge in the Anglo-American zone of occupation. Vidal has already approached Steengracht on the subject, but Tovar feels that it would be rather tactless to do so. Most of his foreign colleagues, by which he obviously means the Swiss, the Swedes and the Danes, have, he says, been instructed not to fall in with any plan of general exodus on the part of the German Government. If our government moves to south

Germany, the missions of these countries wish to remain in Berlin, which would create an unprecedented situation. The Japanese, who do not wish to fall into the hands of the British or the Americans, have apparently asked to be allotted emergency quarters in East Germany. They feel that they will be safer in Russian hands!

Tovar was very amusing on the subject of senior officials of the Foreign Ministry, who received him with such affability and painted so rosy a picture of the situation that he really could not take them seriously. The most difficult period of his career, he said, had been the weeks following the meeting between the Führer and Franco at Hendaye. At that time Portugal had been certain that a joint action by Spain and Germany was afoot to take Gibraltar and close the western exit from the Mediterranean. He hinted at the secret measures which Portugal would in that case have taken in order to preserve her neutrality. Tovar remarked, with some satisfaction, that God had given power to some peoples and intelligence to others and that for eight hundred years of her history Portugal, weak as she was, had succeeded in preserving her independence and retaining her colonial possessions. Finally he wanted to know, he said, why the Foreign Minister was absolutely never to be found in Berlin and seemed to go out of his way to avoid any contact with the heads of missions and the diplomatic corps.

On September 11 we dined with Oshima, a social engagement which had been postponed many times. The Japanese were already in a fairly merry mood when we arrived at their half-destroyed Embassy in the Tiergarten at 7.30 p.m. Oshima received us on the second floor. As he had been with the Führer a short time before, he asked Schmidt, Braun von Stumm, Bassler and myself fewer pointed questions than we had feared. He was, on the other hand, most lavish with the drinks. Bottle after bottle appeared of the famous kirsch of which Oshima is so proud. We had hardly sat down to dine when the alarm sounded. After dinner, which consisted of game soup, trout, roast hare, green peas, and an ice-cream souffle, the Ambassador and his staff were extremely jovial. Oshima went to a bookcase full of collections of students' songs and took out some volumes of German drinking-songs and love-ballads. But since the Japanese pronounce their vowels very differently from us, we were regaled with renderings of such old favourites as *Draussen vor dem Tore* ... and *Heidelberg, Du Feine* ... which sounded more like the monotonous chanting of Malayan boatmen as they ply the oars.

I managed to slip away at 1.00 a.m., followed closely by Strempel, who had exactly the same idea. Unfortunately, however, our informal departure did not escape Oshima's notice. He made a complaint to the Ministry, and we received a not unmerited reprimand. The Japanese Ambassador is a convinced Germanophile; his second-in-command, Minister Sakuma, views German circumstances more coolly.

Oshima had asked for an audience of the Führer in order to offer the good offices of the Japanese for the initiation of Russo-German negotiations. In this he met with a blunt and unequivocal rebuff. However, it was conveyed to him the next day that, if Russian intentions appeared to be directed along these lines, we would be interested to hear what they proposed. Since Hitler, however, would certainly regard any desire by the Russians to conclude a peace by negotiation as a sign of weakness, he would therefore see no reason to initiate any such negotiations. So an understanding with Moscow seems out of the question.

Our attempt to take the Finnish island of Hogland has failed. The military had recommended the seizure of the island on strategic grounds. But this fiasco has given Mannerheim the excuse to change sides. The tone of the Finnish press, which even yesterday was friendly, is now embittered and accuses us of indulging in an underhand military trick.

This episode is a typical example of our inability to foresee the political consequences of *coups de main* and adventures of this sort. If, as must now be feared, Finland declares war on us, Sweden, too, will break off diplomatic relations with us, and our whole position in Scandinavia will be lost. A façade of friendly relations with Sweden was essential for the maintenance of our position in Norway and Denmark.

When things like this happen, we are only too prone to curse the bad luck that dogs us. Goebbels in his articles refers again and again to 'the temperamental whims of the Goddess of War'. This German habit of blaming others for one's own mistakes has seldom had such fateful consequences as at present.

Among the people a new 'stab-in-the-back' legend is being circulated with great skill. After the last war it was the Social

Democrats who were castigated and on whom the blame for our collapse was placed; now they say it is the generals who have let the country down and that, but for July 20, we should not now be in the deplorable situation in which we find ourselves. People are all too ready to believe this nonsense. In the countryside, where people have even less chance than in the towns of hearing what is happening, one constantly hears stories of senior officers who are to blame for everything, of the abscess which burst on July 20, and of the inner healing which has subsequently taken place. How many of these people know that the military leaders exercise no political influence and are allowed to take no military measures other than those which Hitler has ordered them to take? They are simply happy to have found scapegoats.

With each day that passes it is becoming clearer that July 20, 1944, has altered many things and must be regarded as a milestone in the history of National Socialism and of the country. Technically, the *coup d' état* was foredoomed to failure for a variety of reasons. The fact that the Führer escaped assassination is not the decisive factor. A little more steadfastness in their own ranks could still have brought success to the conspirators. The enterprise could not succeed, because the heterogeneous nature of the Corps of Officers precluded the possibility of concerted action. The mechanism of the instrument of command which was essential to a successful execution of the plot broke down almost at once. Doubts and hesitancy among the more senior officers involved, and lack of enthusiasm, if not even opposition, among the smaller fry brought down the whole enterprise. The attitude of the High Command was moulded by the scenes in the Bendlerstrasse in exactly the same way as the attitude of the majors, captains and lieutenants who were the offspring of National Socialism was moulded by the conduct of Major Remer. The existence of the SS constituted only a very minor obstacle to the success of the plot, as is proved by the participation in it of a whole number of SS leaders and SS officials. Responsibility for the failure rests with the Army itself, the same army which without a murmur of protest tolerated the disgraceful treatment of Fritsch and Blomberg and which for years has stood meekly by, while its Field-Marshals, even in military matters, were being treated like lackeys by the political leaders of the country. Had Stauffenberg and the other intellectual instigators any clear idea at all of the mental attitude of the troops whom they hoped to carry along with them?

It is significant that, with few exceptions, the prime movers in the conspiracy were noblemen who, placing their trust in the armed forces, once again tried to do what Von Papen, placing his trust in Hindenburg, the armed forces and the middle class political parties, had tried to do in 1932. The knights in uniform of 1944 committed the same mistake as did the 'Government of the Barons' in 1932. Both hoped to be able to rally a formidable following against Hitler and both failed. In 1932 it was too late. Now it is too soon.

It is nonsense to talk about a movement against Hitler which had commanded wide popular support. No one will dispute that the number of those dissatisfied with the régime has grown steadily from year to year, that it increased tremendously when the war came but diminished with the victories of the opening years, only to increase again greatly as a result of latter-day defeats, and it is equally true that the educated are far more prone to give expression to their misgivings than are the masses and that imprudent talk caused many of them to feel the heavy hand of the Gestapo. But to speak of an organised movement against Hitler, such as those which have come into being in some of the occupied territories, is a distortion of fact. On the contrary, it is just one more proof that no cohesion whatsoever existed between the various individuals or groups who have given free rein to their dissatisfaction and have consequently been penalised. Apart from those implicated in the July plot, throughout all these years there has not been a single centre of resistance which could be said to have constituted a threat to Hitler's régime. That the Gestapo has now and then attempted to draw a different picture – its revelations regarding the activities of the *Rote Kapelle* is a case in point – proves nothing. Every secret police service seeks to justify its existence by dabbling in potential threats and dangers.

The day may well come when people, who have insured themselves nicely against both a Hitler victory and a Hitler defeat, will later seek to prove that they were secret rebels against the régime, and when some of our contemporaries who listened in to enemy broadcasts with the bed-clothes over their heads will magnify their actions into a glorious act of opposition against the Third Reich. In the field of brazen opportunism the German is a difficult man to beat. Even now it makes me shudder to think of those shameless hypocrites who have never lifted a finger for years, and yet dare to sully Stauffenberg's sacrifice by spurious claims to paternity.

A third question continues to confront us during these weeks following July 20. What sort of peace would the overthrow of the régime have brought us? Speculation on the subject is limitless. Would it have been possible to work out separate settlements with the West and the East? There are some who believe that, had the régime been overthrown, the western powers would immediately have made common cause with us and joined us in a crusade against bolshevism and the advancing Russian armies. Others think that Stalin would have forgiven us all our sins and would have joined with us to throw the Americans out of western Europe.

Speculation of this nature is of little value. The British and the Americans are far too obsessed with the idea that Hitler is merely a tool in the hands of 'the *Junkers* and the Generals' to grant tolerable terms to a government composed of '*Junkers* and Generals', even with a few trade unionists thrown in for good measure. The feelers put out by Trott in this context are said to have produced most disappointing results. As for the Russians, whose war aim is the extension of their territories into central Europe, we can be sure that they would show even less insight and certainly less moderation. That a shortening of the war would save both men and material – both vital for the post-war reconstruction of the country – is obvious. What is questionable is whether the mass of the people would be grateful to Hitler's successors for a negotiated peace. There are still plenty of people who believe that victory is imminent and that we must not slacken our pace during the last few yards of the race. So, all in all, I fear that we shall not be spared a plunge into the darkest abyss of the *Historia Germaniae*.

My article, 'The Third World War', is still having repercussions. Vidal asserts that people are calling it 'Ribbentrop's political testament'. In fact, it has not been submitted either to Schmidt or Ribbentrop, and I am quite sure that the Foreign Minister has still not read it. Mühlen of the Supreme Headquarters reports that the British have made extracts which they are dropping as leaflets, to prove that on my own confession we have lost the war. On the other hand, the American medium-wave radio has condemned 'the brazen impudence of this typical Nazi effusion'!

In Hungary friction between the Government and the various

German missions is still acute. Secret attempts to opt out of the war and follow the example of Rumania, Bulgaria and Finland continue. In Slovakia Tiso is demanding the provision of emergency quarters in Germany, which does not say much for his self-confidence.

Enemy pressure in the west is strongest in the area of Aachen and the Burgundy gateway. The enemy air-drop in Holland is designed to secure the Maas, Rhine and Scheldt bridges, so repeating the manoeuvre which we ourselves carried out in the Netherlands in May 1940. If the enemy manages to pounce upon our industrial complex from the rear, by way of Cologne and Aachen and then sweep up the Rhine valley from Mülhausen to Frankfurt, the war in Western Germany will be lost. The British obviously will fan out across northern Germany, while the Americans will thrust straight down the Main river into Bavaria and Saxony.

On Sunday, September 10 central Vienna suffered a heavy air raid, which Marietti was able to watch from her mother's fourth-floor apartment in the Kirchengasse. Many beautiful old buildings were hit, including the Kaunitz mansion in the Ballhausplatz, where Metternich once had his office, Berchtold declared war in the First World War and Dollfuss was assassinated. Konstantin Liechtenstein's young wife, who was Maritza's daughter-in-law, and her mother were both killed while sheltering in the cellar of a residential building in the Bankgasse. The Viennese are dumbfounded by these unexpected events.

The French Pétain-Laval Government has been transferred to Schloss Sigmaringen, which the Hohenzollerns have been forced to evacuate. Struve has also moved in there, in order to keep in touch with Doriot. Baden-Baden, which had previously been selected as the French Government's headquarters-in-exile, was abandoned because of its increasing proximity to the front. The Spaniards, to whom Schloss Sigmaringen had been promised as an emergency headquarters, are therefore left in the air once more.

I have just received the following report dealing with the exalted exiles at present installed at Sigmaringen: 'Yesterday we returned from Sigmaringen, where we have spent two quite incredible days in a castle filled with figures straight out of a fairy-tale. It was astonishing that such dissimilar human types could conceivably exist together under one roof. Huge though the house is, it is still not big enough to prevent everyone running into everyone else the whole time.

'Only Philippe Pétain, his wife and his personal physician are surrounded by an atmosphere of icy withdrawal. Laval is very cheerful again, and winks merrily whenever Abetz now and again offers him a sweet or chocolate. The Marquis is more elegant than ever, full of self-confidence and finding everything – the schloss, the neighbourhood and the task of governing from a place of exile – just too *charmant*. He has brought two ladies with him who are, no doubt, a great comfort to him. Otherwise, there are far too few women in the place. They say that a theatrical company is arriving soon. Madame X will have her hands full. She now runs round the streets with a baby in her arms, to the jaw-gaping astonishment of the local yokels. A handsome Air Force captain, who is said to be the father of the child, is constantly at her side. At every street corner there is a French Minister, '*en somme*' or '*en action*' in the sun, hesitating and not quite sure how to spend the next half-hour. The Marshal progresses through the streets on the way to the neighbouring woods, seated in an enormous car which is driven slowly to eke out its ration of fuel; he is accompanied by one of Prince Hohenzollern's bodyguards and by a police escort. On one point everyone agrees: that Madame Z is quite impossible. The ceiling is either too high or too low. Her husband's writing-desk is smaller than that of one of his colleagues. The food does not agree with her. Madame Y has a better room than she has, although Y is only the Marquis' paramour. She has obviously never stayed in a chateau before!

'In the evenings one gropes one's way through the ill-lit Schloss. The various halls provide ten dining-tables. Abetz honours a different table with his presence each evening. Wherever morale is low, up he pops to put heart into the faint-hearted. Thus one evening we sat with the Ministers '*en sommeil*', who made no attempt to conceal their gloom. No amount of animated conversation about the lovely mountains, the beauty of the Danube or the superb apartments they occupy can rouse them from their lethargy. One of them said: '*Il me faut une femme, ou une manucure au mo ins*'. When I tried to change the subject I quickly realised that it was quite useless, for that was the mood they were in. Finally one solitary man talked, while the remainder silently gobbled the very excellent meal served to them by members of the Hohenzollern household staff. When we retired into the drawing-room after dinner, we passed by the other tables with their rows of ghost-like, familiar faces; Philippe Pétain dodged across the corridor, accompanied by his physician and by von Renthefink of the Foreign Ministry. An astonishing spectacle. Hoffman is in charge of the whole show, and Frau Hoffman looks after the details – and does so very well, apparently. Everything goes smoothly, because it is a Schloss which is used to every type of guest and the staff and servants are well trained. These latter have been reinforced by French valets, ladies' maids and chauffeurs. In addition, there are the many refugees. Curiously enough, the gentlemen of the press have not yet sniffed out this idyllic haven.'

Wednesday, September 20, 1944
Schmidt returned from Headquarters today filled with a newborn confidence. All we have to do, he says, is to hold out till the spring. Arrangements to do so have already been completed on the eastern front, and now we must take similar steps in the West. By the spring, assault armies equipped with the most modern arms will be poised on both eastern and western fronts, ready to strike at the enemy's flanks. Our reserves of raw materials are apparently ample to enable us to implement this plan. The defeats in both East and West have been the result of treason, sabotage and the incompetence of the senior commanders. Kluge is to blame for the evacuation of France and the break-through at Avranches, and at the appropriate moment there will be an official statement on the subject, it seems.

If only things really were as Schmidt has portrayed them! Ever since Stalingrad, views of this kind have been put forward. Time and again some date has been given, by which we have been promised an improvement or a turn in the tide; but nothing of the sort has ever happened. I am afraid I find it impossible to alter my sceptical judgment of the situation. Still, we have been given something to talk about with foreigners; and, after all, putting fresh courage into others is part of our job.

Early this morning I telephoned Marietti in Reelkirchen. The operator refused to accept a private call, so I had to say this was an official call. As I began to speak, I heard the listening-in device come into operation. Then the exchange came on the line to say that my conversation was being monitored and was obviously not of an official character. I was warned that this was contrary to regulations.

Subsequent enquiries disclosed that some little while ago a staff, consisting of a Minister, a senior Counsellor and three telephone operators, had been set up at the Foreign Ministry switchboard, to check which connections were indulging in private calls. This ruling applies only to personnel of Legation Counsellor status downwards and to non-established officials like myself; a typical example of the social outlook in a National Socialist Ministry. Here is another: two hundred and fifty senior officials have been absolved from carrying out air raid warden duty, the junior staff, who have received no such concession, are presented with a small cake of foreign soap on completion of twenty nights on duty (for women, fifteen nights!). Ambassadors, Ministers, Privy Councillors and Consuls General are as hard to discover among the ranks of the fire-watchers as the proverbial needle in a haystack. On the other hand, the chief air raid warden on duty is required to telephone at once to these dignitaries at their homes, the moment there is danger of a raid! Needless to say, junior staff are forbidden to ring up themselves and ask what the air raid situation is.

A little while ago, all letter-boxes were closed, in order to save the petrol involved in emptying them by van! That millions of people will now have to wear out their irreplaceable shoes, walking to a post office to post their letters, does not seem to have occurred to anybody in authority.

Thursday, September 21, 1944
Since early yesterday all westbound trains have been cancelled. The official reason given is that it is because Soest has been heavily bombed and enemy paratroops have been dropped in the vicinity of Osnabrück.

I lunched with Eberhard Oppenheim at the Adlon. He is said to have been held under arrest for a fortnight, but he did not say a word about it. As usual, he had brought a suitcase with him, containing food, which he unpacked quite unconcernedly in the dining-room. When, later, he complained about being kept waiting for the wine he had ordered, the head-waiter said majestically: 'Don't you know there's a war on?' To which Oppenheim with equal hauteur retorted: 'I would draw your attention to the fact that the distance from the wine-cellar to the restaurant is not an inch longer in wartime than it is in peacetime!'

In the evening I went to see Dicki Wrede, who has installed herself in a tiny cellar under the Alberts' old house which has been destroyed by bombs. The house itself has been burned down, all except a verandah, where we dined by candlelight. The surroundings were quite fantastic – a cross between a cave-dweller's hole and a porter's lodge.

Monday, September 25, 1944

Spent the weekend with Ette Kottwitz in Reinersdorf (Silesia). How benevolent the clean atmosphere of the countryside is, in comparison with the horror-world in which we have our being. An hour's drive through the woods, and all horrors disappear. An officer on leave from France, from his Panzer unit in Sagan, a Captain von Portatius, told us that the officer complement of his unit had been wiped out three times over during the course of the war. Most of the Panzer officers died, apparently, in the same manner, shot through the head while observing from their open turrets. On Sunday evening the peace of the countryside was broken by violent gunfire. On the return journey we passed a train at Cottbus full of refugees. As in the early days of war, the carriages were covered with slogans scribbled in chalk. On one of them was written: 'Sieg Heil's a bore, Down with the war!'

We had a visit from Helene Biron. She has been working in Paris for one of our departments which, war or no war, deals with colonial problems. Friedrich Sieburg remarked 'German colonial policy consists of Helene Biron and a pair of scissors!'

The main events in the military field are the loss of the Balkans, the occupation of Reval (Tallin) by the Russians, their advance on Riga and the battle of Arnheim, which the neutral press describes as one of the greatest decisive battles of the war. If we succeed in preventing the British land forces that are now pushing forward out of Eindhoven from joining up with the paratroops dropped at Arnheim, we shall have survived the first phase of the war in Holland.

Thursday, September 28, 1944

Dieckhoff (Madrid) and Hüne (Lisbon), who have been here for the past few weeks, are not to return to their posts. They have been blamed for the cancellation of the wolfram deliveries and the other difficulties which have arisen in our trade with the Iberian countries. In reality, allied pressure on Spain and Portugal has been so strong that nobody could have done anything about it. Politically, the recall of the two Ambassadors at this juncture is a mistake which may well jeopardise our future diplomatic relations with the Iberian countries. We must now face the possibility that Spain and Portugal, urged on by Britain, will refuse to accept any new ambassadors we may appoint.

Dr Schmidt-Leonhardt of the Ministry of Propaganda has, at the request of the Directorate for Implementing the Total War, submitted to the Foreign Ministry a memorandum regarding the duplication of work by the various departments of the two Ministries concerned. The Ministry of Propaganda demands that the Politico-Cultural, the Broadcasting and the Press Sections of the Foreign Ministry be closed down. In support of the demand, the memorandum quotes a Führer directive of 1933, which lays down that, while the Foreign Minister retains the right to prepare foreign propaganda, the Ministry of Propaganda will be responsible for its dissemination.

A police control has now been imposed on the tramway service over the Halensee bridge. All vehicles whose route takes them through the Grunewald are now being stopped and searched for escaped British prisoners of war.

From today, all journeys abroad by members of the Foreign Ministry will have to receive the prior authorisation of the Foreign Minister himself. Up till now, the approval of the head of the section, countersigned by the personnel department, sufficed. Only diplomatic couriers are exempt from this new regulation.

October 1944

The Axis crumbles – Hungary lost? – Führer Headquarters forced to vacate East Prussia

Tuesday, October 3, 1944

The French Government-in-exile in Sigmaringen has issued a proclamation, declaring Pétain to be the sole legal head of the French State. The transfer of Pétain and Laval to Germany was one of those checkmate moves of the directors of our 'political warfare department' that are quite incomprehensible to anyone with ordinary common sense. Any 'political warfare department' worthy of the name would have left Pétain in France and allowed Laval to flee to Spain or Portugal. De Gaulle would then have been forced to join issue with Pétain on his own ground. As it is, we have relieved him of this disadvantage. Equally, the presence of Laval in a neutral country would have been a bone of contention between the allies. In any case, the presence of Doriot, Darnand and Deat in Germany is a perfectly adequate facade for a French government-in-exile.

A German 'war of nerves' exists only in the enemy's imagination. In reality, nothing worthwhile is being done in this direction. Abroad it is being asserted that Papen is in Madrid. He is not. Papen in Madrid and Schulenburg in Stockholm would have needed to do nothing more than show themselves in public once or twice: for the Russians, Papen in Madrid would be a nightmare, and the presence of Schulenburg in Stockholm would be an equal nightmare for the western allies. Instead, old Schulenburg is being kept in reserve because his name is apparently on some list or other as a possible future Foreign Minister, and Papen is simply sitting here twiddling his fingers.

Saturday, October 7, 1944

Under the title of 'They'd be Surprised!' the *Schwarze Korps* of October 5, 1944, published a leading article on the plan for partisan warfare in Germany. The *Stockholms Tidningen* comments: 'This bloodthirsty article is, of course, mostly propaganda, designed to deter the allies from an occupation of Germany and peaceful Germans from any co-operation with them in the future.' That, I think, is a correct interpretation of the object of the article. But I doubt very much whether it will have the desired effect. Partisan warfare cannot be simply 'staged', like an opera. If we really have any serious intentions in this direction, then it is militarily disastrous to draw enemy attention to the fact. Had Germany had prior warning of a partisan movement in Russia, the security measures on our lines of communication would, presumably, have been better organised. As it was, the absence of any preliminary precautionary measures proved to be a great handicap to us. The assertion that a German partisan war would be the most dangerous of all, because it would have the support of our current leaders, does not carry conviction. An occupation of the country by the enemy and the initiation of partisan warfare are synonymous with the loss of the war. In none of the countries in which a partisan movement has emerged – France, Yugoslavia, Italy, Greece – was partisan warfare initiated and directed by the government which had lost the war. The only exception is the Soviet Union. But the Soviet Union had not yet lost the war, but had merely suffered a series of defeats, which did not prove to be decisive. It is conceivable that the régime might be able to organise a partisan war left of the Rhine. But if a major portion of the country were occupied, I find it hard to believe that Hitler would still retain the strength and the authority to create a partisan movement. In that case the reign of terror against our fellow-countrymen called for in the *Schwarze Korps* article would be ineffective. The individual German is not going to continue as a private war a war that has already been lost by his government. The article does us a great disservice, since it makes a contribution to confusing our thought regarding the needs of the future.

Side by side with rumours about the effects of the new Secret Weapons, prophecies calculated to raise morale are being launched. The latest is:

At the beginning of November the allies will suffer the greatest defeat in their history. A new German weapon will plunge Britain into a chaos from which she will not be able to emerge without Germany's help. In April 1945 the whole weight of the

German war effort will be directed towards the East. Within fifteen months Russia will be in German hands. Communism will have been eradicated, and the Jews will have been cleared out of Russia. In the summer of 1946, German U-boats with a new weapon will destroy the remnants of the British and American fleets. By September 1946 Japan will have established sovereignty over China, Australia and south-east India. Under German leadership Europe will enter upon an era of new and unprecedented glory.

Thursday, October 12, 1944

The western front is still holding for the time being, but in the East the Baltic armies have been cut off. In southern Hungary, Russian armour and Cossack brigades are overrunning the lowlands, and Cossacks are reported to have come within forty miles of Budapest. Veesenmeyer seems to be showing as little appreciation of the internal political developments in Hungary as did Killinger in Rumania and Beckerle in Bulgaria. He had disbanded portions of his legation, an act which is regarded both by his own people and by the Hungarians as a sign of loss of confidence. In moments of crisis, most of our Ministers seem to lose their heads. Ettel in Teheran, Killinger in Bucharest and Beckerle in Sofia all allowed their own personnel and the entire German colony to fall into the hands of the enemy. Not one of them thought of organising a motor convoy, ready to move out of one end of the city as soon as the enemy entered at the other. So far only Rahn in Tunis has accomplished this measure.

The bombing season reopened on October 6 with daylight raids on Spandau, Tegel and Charlottenburg. Mosquitoes appeared overhead at 4.00 a.m. today.

Friday, October 20, 1944

Today is the first anniversary of Bose's 'Free India' Government and a reception was held in the Esplanade Hotel. Habib ur Rahman, the president of the local Indian Association, greeted those present, among whom were Oshima, Six and Lorenz. The SS, which has bodily taken over the Indian Legation, were very much in evidence there. The Indian volunteer brigade, which had an adventurous march from the Bay of Biscay to Alsace, is now three thousand strong. In contrast to many German units, who return home without arms, the Indians have all brought their small arms with them. This feat, performed under the most difficult conditions, and the loyalty they display to their German officers in spite of enemy leaflet-propaganda, have come as a pleasant surprise, since no one had placed any great value on these troops. The Indian reception, incidentally, was rather like a spiritualist seance. Erdmannsdorf, for instance, expressed on behalf of the Foreign Ministry the hope that next year's ceremony would take place in India itself! Now that the enemy is on the very frontiers of Germany, that the Home Guard has been called up, that the Japanese are suffering defeat after defeat and that the Americans have landed in the Philippines, the prospects of any 'liberation' of India seem to be somewhat meagre. But those present seemed hardly aware of this painful situation. It seemed almost as though the clothes of a man who had been buried that morning were now sitting at table with us.

I was overwhelmed with a similar feeling of unreality at a battue shoot in Jahnsfelde. The hunters were all aristocrats, despite the fact that since July 20 the persecution of the aristocracy has been proceeding apace. All the beaters were French prisoners of war, although there remains hardly a German soldier on French soil. On the property we saw Russian prisoners of war at work in the fields, despite the fact that the Red Army will very soon be poised on the frontiers of the Reich. At the hunt-dinner that followed were Spaniards, Rumanians and Bulgarians, diplomats whose countries have either deserted us or adopted a very much more reserved attitude towards us. Among the bag was a wild boar, which also seemed to have come from another world, so mighty were its proportions. The sportsmen were dumbfounded at having put up so magnificent a specimen only thirty miles from Berlin. But that was the only thing that we had to be enthusiastic about; we preferred not to think about other matters.

I spent four days in Reelkirchen, where on Sunday, October 15, a low-flying attack on Horn killed fifteen people. Twenty machines cruised over Reelkirchen, bringing the whole area under fire and damaging severely the small railway junction of Schieder. On the way back we ran into an air raid in Hanover. In the station shelters there were scenes which reminded me of Gorki's Night Asylum. Dozens fainted. At the shelter entrances complete panic, because the people believed that tonight Hanover would be razed completely to the ground. We arrived in Berlin at 3.00 a.m. The Zoo station is crammed with refugees and homeless who spend the night there, whether there is a raid or not. There are clear signs that the nerves of the people are cracking; inexpressible anxiety, horror, bitterness and fatalism are stamped on all their faces.

The Government in Hungary has fallen. The downfall of Horthy was no more surprising than was the *coup d' état* carried out with our help by the Arrow Cross Führer Szalasy. It had been known for a long time that Horthy possessed a secret transmitter. But this makes all the more inexplicable the fact that Horthy's request for an armistice and his orders to the Hungarian troops to cease fire should have been ignored. At the last moment Rahn was sent to Budapest and, in conjunction with Veesenmeyer, succeeded in persuading Horthy to cancel his proclamation and to abdicate. The prospects of the new Government in Hungary will depend on the military situation. If the Russians reach Budapest, it will hardly be possible to protect Vienna.

Tuesday, October 24, 1944

During the last few weeks, Belgrade, Aachen and Debrecen have fallen. In East Prussia a new Russian offensive has been launched. Führer Headquarters is being forced to vacate East Prussia.

A captured American journalist, Beattie, who was interrogated by Schmidt and Strempel, thinks that there is still a possibility of negotiations between the Anglo-Saxon powers and ourselves – an opinion that I cannot share.

In the Hotel Adlon the French emigrants are a combination of forlornness and feverish activity. Many of them are running round in German uniforms, some with badges of high rank. Leon Degrelle, too, can be seen sitting around in the lobby of the Adlon. Another Adlon figure is the Croat, de Monti, erstwhile diplomat, tennis champion, film producer, political agent and self-styled count. He drives around in an enormous English film director's car and cuts a great dash. Where he gets his petrol and the succulent delicacies which he presses upon his friends remains his own well-kept secret.

Gottfried Bismarck, who was standing his trial before the People's Court in connection with July 20, was yesterday found not guilty. Whether he will be released remains to be seen. The verdict at least spares the régime the macabre spectacle of the execution of one of Bismarck's grandsons. But so far we have not heard of any of the other conspirators being granted a pardon.

Wednesday, October 25, 1944
The London correspondent of *YA* quotes a declaration which Mussolini drew up after his arrest and sent to Admiral Franco Maugeri through Badoglio. Mussolini is said to have declared that the Germans had never appreciated the significance of the Mediterranean problem, and that his repeated efforts to convince the Führer had invariably ended in failure. Hitler's great mistake, according to Mussolini, was his declaration of war on Russia before he had stabilised his position in the Mediterranean. Instead of linking the Near East and Africa by means of land operations and instead of conquering Egypt, Hitler had initiated a fresh front in Russia and thus nullified his diplomatic victory of 1939. After the fall of France, Italy had to come into the war, Mussolini said, if she were not to abandon all her just claims. He, Mussolini, had been convinced that the Germans would land in England. After Stalingrad he had advised Hitler to come to terms with Stalin, even if this meant giving up all the Russian territories that had been conquered.

Saturday, October 28, 1944
Dined at Carl Clemm's with the Italian Ambassador Anfuso and his very attractive wife, a Hungarian from Budapest. Anfuso bears current events with philosophical calm. He has acquired the ability to stand back and contemplate in its true perspective his career, which had just reached its peak when fascism came to an end. Anfuso has no illusions regarding Italy's future. He says that the British have strong strategic and tourist interests there and is quite sure that they will wrest the country from the grip of bolshevism. Politically, he regards Italy as lost. During the last decades, he says, the British have too often been angered by the brash and boastful struttings of fascism to allow Rome once more, as Churchill expressed it, to point an empty pistol at their heads. The Anfusos are living in Schicht's villa on the Wannsee, which Alfieri also once occupied; they have turned the ground floor into an office. Because

of lack of petrol, his wife travels every day into Berlin by *S-Bahn* train to do what she can for the local Italian colony.

Attended an evening reception given by Nadia Nogarowa in Hermsdorf. In addition to a few Hungarians, there was a youthful member of Speer's Ministry, who arrived in his two-seater sports car, driven by a Dutch chauffeur. About midnight he sent into town for five hundred cigarettes. His comments on the war situation were of a nature which, in view of the presence of foreigners, necessitated my intervention. I am told that after I had left he made it clear to the Hungarians that the war was lost. This is a typical example of the complete lack of self-discipline displayed by so many senior representatives of the régime in the company of foreigners.

Some years ago, Louis P. Lochner, the head of Associated Press in Berlin, once told me that in no other country was it easier to obtain information than in National Socialist Germany. Whereas in other countries a network had to be organised and paid for in order to obtain up-to-date news, here foreign correspondents simply could not escape from Party and State officials eager to entrust State secrets to them, without demanding anything in return.

Monday, October 30, 1944
The German envoy in Budapest, Dr Edmund Veesenmeyer, has been awarded the Knight's Cross of the War Service Cross 'for outstanding services to the Reich'. So we read in the *Völkische Beobachter* of October 29, 1944!

Tuesday, October 31, 1944
My plan to fly to Stockholm this morning as a courier misfired. With Six and Lechenperg, who were catching the same plane, I waited for four hours in a mist-enshrouded Tempelhof airport before the flight was cancelled. We spent most of the time in a *Mitropa* restaurant car, which has been installed on the edge of the runway as a replacement for the bombed airport restaurant.

In the *Weltwoche* of October 20 Schuhmacher writes: 'The situation of the Third Reich can be compared to that of besieged Carthage, which was unwilling to make peace and incapable of waging war.'

November 1944

Mission to Stockholm via Copenhagen: anti-German atmosphere – An English report on a 'German extermination camp' at Maidanek – Mission to Vienna: unsuccessful attempts to contact governments-in-exile – Frustrating return to Berlin

Tuesday, November 7, 1944

After last week's false start, the journey by train to Stockholm via Warnemunde, Gedser, Copenhagen and Malmo passed off without incident. At Stettin, a man boarded the train, entered our official compartment and sat down opposite me. The military cut of his clothes, the manner in which he handed his papers for scrutiny by the railway police and his mode of expressing himself betrayed him as a Gestapo man. On the ship between Warnemunde and Gedser I identified him as the bodyguard of our Envoy Best, who was travelling on the same ferry with our Naval Commander-in-Chief in Denmark. There was very considerable nervousness on board on account of U-boat mines and the danger of air attack. Before we even left Warnemunde harbour, we were ordered to put on our life-jackets. The men returning to Denmark from leave are an uninspiring lot. They include many wounded, cripples hobbling along on crutches and elderly reservists. How can they possibly defend the country against invasion!

In Copenhagen, where the atmosphere is extremely anti-German, I stayed at the Palace Hotel, where everything was more simple than two years ago, but still very good. We visited a few bars, which were full of drunks. In the Trocadero half a dozen Security Service men in mufti were carousing in one corner and a prince of Denmark and friends in another. Between them sat a number of prostitutes and 'men of the world'. Police regulations call for an 11.00 p.m. closing.

Malmo harbour was full of brand-new merchant shipping, belonging to Norwegian owners, among them a twenty-five thousand ton tanker. The Norwegian Government-in-exile and the Norwegian Shipbuilders' Association have initiated legal proceedings in an endeavour to secure the release of these ships, which have been built with the object of providing Norway with the nucleus of a merchant navy on the conclusion of the war. The freight assets of Norwegian shipping companies in England are said to be something like sixty-five million pounds. Hence the wealth of the Norwegian Government, which, after the Polish, is the richest of all the governments-in-exile.

In Stockholm I stayed at the Hotel Reisen, but was unable to secure a room for my first night there. All the beds are occupied by refugees from Finland, Norway and Denmark.

Thomsen, the German Minister, as well turned-out as ever and very realistic in his outlook, is carrying out his duties with great skill. One evening we dined together and then went on to the Opera House, where we saw a miserable ballet *Coppelia and Hulabou*. The dancers were dressed as *maquisards,* and the chorus consisted of naked Swedish women, painted a chocolate colour, who hopped round like a herd of apes. One striking figure was a *Walküre* with a superb navel and breasts encased in sequined cups.

In no other town in the world does one see so many nude performances as in Stockholm. The Swedes respond most readily to political propaganda when it is served up to them in conjunction with some form of female nudity. In the last number of *Tysker Roster,* the newspaper published here by the German Legation, an article entitled 'National Socialist Women Workers in the Sauna' was illustrated with four pages of nude photographs. An exhibition here of photographs of children includes a nude study of a female body in a posture which is quite indescribable. The prevalent perversions in sexual behaviour, which result from indulgence in methylated spirit as an alcoholic drink, the impotence of a large proportion of the men and the great superfluity of women have all combined to give a fillip to the lure of sexually exciting spectacles. Despite this, however, women returning home alone late at night are frequently molested by hordes of ruffianly adolescents, against whom there is only one form of organised protection: to ring up the Boy Scouts' Headquarters and hire the services of a twelve- or fourteen-year-old lad as an escort. The service remains open until 1.00 a.m.

Anti-German feeling is very strong. In the Foreign Ministry two key positions are occupied by people who have recently returned from Berlin. Post is head of the Political Section, and Essen is the Foreign Minister's secretary. Both talk with great bitterness of the incarceration of so many of their friends in Germany. The Edelstams, who spent eighteen months in Oslo under German occupation, are among the few who take an objective view of things. Dagmar Cronstaedt complains that as the result of her broadcasts from Berlin she has been boycotted by all her acquaintances.

In the German colony here no less than a hundred and seventy-six people have managed to avoid war service. In the Legation intrigues and denunciations are the order of the day. Anyone who is ordered to visit Berlin fears at once that he will be kept there. Many of them, out of fear of what will happen to them in Berlin, have emigrated. The representatives of the German nation abroad, official and unofficial alike, display the same attitude towards their homeland as did nationals of the Soviet Union in the first years after the revolution. They get out and ask for political asylum abroad. This tendency will not be overcome, until the psychological causes of it have been eradicated. Our 'National Group Leaders' abroad are hated and feared by the German colonists, less because they are the representatives of the Third Reich than as a result of their own personal characteristics.

Thursday, November 9, 1944

Roosevelt has been re-elected with a surprisingly huge majority. We sat up following the results until 5.00 a.m.

German attempts to influence the course of the American elections all failed, with one exception. Heintze was sent to Stockholm with the task of persuading the Swedish press to publish a report to the effect that the Russians were about to make common cause with the Japanese against the United States. With this manoeuvre Berlin hoped to be able, at the last moment, to influence the election! Thomsen, Grassmann, Hepp and Dankwort of the Legation staff were aghast. Nevertheless, the report duly appeared in the *Göteborgs Post*. Repercussions were even less than they might have been, because on the eve of the poll Stalin made a speech in which he attacked Japan. Another suggestion was that, should Roosevelt's opponent Dewey win, Germany would at once make an offer to conclude peace.

At a lunch with Tovar we argued about the question of how far one should tolerate stupidities in politics. Schmidt was against and

Tovar in favour of tolerance – when the individual concerned was the press chief of the Foreign Ministry! At a political breakfast with the Swedish envoy, Richert was a complete flop. The Swede with icy reserve refused absolutely to talk politics.

The *Illustrated London News* of October 14, 1944, publishes an illustrated report on a 'German extermination camp' in Maidenek. Schmidt is as much in the dark about this as is everyone else in the Ministry. No one can give any information as to who is responsible for this establishment or on whose initiative it was originally set up.

According to a United Press report dated November 2, 1944, Eisenhower has imposed a fine of twenty-five dollars on any American soldier caught talking to a German. A glass of beer partaken with a German involves a fine of sixty-five dollars. On the other side, the *Schwarze Korps* threatens to impose the death penalty on any German who offers an American a glass of water! All this sort of thing is going to make life in the occupied zones very complicated.

The British newspapers have published photographs of four members of the Hitler Youth – 'baby snipers' – who fired on the Americans during the battle for Aachen. The offenders are eight, nine and fourteen years old and are to be tried by court-martial as 'Nazi beasts'. Had these children belonged to the French partisan movement they would have been hailed as national heroes!

Friday, November 10, 1944

November 9 has passed off without an air raid and without a speech from the Führer! We gave a small party, at which the Danish journalist Steman was one of the guests. Towards midnight, when people were beginning to feel a little hungry and we had nothing to offer them, Steman went back to his hotel and brought food and drink, with which he is amply supplied from Denmark. The occupied countries live very much better than the *Herrenvolk*, despite the fact that all their consumer goods are sent to them from this country. Nevertheless we are accused of looting the smaller countries.

Tuesday, November 14, 1944

At a Home Guard parade held in the Wilhelmsplatz Goebbels claimed that a hundred Home Guard Grenadier Divisions had been raised. His speech was broadcast and was heard by most of the city's four million inhabitants, including the foreign element and the diplomatic corps. An hour later, the German News Agency issued instructions that the number of divisions mentioned by the Minister was not to be published, and the foreign journalists were individually requested not to mention it. This embargo was imposed as the result of representations by the army command. This is typical of some of the bricks dropped by Goebbels, the inventor of the '*Pst*' – campaign. A carpenter who babbles about the packing-cases he is making for V1 missiles is liable to lose his head. A Minister, who is at the same time Defence Commissar and Plenipotentiary for Total War, can give away military secrets without fear of punishment.

Wednesday, November 15, 1944

We joined the Strempels for a weekend with Vidal in Wilkendorf. The Ambassador was less gloomy than usual and did his best to be a genial host. He is living in a country house owned by Frau von Dippe, an Englishwoman who spent six years of her married life in India, buried her husband in Peshawar and in Monte Carlo met and married Herr von Dippe, a diplomat and landowner, who at the moment is a prisoner of war in British hands. Vidal's primary interest is whether or not he will remain Ambassador here. Dieckhoff's long absence from Madrid, and the rumours that he is not to return there, are worrying Vidal. He fears that Spain, too, might decide to be content with a chargé d'affaires in Berlin. In the meanwhile it has been announced that Halem is to relieve Bibra as chargé d'affaires in Madrid. The Foreign Ministry has ordered an enquiry to find how the news leaked out.

As regards the Franco interview, the Ambassador made it fairly clear that he was not happy about it. Shortly before his death, Jordana had assured him that he would rather resign than break off diplomatic relations with Germany. But Jordana is no longer there, and Franco wants to take his place beside the people who, he thinks, are going to win the war.

On Tuesday at the Foreign Press Club we had the Croat envoy Kosak as our guest. After the meat course, conversation turned to political events. Kosak complained that when the Press Section issued its news bulletins he had been excluded from the short list of recipients. Schmidt retorted that in the past heads of missions had all been on the short list, but that then, at a reception, one of them had expressed his astonishment that the Foreign Minister should make available such delicate material to foreign diplomats. The heads of missions were thereupon struck off the short list. 'I can't believe it!' Kosak exclaimed somewhat cryptically. Then – 'Is it really true, sir, that a head of mission would be received by the Foreign Minister?' When he left, he drew Schmidt aside and said: 'Sir, will you please do what you can to ensure that our Croat sovereignty receives less tokens of respect from above and more from those below!'

The sinking of the *Tirpitz* robs us of our last battleship. The *Tirpitz* had tied down a number of British battleships, which were employed as escorts for the Russian convoys and which will now be available for service elsewhere – probably against Japan.

Friday, November 24, 1944
I went to Vienna on November 17 and returned on the 23rd. The outward journey took twenty and the return journey twenty-six hours. All the stations in Vienna, with the exception of the West station, are out of action. The trains arrive and depart from Florisdorf or Stadlau, because most of the Danube bridges have been partially destroyed. Communication between these suburbs and the city is maintained by motor-buses, which are so overcrowded that it is impossible to get a seat. On the outward journey I met Gabriele Kesselstatt and Camillo Haubert on the train. When we arrived they managed to wangle a car from the Hungarian Consulate, without which we should never have succeeded in getting into town. Instead of arriving at 9.00 a.m., it was 6.00 p.m. before I reached the Imperial Hotel. In Angern we were held up for several hours on account of an air raid alarm. While five hundred bombers flew over our heads, we crouched in a hollow in a potato field. The outer districts of Vienna, III and IV, the diplomatic quarter, the Argentiniengasse, the racecourse, the Prinz-Eugen-Strasse, the Schwarzenberg Park and the Belvedere have all been severely damaged. Large cars, filled with exiled politicians, sweep through the streets. In the shops there is nothing to buy except black ties.

Wednesday, November 29, 1944

An attempt to get in touch with the Zankoff, Horia Sima and Neditsch governments-in-exile in Vienna failed. Neditsch has moved to Kitzbühel, Horia Sima to Berlin, and all we saw of Zankoff was his large family in one of the air raid shelters. The whole place, incidentally, is crawling with Balkan nationals, busily engaged in political tittle-tattle or black market activities. The gardens on the Karlsplatz, the self-service restaurant near Meindl's in the Karntner-Strasse and all the big hotels are filled with people peddling ration cards, cigarettes and soap. Ration coupons are being filched in the Rhineland towns by corrupt officials and sold in Vienna. A black coupon for a month's meat ration sells at eighty marks. One of the racketeers has dressed up as a bridegroom in frock-coat and top-hat, and thus attired carries on his business, with the ration cards concealed in the bouquet of flowers he carries. In the Grand Hotel, the Gestapo prohibited the auction of a lady's costume. Since then the hotel lobbies remain closed to the public until midday. The foreigners loafing round the town are not being called upon either to serve in the Home Guard or the Labour Force or to assist with the clearing away of debris. All the girls in Vienna, on the other hand, have been called up for work in the munition factories. Missi Wassiltschikoff and Antoinette Croy were made to help dig out the corpses of the victims of the last air raid. While our troops are defending Budapest, thousands of Hungarians are just loafing about in Vienna. In Florisdorf we passed a column of Hungarian Jews who had trudged on foot all the way from Budapest, laden with bedding, the women in trousers and carrying emaciated little children in their arms, and all of them wearing an enormous yellow star on their clothing. It was indeed a shattering spectacle.

On the way to Pressburg we had to make several detours, because the main road was riddled by innumerable bomb craters. The Slovak capital seems to look much the same as usual. Slivovitz still flows by the gallon, but in front of my hotel was a notice-board, saying: 'This is NOT a recreation area!' An air raid shelter has just been completed for the German legation. Every time a bomber formation flies over Hungary on its way to Upper Silesia, the alarm is at once sounded in Pressburg, and the all clear does not sound until the last bomber on its way back from Silesia has disappeared.

Wednesday, November 29, 1944

As a result, the city's life has been paralysed. No bombs have so far been dropped on Pressburg itself.

On Tuesday morning I went to see Tido Gaspar, who, like most Slovaks, gives the impression of being very depressed. The revolt has been suppressed, but it did show the weakness of the foundations on which the Slovak State rests. Although Slovakia is at least as well off as Denmark and although the country has become an economic oasis in Hitler's Europe, the number of discontented people is legion. The political climate will improve only if we achieve some military successes. There are always hundreds in the queue for any appointment in Switzerland; but a job in the Slovak State administration interests nobody. The general atmosphere is redolent of plots, corruption and ill-discipline. Petreas, the Press Chief of the Slovak Foreign Ministry, complains about the Slovak press attachés abroad, who, he says, write articles to the detriment of the Slovak State and are never called to account. In Slovakia, as in Hungary, the opinion is gaining ground that the Russians are not nearly as bad as German propaganda makes them out to be and that the atrocities committed by the Germans are far worse than anything the Russians have perpetrated. People point out, for instance, that in many of the Slovak cities the Russians have not laid a finger on private property and possessions. In Hungary, the Red Army is said to have installed a son of the late Premier, Count Telecki, as a provincial administrator *(obergespan)*.

Count Tisza, they say, has been allowed to return to his castle and to bring his family back from Budapest. The Esterhazys are reported to have held a family council in Galantha and to have decided not to flee if the Russians come. It is rumours such as these, which no one can verify, that give impetus to the anti-German whispering campaign.

For the return journey to Berlin, after a day of frustrating search, we managed to hire a taxi for the sum of fifty marks, to take us from the centre of the city to Stadlau on the opposite bank of the Danube, where the train is due to start from. On the way there we had to stop to fill up with petrol. There was a queue of forty cars ahead of us, and I had to bribe each one of the forty drivers with a cigarette and enlist the help of a policeman, to get served first. On the Danube bridge our taxi was stormed by a pair of hysterical women who, laden with innumerable parcels and string bags and shrieking madly, tried to force their way into our car. When we reached Stadlau at 6.00 p.m., the sleeping-car train, which was due to leave at 7.36 p.m., had not even arrived. The last news of it was that it was running three and a half hours late out of Oppeln, and since then it has simply disappeared somewhere in Slovakia. Another train arrived at about 11.00 p.m., from Berlin, which was also equipped with sleepers. We managed to find a couple of seats in a passenger compartment, over which Kircher stood guard while I went off to find the sleeping-car conductor and try and get berths. About thirty other passengers, among them Czornig, had had the same idea. After waiting in vain for a couple of hours, we heard that the sleeping-car conductor had been left behind at Marchegg, having got off the train to try and obtain hot water from the station buffet. So we buckled to ourselves, grabbed a compartment and prepared to settle down in the crumpled, unmade beds, when someone hit on the idea of getting clean linen from the conductor's linen cupboard. Someone else discovered a case of beer and a store of bread in the service galley. Next we managed to get the heating going again in the sleeping-car. At Marchegg the missing conductor boarded the train and was speechless with indignation at our high-handed behaviour. The next morning he served tea, which he had brewed in a soup tureen and which tasted so strongly of fat and condiments that Czornig had to make it more palatable by adding schnapps to it. The conductor uses the same tea-leaves for five brews, and charges two marks a glass!

I had a long conversation with Anfuso, Rogeri and Torso. Why is it, I wonder, that we employ so many Italians on road construction and none in the diplomatic field? Even the least gifted among them is far better suited for the job than many of the Germans who are regarded as being first-class. Frederick the Great knew this, and for preference always employed Italians, of whose subtlety, vision and experience he had a high opinion.

At midday my companion at a late breakfast was Count Monoto, the new Counsellor of the Japanese Embassy, who has just arrived from Vichy and who speaks better French than any other Asiatic I have ever heard. His German is equally good, though he has never lived in our country. Nearly all the heads of missions were present. Steengracht presided, The Reichs administration was represented by Meissner and Kaltenbrunner, the latter being the Chief of the

Security Services. Regarding the reshuffle in the Bonomi Government, Anfuso remarked that they had had to open the graves in the Via Appia in order to find people to form a government – an allusion to the advanced age of Orlando, Sforza and the other leaders.

Thursday, November 30, 1944

The press has published the details of the new regulations regarding the employment of domestic personnel. At a time when, except in a few, precisely specified instances, there is a general embargo on the employment of servants, we go and issue rules which are to govern the working hours and rest periods, days off and meal-times, restrictions on giving notice and the reciprocal 'loyalty pledge', and all this rigmarole as it applies respectively to cooks, parlour-maids, nannies, wet nurses, housekeepers, female secretaries, private tutors, chauffeurs and gardeners, is precisely laid down in minute detail! With typical German fondness for banalities, the concept of 'domestic partnership' is set forth with comic finality. Servants are to work for ten hours a day, must sleep for at least nine hours; the repose of an eighteen-year-old maid must not be interrupted during the night by her employer; the authorised two free afternoons a week may be converted into one free day instead – and a whole heap more such nonsense! While Government officials with thirty years service no longer have any right to specific periods of leave, domestic servants may, under the new regulations, claim eight days leave in the first year of service, ten days on the completion of three and fifteen days after four years. Have the authorities taken complete leave of their senses? One might just as well frame regulations governing the social rights of moon-worshippers, centaurs and baseball players.

The day before yesterday the Premier, Hansson, and the Foreign Minister, Gunther, gave the Swedish Parliament an account of the German-Swedish negotiations on the evacuation of refugees from Norway. The text of the German note drafted by the Legal Department, to which the Swedish statesmen referred, was not released to the departmental chiefs of the Foreign Ministry until midday today.

December 1944

Home Guard regulations – We launch an offensive in the West – H.G. Wells on Churchill, according to Tribune: an example of British press freedom

Tuesday, December 5, 1944

For the Home Guard, our last line of defence, dress regulations have been issued which might well be notes on etiquette for a Court Ball. Our overburdened German language has been enriched by a new word – *einsatzbrauri* – field-service-brown. Here is a quotation from the *Neue Wiener Tageblatt;*

'As far as the Home Guard is concerned, what a man wears and how he is armed are questions to be settled by the individual himself. In this sixth year of war and in view of the terror in the air, most men must be modestly content to go around in their ordinary civilian clothes. For this reason a number of auxiliary measures have been introduced, with the result that quite a number of Home Guard units are already uniformly dressed and equipped.

'The *Reichsführer-SS*, in his own sphere and in so far as the priorities enjoyed by other services permit, has already been able to make good many deficiencies. The contents of SA, NSKK and SS stores can, with the prior sanction of the Party treasurer, now be made available for issue to the Home Guard.

'Uniformity of clothing in the Home Guard is, of itself, of no importance; but camouflage is. To wear bright or very light-coloured clothing is inadvisable. It has therefore been decided that light-coloured clothing, such as the Party uniform, shall be dyed the new standard '*einsatzbrauri*'. The dyeing of civilian suits, however, will only be carried out if the original colour is unsuitable for field service and provided that the suit, after being dyed, can still be worn by its owner for his lawful, civilian occasions.

'Payment of clothing compensation to members of the Home Guard is to be avoided. In cases of particular hardship, an appeal may be lodged with one of the above-mentioned authorities.

In all these questions of clothing, the object in view is not to achieve uniformity within companies and battalions, but rather to ensure that every man in the unit is dressed in a manner which will enable him efficiently to perform the duties allotted to him. Outfitting of individuals who have been bombed out is one of the tasks which must be given priority. In the Home Guard, that uniformity which will formally confirm its status as a combatant formation and thus confer upon the individual the same status as that of the regular soldier in accordance with international agreements, will be ensured in a different manner. The improvised white and yellow armbands at present in use will be replaced by an armband, uniform throughout the Reich, bearing the words: *'Deutscher Volkssturm – Wehrmacht'* on a dark background. Each man will also be issued with a regulation Pay Book. The issue of these is already in hand.

'Finally, it is intended that the Home Guard should wear some distinctive crest, although all of this cannot, of course, be done with equal speed throughout the country. Badges of rank will consist of silver stars, of which a section leader will wear one, a platoon commander two, a company commander three, and the officer commanding a battalion four; these will be worn either on the lapel or the collar. No other badges will be worn by members of the Home Guard, but those who are already entitled to do so will continue to wear the national emblem. Special régimental colours for the Home Guard will not be introduced. Instead, a modification of existing local NSDAP Group colours, consisting of the addition of a small black flash with the battalion's number in arabic numerals, will be used to denote that the Group in question has been transformed into a Home Guard formation.'

On Saturday I went to Buckow with Freddy Horstmann. The Manchukuo envoy, a Japanese, who was to pick us up at 5.00 p.m. at the Steinplatz, failed to appear until 8.15. He apologised and explained that he had had to attend a lunch given by the Japanese Ambassador to mark the anniversary of Pearl Harbour, and this had continued until 6.00. During the drive we listened on the car radio to news of what was happening in the air. Every time danger threatened anywhere near where we were, the envoy stopped the car, hopped out and took cover. When we at last reached Buckow at about 10.00 p.m., we were at once greeted with the air raid warning.

Alfred Rukawina and Geza Pejacsevich, both of whom were brought up as Austrians, have been posted to the Croat Legation.

At the APC we saw Garbo's film, *Ninotchka,* the showing of which is only allowed to 'selected audiences', obviously because many of the 'scenes from Russian life' depicted in it might well have been filmed in the Germany of today.

The last numbers of the American *Vogue* and *Harper's Bazaar* both claim that American fashions have tended to become dull and dowdy as a result of the prolonged absence of the traditional Parisian influence. Certainly, France will very quickly re-establish its hegemony in the sphere of *haute couture.*

The conclusion of a pact with Russia is a great triumph for de Gaulle. It is also a good example of the fact that in politics persistence pays.

Churchill's speech on Greece in the House of Commons is one of the most interesting declarations of British foreign policy to be made in recent years. For the first time, Britain has taken a definite stand against her Russian ally.

Tuesday, December 12, 1944

On December 5 we were subjected to a heavy daylight air raid for the first time since June 26. Spandau, Siemensstadt, Wittenau, Oranien-burg, Hermsdorf, Schoneweide, Rosenthal, Pankow and Weissensee suffered heavily. The centre of the city was not attacked this time.

The military situation is very serious. We have withdrawn from the line of the Vosges. Budapest is expected to fall any day. In East Prussia heavy enemy concentrations of men and materiel are reported. The ring is steadily closing around us. Meat is being distributed in suspiciously generous quantities. I am told that this is due to the great influx of 'refugee' cattle, which must be slaughtered.

Thursday, December 14, 1944

At the British Labour Party conference, the only man who broke a lance on behalf of Germany was the Jewish Member of Parliament, Strauss, who vigorously opposed any plan which envisaged transforming Germany into a purely agrarian country. He said: 'Europe will have no cause to rejoice, nor will we here in England, if the industrial heart of Germany ceases to beat. All these proposals will simply create discontent, bitterness, hatred and unrest, which will inevitably lead to a resurgence of new fascist parties and new wars.'

Wednesday, December 20, 1944

Newspapers carrying the news of the western offensive we launched on Saturday are being snatched out of the hands of the vendors while they are still damp from the press. For the first time in this war the launching of a major military operation has successfully been kept completely secret and has come as a complete surprise to the enemy. Since both sides are refusing to release details, it is not known whether this offensive has been launched to relieve pressure, or whether it has some broader objective, such as, perhaps, the retaking of Antwerp. In his appeal to the troops, Model mentions 'the sword of retribution' and 'the spirit of Leuthem'.

At a Christmas party at the Foreign Press Club, attended by members of the Press Sections of the Ministry of Propaganda, the SS, the armed forces and by foreign journalists, Frau de Kowa, *née* Mitchiko Tanaka sang, while her husband recited poems by Wilhelm Busch and Christian Morgenstern. Schmidt made a speech, half Christmassy and half political, of which my only criticism is that there are too many references to the 'winter solstice'. One of the stupidest phenomena of our times is the fact that we are not permitted to refer to Christmas by its own name!

In Vienna the annual conference of the International Congress of Journalists from which nothing but hot air emerges, is now taking place. By order, great prominence has been given in the German press to a speech by Dietrich. Seeing that the Ministry of Propaganda has ruled that all these conferences are superfluous, I cannot help wondering why they are held at all.

The following assessment of Churchill by H.G. Wells in the socialist *Tribune* of December 15, 1944 is an illustration of the degree of freedom of expression allowed in Britain:

'Winston Churchill, the present would-be Führer, is a person with a range of ideas limited to the adventures and opportunities of British political life. He has never given evidence of thinking extensively, or of any scientific or literary capacity. His ignorance of contemporary social and physical science is conspicuous ...

'His ideology, picked up in the garrison life of India, on the reefs of South Africa, the maternal home and the conversation of wealthy Conservative households, is a pitiful jumble of incoherent nonsense. A boy scout is better equipped ...

'He has served his purpose and it is high time he retired upon his laurels before we forget the debt we owe him ... We want him to go – *now* – before he discredits us further, for his own sake as well as ours, and if he takes all the Royalties in the world with him – so much the better for human hope. The matter is urgent ...'

January 1945

Results of our western offensive dubious – Increased enemy air activity over Berlin – Collapse on the eastern front

Monday, January 8, 1945

The hopes raised by our western offensive have not been fulfilled. The failure to achieve a decisive victory after very considerable initial successes is ascribed to a change in the weather, which suddenly improved and allowed the enemy to deploy his strong air power, against which Model could muster only one thousand aircraft. There is no doubt that our offensive came as a shock to our opponents, who already regarded us as finished; but they reacted in a manner typical of the Anglo-Saxon mentality. In Britain 350,000 new recruits have been called up. America is preparing to introduce conscription. It is unlikely that we shall be able to maintain the bulge we have made in the front if attacks are launched against our flanks. It would appear, therefore, that a boldly planned operation has failed prematurely on account of our lack of reserves.

Christmas in Reelkirchen. Westbound trains now run only under cover of darkness. One can leave Berlin at 8.30 p.m. or 10.30 p.m., arriving in the industrial area in the early hours of the following morning, to catch connections which get one away before the daylight attacks begin. Dr Tram of the Dr Otto industrial organisation brought us back in his DKW car. Shelters have been hollowed out all along the *autobahn* for the protection of the few motorists on the road, whereas shelters for the populations of the great cities are woefully inadequate. The National Socialist '*Volksstaat*' is full of such anomalies. The preferential treatment which it accords to the few far transcends the privileges enjoyed by the ruling classes in any other country.

In Berlin, the new year announced itself with a shower of bombs, while the old year was seen out with a New Year's Eve attack.

The *English Digest* publishes the following extract from the *Evening News*: 'In a restaurant in a town somewhere in the south of

England the following notice is displayed: "Please don't talk about your bombs!" In a Government office, also in southern England, I saw this notice: "Anyone talking about bombs and bomb damage will be fined one shilling". I am told that lots of people gladly part with that sum just for the pleasure of getting their bomb stories off their chests.'

Tuesday, January 16, 1945

The Russian winter offensive was launched on January 12. By early this morning the spearheads of Soviet armour were within thirty miles of the Upper Silesian industrial complex. Without coal from Upper Silesia, our war industries in central and eastern Germany will hardly be able to function. Why did we use our forces for an offensive in the Ardennes, when they were so urgently needed at the decisive point, on the eastern front? Is the same situation to arise in Silesia as has already arisen in the Rhineland? Now that we have lost our freedom of movement on both eastern and western fronts, we appear to be confronted by a hopeless prospect of trench-warfare and house-to-house fighting. A London press release today points out that Moscow is now twice as far from the front as Berlin, and that London now lies nearer to the Russian eastern front than does Stalingrad.

Enemy air activity over Berlin has again increased very considerably. During the weekend alone, there were four alarms. During one of the attacks we were with Dicki Wrede, who provides accommodation, night after night, in her 'catacomb' in the Rauchstrasse for men on leave from the front, and on this occasion was celebrating the arrival of some of them with a bottle-party. Twenty guests, nearly all of them badly wounded officers, some with a wooden leg or on crutches, and decorated with the Golden Cross or the Knight's Cross, turned up, laden with bottles; among them were Knyphausen, Hanstein, Brandis and Rumohr. When the alarm sounded, not one of them showed the slightest sign of nervousness. The flak in the Zoo opened a furious rapid fire. Then down crashed the bombs, and there ensued the heaviest gunfire and the most concentrated bombing that I have ever witnessed in the Tiergarten area. The greater the fury of the explosions, the merrier became our mood. The music did not stop for a moment. When one young girl in a moment of panic wanted to rush out into the street, the roars of laughter quickly brought her to her senses and she returned to the party. But how very stupid it was, to have closed the night clubs in all the large cities. I wonder if any of the reunions held by order of the régime would have shown the same spirit during a heavy air raid as did these young people, whose love of life had been unimpaired by their terrible injuries and who laughed at the threat of death.

Monday, January 22, 1945

The situation on the eastern front is now so catastrophic, that it is impossible to see how it can possibly be mastered. There appear to be three main Russian thrusts in progress – through south-east Prussia on Danzig, from Warsaw on Poznan, and on Breslau. In Silesia the Russians this morning reached Gross Strehlitz, which belongs to the Castells. All the property of the Studnitz family in Upper Silesia is now in enemy hands, and Schönwald has even been mentioned in a Russian army communiqué. Ten days ago, no one would have dreamt of such a possibility. Feelings here vacillate between belief in a miracle, resignation and panic.

Russian reports say that the army columns advancing on Poznan will push straight on to Berlin. They are already announcing the number of miles which separate the Russian spearheads from the German capital. We shall be faced in the immediate future with the problem of what is to become of Berlin and of the members of the administration still stationed here. At the moment any mention of the problems of evacuation brings an immediate charge of defeatism. In Berne, as early as August 1943, Urach asked me to raise the subject, because the technicalities of establishing communications between a German redoubt and the outside world could not be carried out overnight. Schmidt, however, thought at the time that it would be impossible to raise the question. The Foreign Ministry proposes to establish emergency quarters in the vicinity of Buckow. This move, however, was envisaged only as an insurance against any increased severity of the war in the air. No one even considered the possibility that our eastern front might start shrinking. It is true that the ministerial staffs could be moved comparatively swiftly to Berchtesgaden and Salzburg areas, but to move the whole compli-cated machinery of national administration would be infinitely more difficult. If the Russians get as far as Frankfurt (Oder), it will be too late. One might, of course, take the view that in that case the war would be over, anyway. But that is a viewpoint which our National Socialist leaders, determined to 'fight to the end', would not tolerate for one moment.

Tuesday, January 23, 1945

Today the Foreign Press Club had as their guests the Danish envoy, Mohr, and one of his colleagues. He is a friendly old gentleman, who warmed up quickly and seized the opportunity of getting all sorts of things off his chest; he made no secret of his bitterness over the deplorable state of Danish-German relations. Mohr regards Clausen's Danish Nazi Party as being primarily responsible for the deterioration of relations between the two countries. He went on to complain about the overlapping and duplication of the large number of German authorities in Denmark. There was absolutely no central authority such as that which the British always succeed in setting up in the territories they occupy. The SS and other administrative groups did not consider themselves bound by any agreement which Best or the military Commander-in-Chief might have made with the Danes. The lack of co-ordination between the various German authorities had led to the military authorities constructing coastal defences without consulting the Navy. The whole of Denmark was laughing, because massive forts had been erected in places were sandbanks or swift currents made any landing quite impossible. In other places, on the other hand, where there really was a risk of invasion, the authorities had refrained from constructing any defences because they wished to spare land which was agriculturally valuable. Instead, a defensive line had been constructed diagonally across North Schleswig, the only possible use for which would be for the defence of Denmark against Germany! Lunch, which started at 2.00 p.m., was still going on at 4.00, because Mohr showed no sign of coming to the end of his long list of complaints. The old gentleman, obviously, was determined to make the most of this unique opportunity of getting a hearing for the Danish point of view.

It is a tragedy that Best should be resigning his post in Denmark. He is a man of absolute integrity, actuated by the highest motives, and is – like Abetz – one of the few National Socialists who have learnt from experience.

Thursday, January 25, 1945

The situation in the East has deteriorated so greatly that one must frankly admit that our front has collapsed. East Prussia is cut off from the rest of the Reich. At Elbing, the Russians have reached the coast. Russian armoured assault spearheads are advancing on Frankfurt (Oder). Breslau has been surrounded, and the attack on the Silesian industrial area is in full swing. Between Breslau and Oppeln the Russians have established a number of bridgeheads on the west bank of the Oder. Our panzer armies surrounded in East Prussia and Courland have no petrol. The enemy offensive has been in progress for a fortnight and still shows no sign of losing its impetus. It is estimated that three million refugees have fled from the eastern provinces and are choking roads and railways alike. The streams of refugees are interfering with military operations, disorganising the lines of communication from which some counter-stroke might be launched, and are denuding the East of its German population. In the midst of all these terrible tragedies childish actions still abound. For example, German troops were ordered to destroy the Tannenberg memorial, in order to prevent the Russians from demolishing it! Whether they would have done so or not, God only knows! But in any case, the Russians can now with justice assert that, by themselves destroying the Tannenberg memorial, the Germans have admitted that they cherish no hopes of returning to East Prussia. The goods-wagon in which Hindenburg's body is being brought back would have carried sixty refugees to safety. We would have rendered a greater service to the future of Germany by rescuing that number of refugees than by sending the Field-Marshal's corpse on a tour round the country.

Events in the East have robbed many people of their last shreds of composure. I long ago remarked that people took the stability of the eastern front just as much for granted as the appearance of fresh rolls on their breakfast-tables. Not a soul had dreamed of the possibility that the enemy might break through to the Oder or come knocking at the gates of Berlin. Now, however, even the present generation, which has not hitherto given much thought to the war, realises that our agony has begun. Yesterday evening the Adlon was full of people who had been awarded the Party's Golden Badge and had won the highest decorations for valour. The dining-room, which has been the scene of so many memorable sights, was filled with an atmosphere of such gloom that one might have thought the end of the world had come. The Berlin Home Guard has not yet been called out, though many factory workers are receiving preliminary training.

The press persists with headlines such as: 'Our determination is unbroken', 'Defensive successes on the flanks', 'We shall turn the tide', 'This is how the Upper Silesian Home Guard fights', 'Bitter fighting in the heart of the battle area'.

Every now and then the electric current is cut off. In houses which have coal grates, the gas supply has been discontinued. The use of sun-ray lamps has been forbidden. Postal services have ceased to function. Many houses are without heating of any kind. The underground, the *S-Bahn* railway and the trams have introduced restricted schedules. At the main Berlin railway stations scenes occur such as have not been experienced since the days of the mass air raids in the late autumn and winter of 1943-44. When I took Marietti to the station yesterday about midnight to catch her train to Hanover, we saw people fighting their way into the compartments and trampling over anyone who got in their way. Apart from these refugees, thousands of men on leave are squatting in the railway stations. What they are doing here, when the situation at the front is so desperate, nobody knows. The unheated train was composed of a conglomeration of unmatched carriages. Eight of the ten entrances to the Schlesische station were closed, which only added to the confusion. Fresh snow and low temperatures have heralded the advent of winter.

Friday, January 26, 1945

Yesterday evening, while I was having a drink with Leo Fürstenberg, we suddenly got a message from Uscha Geyr, who had fled from the Warthegau. She was stranded at the Zoo station, laden with two heavy suitcases and two small children, homeless, hungry and frozen. We set out in the icy cold and driving snow to go to the assistance of these refugees. As the trams were not running and no vehicle of any sort was to be had, we had to make our way on foot with the two infants from the Zoo station to the Kielganstrasse. We towed the two heavy pieces of luggage over the snow by means of a tow-rope made up of my handkerchief, Leo's belt and a bit of rope. Uscha had reached Berlin in a Party welfare truck. She had left Luisenau in the Warthegau eight days ago by one of the last trains to run. Then she had made a halt in a forest bungalow near Sagan, and then, as the front drew nearer, had set out on the second stage of her flight to Berlin. Tomorrow she proposes to go on to the Rhineland. Her husband, Teddy Geyr, could not be persuaded to accompany his family. Although he is a Rhinelander with nothing that binds him to his wife's properties in West Prussia, and his diplomatic rank would have made it easy for him to get away, he felt that his place was on the estates, which were now directly threatened by the Russians.

Monday, January 29, 1945
We spent the weekend with the Pfuels in Jahnsfelde, probably for the last time. Pfuel's father-in-law, Leo Geyr, Guderian's successor as Inspector-General of the Panzer Forces, drove us out there. On the icy, snowbound roads and against a strong east wind we made painfully slow progress. The streams of passing refugees and retreating troops made a sorrowful sight. The roads were full of open carts drawn by decrepit nags, in which people huddled together under blankets and bundles of straw, seeking protection against the freezing cold. At the crossroads in Müncheberg we skidded and came into collision with an Air Force heavy lorry; Geyr's car emerged from this encounter with a handsome dent and his daughter with a bloody nose. In Jahnsfelde a group of fifty were camping on the straw-spread floor of the Schloss's dining-hall. On Sunday an army Staff Quartermaster arrived to commandeer the property. At the same time the Foreign Ministry asked us to arrange accommodation for Keppler, who had fled from Krummhübel. Chaos and confusion everywhere. We spent Sunday packing. Terrible, having to quit a great house in which the same family has lived for five centuries, none of whom know whether they will ever see it again. On Sunday evening, enemy reconnaissance armour was sighted near Schwiebus and Meseritz. This afternoon three hundred Russian tanks reached Landsberg. The cold is increasing; so is the wind. All who can are leaving the town.

February 1945

The emergency: official wangling – Impossible to evacuate Berlin – The Government awaits 'a miracle or annihilation' – A Russian frontal attack on Berlin expected – A British breakthrough at Kleve? – Our official news services collapse – Deserters swarm around – The Diplomatic Corps leaves Berlin – The Black Market flourishes – Thirteen night raids in succession – Cologne about to fall?

Thursday, February 1, 1945

From today, Berlin policemen on the beat will wear steel helmets and carry carbines. Last night the Home Guard was alerted. Many are failing to turn up at our Ministry press conferences. Strempel was put on guard duty at the Charlottenburg station, as enemy paratroops were said to have been dropped in the vicinity. As a keen sportsman he was detailed to the snipers' section. He spent the night in the dilapidated driving cabin of a lorry, smoking and sleeping.

Like everything else, wangling has been organised on a planned official basis. The staff of the principal offices of State and other departments 'of importance to the war effort' have been issued with a white 'Z-card', which places them in Category Two in the event of a call-up. Should they, by any chance, be called up with Category One, they must be immediately released. But the really privileged are the holders of red Z-cards, who belong to Category Three. These red cards have been issued to State propagandists and intermediary and senior Party functionaries. The sick and the crippled have been placed in Category Four. On January 30 the Führer declared that he expected every sick man to do his duty.

What will Goebbels do? As *Gauleiter* it is his duty to supervise the defence of Berlin, yet as Propaganda Minister he must leave the city if the Government decides to move to some other place.

During the night the Russians have crossed the Oder between Wriezen and Küstrin. The threat to Berlin grows hourly. The population remains calm. That 'General Thaw' will come to our assistance is unlikely, for the soil in the Brandenburg district is of too light a texture to be transformed by a thaw into a morass that would be an obstacle to tanks. In any case, the enemy will find an excellent network of roads at his disposal.

Even now the Berliners have not lost their sense of humour. The situation cannot be regarded as really critical, people are saying, until you find you can get to the eastern front by underground! Another sarcastic observation runs: *'Eh det ick mir hängen lasse, jloob ick liba an 'n Endsieg'* ('to save myself from getting strung up I'd better go on believing in a Final Victory'). The last Führer speech evoked remarks like: 'So now our Adolf has declared war on *us!'* The barricades, they say, will save Berlin, because, when the Russians see them, they'll die of laughter!

The efficacy of the Home Guard is likely to be jeopardised by lack of weapons. At a roll-call of a thousand Home Guardsmen, only eighteen were found to possess rifles. In the eastern sector of the town, road blocks are going up for the first time, constructed from rubble. The stream of refugees to Berlin continues.

Spent the evening at the Croat Legation. The chargé d'affaires, Alfred Rukavina, has to provide transport for the evacuation of eighty-nine members of his staff and has only twenty cars at his disposal. The Foreign Ministry is not issuing any directives to foreign missions as to where they should move to. Whereas Rukavina is obviously very worried, Geza Pejascevich manages to find a funny side to everything. Having had to flee his estates, first in Yugoslavia, then in Budapest, with the Russians breathing down his neck on each occasion, he is a really practised escape-artist!

A professor of the Gleiwitz Technical High School has told the Red Army: 'We have all lost our heads. One day the *Gauleiter* of Silesia issued an order in which, in the name of Hitler, he emphasised that the district stood in no danger and that everyone must remain at his post; anyone who spread rumours to the contrary, he added, was liable to be shot. The next day the same *Gauleiter* issued another order, directing that preparations for an immediate evacuation should be taken in hand and that anyone who tried to remain where he was would be hanged!'

The most cherished possession is a car with petrol. Unlimited supplies of coffee, spirits and cigarettes are being offered on the black market in exchange for a private car and fuel.

The newspapers now appear as single sheets, with abbreviated headlines and sub-titles.

Monday, February 5, 1945

Last Saturday's daylight attack, directed against the centre of the city, the government district and the railway stations, was the ultimate apocalypse, as far as Berlin is concerned. The attack began at 10.45 a.m. and ended at 12.30. The Adlon shelter is a foot deep in water that has leaked through from the melting snow above. Many people had to wade about underground for two hours in icy water. Under the heavy explosions the massive shelter swayed and shivered like the cellar of an ordinary house. Finally all the lights went out, and we felt as though we had been buried alive. In the Foreign Ministry, one wing of the Minister's suite and house No. 73 were hit. We saw the Foreign Minister and the Japanese Ambassador wandering about among the ruins, surrounded by a crowd of people and being greeted with the Nazi salute by those in uniform. Ribbentrop was wearing uniform, while Oshima was wearing a leather jacket and a deerstalker. Both were carrying stout walking-sticks. Gigantic clouds of smoke hang over the whole city. The Schloss, the Esplanade and Fürstenhof hotels and the newspaper district were all burning. The German Office of Information and the Transocean Agency have been put out of action, and the Antiques Section of the AWAG (formerly Wertheim) Department Store, now located at Lennestrasse have been destroyed. Unexploded bombs, and huge puddles of water fed from burst mains, have made the streets impassable. I helped the Strempels to rescue a few things from the ruins of the Esplanade. The hotel had received seven direct hits, which had destroyed the two upper floors and annihilated a cinema opposite. Above this scene of desolation hangs, night after night, a moonless sky, tinged with streaks of blood-red and sinister, pale yellow.

The new Commandant of the third Military District, General von Hauenschild, has been complaining on the radio about the amateurish tank obstacles that have been set up. The area political command comes on the air each evening at 8.15 to deliver a pep-talk at the hour when the nightly air-raid starts. Ration cards are now to be made to last for a week longer. Goebbels, who is trying to encourage the Berliners to a supreme effort, announces that he gives the surrounded garrisons of Konigsberg, Thorn and Poznan daily advice by telephone on how they should defend themselves against the Russians. Never has the city looked so devastated as it does in these days, when rain and water from the melting snow bespatters its ruins with muck, and streams of filthy water flow through the streets.

Rabbles of soldiers fleeing from the front have demolished C.C. von Pfuel's Schloss in Jahnsfelde, smashing the doors, windows, glassware and porcelain, pillaging the linen and silver, stealing the cars in the garage, and killing all the pigs and poultry. They have riddled the beautiful Danzig wardrobes with bullets in the process of shooting off their locks. One night, eight hundred camped out in the living-rooms and, on a following night six hundred. The Strempels have been forced to evacuate their hunting-lodge in Münchehofe.

Evacuation plans which had been taking shape during the last few weeks have now again been overtaken by events. The State Defence Council has decided that the Government must remain in Berlin, and there await either a miracle or annihilation. The decision was taken because the evacuation of four million Berliners was seen to be technically impossible, and it was felt that the population could not be compelled to resist to the end if the Government deserted them. If the Russians thrust into Berlin itself, the city defences are to be organised in three rings, the innermost of which will be the government district. Local Home Guard units are to set up an organised defence of their own sectors of the city.

In this way the hopes of many that they would be able to escape to the West have come to naught. Anyone who attempts to leave risks being picked up in the provinces, where the machinery of the régime is still functioning, and shot as a deserter. Those who remain here have the choice between death and capture by the Russians.

Tuesday, February 6, 1945
The Russians, who are concentrating their main forces on the Oder, have paused in their advance. For the next twelve days the Oder will be swollen with icefloes and floodwater and will be difficult to forge. But it is anticipated that the offensive will be resumed about ten days or a fortnight from now. Will this turn out to be a costly reprieve? On the Lützowplatz, furniture vans are being moved into place as roadblocks.

Wednesday, February 7, 1945
Foreign Ministry Departmental Order No 3 states:

It is possible that in the very near future travel within the city and suburban areas served by electric and steam-engine forms of transport – the Circle railway, suburban services, underground and tramways – will have to be curtailed to a degree which will necessitate the introduction of regulations, under which only those persons will be permitted to use public transport whose journeys are shown to be of vital importance to the national war effort. With this possibility in view, the State Railways and the Berlin Transport Authority envisage the introduction of curtailment in three stages:

Stage 1 Curtailment to fifty per cent of current services
Stage 2 Curtailment to twenty-five per cent of current services
Stage 3 Curtailment to ten per cent of current services

On the introduction of these curtailments, only those persons in possession of a special pass will be permitted to use public transport.

In anticipation of these measures, the State Defence Commissar proposes to issue special regulations governing the use of public transport, within the defensive area of the capital. To enable this decision to be put into force, the attached questionnaire is to be distributed by members of the Office of Statistics and by those units working in collaboration with the above Office, and the completed forms are to be returned to the Director General of the Office not later than 1300 hours on 6.2.45.

Friday, February 9, 1945
It has only now become known that in the daylight attack last weekend the President of the People's Court, Dr Freisler, and most of his colleagues were killed. Freisler's death has aroused considerable excitement in Berlin and is regarded as an act of just retribution for the revolting manner in which he conducted the case against the July 20 accused.

In the Foreign Press Club in Dahlem we sit around every evening in candlelight, which has a comforting and soporofic effect and makes members forget that the Russians are only about thirty miles from the city and that their entry will mean the end of their activities for most of the foreign journalists in Berlin. Some of them, like Jaderlund, who wrote reports on Katyn and Vinnitsa, are probably on the Russian black list.

In the cellar of the Ministry of Propaganda's Press Centre an unexploded bomb weighing five thousand pounds has been found. It had torn a great hole in the wall of the house, but for some days no one took any notice of it.

Of the diplomats, Vidal has gone to Salzburg and most of his staff to Switzerland. Nearly all the Legations have sent their women and children away. Tomorrow the Swedish women and children are leaving. Tovar has moved out to some place near Neu-Ruppin.

Friday, February 16, 1945

Now that Koniev's Army Group has crossed the Oder on a broad front between Oppeln and Küstrin, the 'Oder Line' is a thing of the past. Koniev's forward elements are already approaching Sagan. They have occupied Bunzlau, Grünberg and Sommerfeld and are now only fifty miles from Dresden. We are wondering whether he will continue his advance in a north-westerly direction on Berlin or westwards on Dresden. In the northern sector of the Oder area, the Russians are trying to reach Stettin and cut off Pomerania. The situation on the flanks is very fluid. In the Frankfurt-Küstrin area, where Zhukov is preparing a massive advance, things are deceptively quiet. Once Schneidemuhl has fallen and resistance in Poznan has ceased, the Russians will be able to free very considerable forces for the Oder central sector. An attempt to wipe out the enemy bridgeheads on the western bank of the Oder has failed. The frontal attack on Berlin can now begin any day. Regardless of this fact, there is plenty of talk about a German counter-offensive which is to be launched against the Russian flanks.

I was at Eberswalde station when a trainload of troops arrived and disembarked. The country all round is peppered with tank traps, roadblocks, minefields and gun-emplacements. These installations are guarded by a few elderly, unarmed Home Guards. The French and Russian prisoners on the Stein estates have received orders to be ready to move at a moment's notice. In the villages the peasants are preparing to evacuate. Leo Fürstenberg and his family intend to stay in Lichterfelde. The Steins, who are relatives of his and already have the long journey from East Prussia behind them, have no desire to take to the country roads once again. They would rather die, they say, than undertake another such forced march.

Between Bernau and Eberswalde Leo and I got a lift on a fuel tank train which was bound for the front and so had right of way over all other transport, which allowed us to reach our destination comparatively quickly. For the return journey we had the choice of five goods-trains which were about to leave for Berlin. The problem facing us was to find out which of the five would start first. Burdened as I was with a carpet and a large mirror, I did not look forward to the prospect of having continuously to change trains. In the end, we and three soldiers found space in the brake compartment of a cattle-truck. But the train went only as far as the Rüdenitz mar-shalling-yards, and we had to hump our heavy loads the remaining three miles to Bernau – in the middle of an air attack, for good measure.

In Eberswalde stood a goods-train with a régiment of child-soldiers, kids of twelve to sixteen years of age in baggy Air Force uniforms, who glared at us with animal-like eyes set in emaciated, prematurely knowing faces. They were in charge of a bunch of surly NCOs. A train drew up on the next track, filled with members of the Women's Auxiliary Anti-Aircraft Force, pretty girls in uniform with open faces, broad smiles and beautiful long hair. In contrast to the small boys, these girls look obviously well-nourished. On the other hand, their vulgar behaviour – shrieking and mouthing obscenities – struck a particularly jarring note. Since the goods-trains had no latrines, boys and girls alike had to use the permanent way, and the space between the two trains was a mass of excreta, old tins, paper and rubbish of every kind.

Monday, February 19, 1945
On Saturday there were stories of a British breakthrough at Kleve. It is becoming increasingly difficult to find out what is really happening, since the Foreign Ministry's news service bulletins only arrive sporadically nowadays. The official news service's *'DNB-weiss'*

bulletins are hardly to be seen any longer, although it is the only useful publication issued by that agency. Lack of paper is said to be the reason. Although two weeks have passed since the last air attack, the 'DNB' facility is still only partially restored. Newspaper distribution is equally unpredictable.

Chaos is spreading rapidly. Stapf has been missing for fourteen days. He set out for Kassel and has not been seen or heard of since. Nobody knows whether the man in charge of *Mundus*, with two hundred foreign editors and their staffs working for the press department under his command, is dead, conscripted into the Home Guard or taken prisoner by the Russians. Even a government department such as the Foreign Ministry no longer has the means to obtain swift and reliable information.

The newspapers of February 16 carried a proclamation regarding the institution of standing courts-martial: 'Any person who attempts to avoid fulfilling his obligations towards the community, and in particular any person who so acts from cowardice or for selfish reasons, must at once be punished with appropriate severity, in order to ensure that the State suffers no harm through the failure of the individual citizen.' This is a very elastic formula. The findings of the courts-martial will require confirmation by the State Com-missar of Defence. If the latter cannot be reached and 'it is in the public interest that the court's finding be immediately confirmed', then the prosecuting counsel will have authority to act on the Commissar's behalf. The Public Prosecutor thus becomes both judge and the authority which exercises the prerogative of mercy – a truly astounding precedent in the legal history of civilised peoples!

Placards on the hoardings of underground stations announce that the twenty-five-year-old deserter Lieutenant Karl Ludwig has been shot while resisting arrest by a military patrol. The notice goes on to say that any soldier who leaves his country in the lurch in the hour of danger forfeits his right to live. This is intended as a warning to the many thousands of deserters. Everywhere one sees weaponless soldiers who are nevertheless correctly dressed in field-service uniform: no one knows where they have come from or where they are going. The stories one hears of the lack of discipline and excesses of German troops at base camps near the front defy description. The signs of disintegration are multiplying every day.

At the same time the press is publishing little paragraphs about the millions subscribed by the troops of beleaguered garrisons to the Winter Aid Fund. The commander of a Cossack division, for example, is said to have sent a million marks to the Minister of Propaganda, to be used 'in the public interest, as he thinks fit'. A Cossack division consists of ten thousand men. I find it hard to believe that every Cossack has sacrificed a hundred marks of his pay as a donation to the benevolent funds of a community to which he does not belong and whose language he does not speak!

Almost the whole of the Diplomatic Corps has now left Berlin. While the Foreign Ministry denies that the Government intends to move from Berlin and says that no further steps are being taken to move State archives – a few days ago Schroeder, Administration Head of the Foreign Ministry, stated that the removal of a few files did not indicate that the whole of the State archives were to be evacuated! – the foreign diplomats are nevertheless being unofficially encouraged to leave the capital and alternative accommodation is being found for them. For instance, accommodation in the Osterreichische Hof in Salzburg has been requisitioned for the Irish, Portuguese and Manchukuo Legations, and for the Spanish Embassy.

The Swedish Legation has vacated Schloss Alt-Dobern, the property of Prince Lippe, because of the increasing proximity of the front, and has moved to Schloss Schönhausen on the Elbe, which belongs to the Bismarck family. The Swiss Legation, with the approval of the protocol department, has evacuated to Saulgau its section which looks after the interests of some of the belligerent States. In Wudicke we saw for ourselves that the Swiss were loading their archives on to lorries. At the same time, foreign representatives are being requested to leave token Legations in Berlin. Charlie Mills, the Irish race-horse trainer, for example, whom Strempel and I visited in Staffelde, told us that the protocol department had approved his taking up the post of Irish chargé d'affaires in Berlin.

In Schönhausen, where we had breakfast yesterday, there is little sign of war. The Schloss, Bismarck's birthplace, is a rather tumble-down building with clumsily angled roofs and walls and is crammed with rubbish which, for pious reasons, may not be thrown away. The Swedish envoy, Richert, is delighted to have been allotted this historic building as a place of exile.

The main events on the eastern front have been the fall of Sagan and the operations in the Forst, Guben and Kottbus area. Military circles assert that in this area the High Command intends to fight a decisive battle which will change the whole aspect of the eastern front. After the disappointments of the last few years, no one is bold enough to believe in any such turn of the tide.

Last week Dresden was destroyed from the air. Although people have now become accustomed to the horrors of war, the destruction of Dresden has given rise to greater consternation than perhaps any other event in recent times. As the town had so far not been attacked, people had come to presume that it would be spared – an illusion that has been shattered in the most brutal manner.

Wednesday, February 21, 1945

Dined with Guido Schmidt, the former Austrian Foreign Minister who is now the director-general of the transport interests in the Hermann Goering Works. He has been greatly shocked by a horrible thing that has just happened. The day before yesterday in Fürstenberg (Oder) twenty-eight of his best bargees were court-martialled and shot, because they had refused to take their barges along a stretch of the river which was under Russian artillery fire. Had the Oder bargees, like those on the Danube, been called up for military service, they would not have refused to obey an order. But these simple fellows, who for years had lived on their barges with their wives and children, quite detached from events in the outside world, did not for a moment think that, as private citizens, they were under any obligation to do what they were told. This is just one more example of the ever-increasing rule of frightfulness to which we are being subjected by the authorities.

C.C. Pfuel has given me another example of this kind of brutality. With the permission of the Frankfurt district administration and the Brandenburg provincial governor, he had sent some of the more valuable pieces of his furniture from Jahnsfelde to the Oder, whence they were to be shipped to safety. The local Group Leader in Jahnsfelde, in civilian life a stable-boy, had tried to prevent the move on the grounds that in Jahnsfelde he, and not the *Gauleiter*, gave orders. When, despite this, the furniture was moved, he called upon the District Leader of the Oder harbour area to intervene, and threatened his employer with a court-martial!

Since the Dresden attack there has been a lot of talk about reprisals against prisoners of war. The idea is said to have emanated from

Goebbels and to have been submitted to the Führer as a serious proposition. The Foreign Minister and Supreme Headquarters have opposed the idea, on the grounds that it might well place in jeopardy the lives of the million German prisoners in British and American hands and even lead to the introduction of further horrors, such as the use of gas. Furthermore, any such move on our part would inevitably cause the remaining neutral countries to break off diplomatic relations with us. Strempel has prepared a memorandum warning of the disastrous consequences of such measures.

Thursday, February 22, 1945

The Oder line between Frankfurt and Küstrin has been under continuous Russian artillery fire for the last two days, and this is presumed to be the overture to a major attack. Nothing more is being said about our counter-thrust in the Dresden-Kottbus area. Our counter-offensive in Pomerania has come to a halt. The Russians report that German counter-attacks have taken place all along the line, without, however, revealing any sign of a co-ordinated offensive. Some people declare that the army engaged in the recent Ardennes offensive is to be transferred in the course of the next few days to Litzmannstadt, with the object of cutting the lines of communication of the Russian forces in Silesia. These troops of ours are apparently armed with new weapons. The success of any counter-offensive depends, ultimately, on the ability to feed it with reinforcements of men and materiel. But we are short of everything. If the heavy weapons are available, there are no tractors; if both are available, then there is no fuel; if fuel is available, ammunition is lacking; if ammunition is available, then there is no transport to take it to the front. The State Railways have been made the scapegoats for the failure of our offensive in Pomerania. Dorpmüller is to be sacked and to be replaced by Speer. And Dorpmüller and Backe, incidentally, are two of the few efficient technical experts still in positions of authority.

While the troops go short of fuel, the petrol black market in Berlin is doing a roaring trade. Thousands of private cars are still cruising about. A litre of 'black' petrol costs forty marks or twenty cigarettes. Twenty litres cost a pound of coffee or a kilo of butter.

Tyres can be bought for two or three thousand marks. Small trailers are being offered at twenty thousand marks each, and even an old car cannot be had for less than fifteen or twenty thousand. There is also a brisk trade in false number-plates and diplomatic CD plates. A complete set of false papers, consisting of a travel permit, a military pass, an employment card and a Home Guard Z-card, costs eighty thousand marks. Recently a soldier was arrested while carrying a suitcase filled with bogus official rubber stamps. They were better cut than the official originals, and the SS department which arrested the man immediately confiscated them for their own use. Large sums are also being offered for Jewish Yellow Stars!

During both of the last two nights we have had two alarms. Yesterday afternoon there was a preliminary warning when six reconnaissance planes appeared over the city, taking aerial photographs. These reconnaissance planes are always regarded as the forerunners of a major attack and make people very nervous.

The latest novelty in the food line is 'desiccated oatmeal jam'. In the restaurants half the meals served consist of substitutes. The worst imitations are puddings and sweets, souffles, fruit sauces, semolina, peasoup and pancakes, which are made of potato starch and then coloured. That butter can be extracted from coal, margarine from tar and that the Italians weave cloth made from milk is nothing new. Two years ago *Punch* had a drawing of a man saying: 'Ladies and gentlemen, may I introduce to you Professor Schickedanz. He is a very famous scientist. He claims to be able to make butter out of cream.'

Friday, February 23, 1945

For those representatives of foreign powers who are sticking it out in Berlin the Foreign Minister has now inaugurated informal tea parties. The first of these is to be held on Wednesday 28, and the guests will be the foreign diplomats and German and foreign journalists. Refreshments will consist of tea and of an *Eintopfgericht* (that famous 'patriotic' war-time stew). All this is being introduced twelve years too late. Had it been done earlier, the Foreign Minister would have been able to establish with the diplomatic representatives the liaison which has been lacking for years. The only social contacts between foreign representatives and the Foreign Ministry still existing are the fortnightly luncheons given by the Secretary of State in the Adlon Hotel. Unfortunately, ladies are not admitted, and it is always the same politically insignificant and socially boring members of the political section and the protocol department who are detailed to attend the function.

Wednesday, February 28, 1945

Yesterday we had a night alarm for the thirteenth night in succession. And at 3.00 a.m. the alarm sounded for the second time. The day before yesterday there was a major daylight attack. The city centre, the railway terminals in the east sector, the Minister's own residence and the shell of house number 74, in which I work, were all hit. In the Esplanade Hotel, the kitchens, which had just been restored to working order, were again destroyed. Despite this, the restaurant remained closed for only twenty-four hours. Many more Mosquitoes took part in the night raids than usual. During the attack on the night of 24-25, fifteen bombs dropped in the vicinity of my apartments in the Kielganstrasse and reduced the house to the state it had been in before we had it repaired. All the cracks and crevices which had just been patched reappeared, and rain came pouring through the roof of the sitting-room. During the night of 26-27 a mighty explosion shook the house an hour after the all clear had sounded, and broke such windows as were still intact. A delayed-action bomb had exploded in the Derfflingerstrasse, not fifty yards from our front door.

Recently all the male members of the Foreign Ministry staff have been allotted navvy work once a week. With Strempel, Doernberg, Bergmann, Weber and Geffcken I was detailed to shovel debris lying in the Wilhelmstrasse into iron trucks and transport it into the courtyard of the Ministry, where others were engaged in strengthening the side-walls of the air raid shelter. While we were at work, ankle-deep in muck, hundreds of Russian prisoners of war, also engaged in clearing operations, watched us derisively. For the few people in the Foreign Ministry who, like myself, still have something to do, this shovelling business is a sheer waste of time. At the same time thousands of prisoners of war and foreign workers, whose places of work have been destroyed, are hanging about, doing nothing. It would make more sense if the Foreign Ministry at long last set about making a decent air raid shelter for its staff. The Ministry of Propaganda has had an excellent shelter built in the ruins of the Church of the Trinity, in which Schleiermacher's altar once stood. An undamaged cross is said to have been walled in. Admission to this shelter, however, is confined to members of the Propaganda Ministry staff. Foreign Ministry officials are barred!

In this connection, the text of the following memorandum, issued by the Defence Commissar for the Berlin Defence Zone and addressed to the 'Heads of all Government Departments and Offices', is of interest:

> Repeated inspections of air raid shelters by the Berlin police administration have revealed that among the people who take refuge in the shelters even before the alarm has sounded there is always a considerable number of officials from nearby Government departments and offices.
>
> The working population of the city, who have no opportunity of leaving their posts prematurely and thus seeking shelter, view such unworthy behaviour with repugnance. The whole life of the city carries on even after the preliminary warning has been given, and work does not cease until the alarm itself is sounded.
>
> You are therefore requested to warn the members of your staff that I shall in future take action against any person who prematurely seeks refuge in a shelter or who deliberately loiters in the vicinity of a shelter in anticipation of an alarm.
>
> *Heil Hitler!*
> (signed) Dr Penne,
> for Defence Commissar.

While we were shovelling debris, a second squad of Ministry officials, among them Hammerschmidt and Mirbach, turned up. Like ourselves, they were wearing overalls, and they were sporting Italian military caps. They constituted the Foreign Ministry's 'Security unit', *en route* for the Kronenstrasse, where they were to help with the burning of mountains of office files.

In the Führer's proclamation marking the twenty-fifth anniversary of the Party programme manifesto the foil owing sentences occur:

... They have destroyed so much that was beautiful, elevating and holy to us, that we must now devote our lives to the sole task of creating a State that may rebuild everything that they have destroyed ...

... They have taught us such Rightfulness, that life can hold no further terror for us. What our country has endured is terrible, what those at the front have accomplished is superhuman ...

... Whoever is suffering knows, and must know, that there are many Germans who have lost far more than he has. The life that is left to us must be devoted to making good the things that these international Jewish criminals ... etcetera.

At the moment the military situation is more critical on the western than on the eastern front. Cologne is about to fall. The Americans are talking of a breakthrough.

March 1945

American breakthrough on the Siegfried Line – The Croat mission goes down bravely … in a sea of alcohol – Guderian's press conference – Ribbentrop's public optimism – Berlin bombed twenty nights running – Peace offer rumours involving Rundstedt and Hesse – The Government is to leave Berlin after all – I struggle home to Reelkirchen

Monday, March 5, 1945

Mosquito attacks have occurred for the sixteenth night in succession. They arrived at 3.15 a.m. I myself was in Kerzendorf at the time, eighteen miles from Berlin, where the raids are just as heavy as in the city itself. Kerzendorf appears to be one of their favourite targets.

This morning, between 9.30 and 10.00, yet another alarm. The Police radio station, which works on the Rennes, Belgrade, Stockholm and Paris wave-bands, is a first-class organisation. In contrast to the short-wave relay station *Mio*, which transmits the whereabouts of enemy formations only in cipher, the Police transmitter goes so far as to tell us the areas over which the enemy bombers are flying, and even pinpoints the position of aircraft over the various sectors of the city. This enables one to follow the course of the attack and act accordingly.

All is still deceptively quiet in the central sector of the eastern front. The Pomeranian cauldron has been cut in half by a Russian thrust on Koslin and Schlawe.

In the West, the American breakthrough on the Siegfried Line has developed into a catastrophe for us. Within a few days the enemy will be in possession of the west bank of the Rhine. He has overrun Munchen-Gladbach and Krefeld and has reached the outskirts of Düsseldorf.

In the Unter den Linden yesterday I saw a dray belonging to the Schultheiss brewery being drawn by oxen. Many civilians have now equipped themselves with shoulder-straps, to which they can attach briefcases and small suitcases. In these days, bags of bread and lunch baskets have now become part of the standard outdoor outfit.

For the last four months, night after night, the Croats have been giving 'farewell parties' in Frau von Pannwitz's villa in Dahlem. Each banquet is followed by a drinking bout, in which strong spirits flow freely. At about midnight, a Croat choir appears and sings folk-songs. When the all clear sounds, the gunners of a Croat anti aircraft battery stationed nearby for the protection of the Legation come in and give a jazz concert. During these festivities the revellers frequently fire off their revolvers into the air. The porter of the Croat Legation lost three of his fingers as a result of such horseplay. Participants in these 'farewell parties', in addition to the Legation staff, include Germans drawn from every walk of life, stars of stage and screen, representatives of the régime and foreign diplomats. Not infrequently, distinguished but hopelessly intoxicated gentlemen have to be carried away. The Croat Minister, Dr Kosak, justifies these orgies by saying that he thereby acquires valuable inside information!

Tuesday, March 6, 1945

At the corner of the Kurfurstendamm and Joachimsthalerstrasse, next door to the Kranzler *konditorei,* a public notice-board carries messages from people seeking accommodation or offering things for barter, from language teachers, masseuses, and so on. Recently the new Berlin Commandant, Lieutenant-General von Hauenschild, joined the band of advertisers. His 'insertion' promulgates, in accordance with a Führer directive dated February 17, 1945, the execution of an officer deserter and three soldiers who were using false papers. The proclamation ends: 'These sentences were pronounced also in the name of those women whose husbands, brothers and sons are worthily defending their fatherland.'

This afternoon, when we went on air raid duty in the Foreign Ministry buildings, Wenmakers told us what had occurred on February 26. An air raid took place that evening, and that part of the Ministry which overlooks the garden of the Reichs Chancellery was apparently not properly blacked-out. The Führer, on being informed of this, ordered an SS patrol to extinguish any offending light-bulbs by shooting them out. The following evening, exactly the same thing occurred, whereupon the Führer remarked to the Foreign Minister that the Foreign Ministry did not appear to set much store by his life. The Foreign Minister immediately ordered that all electric light-bulbs should be removed from those rooms which overlooked the Reichs Chancellery garden. Even so, lights continued to burn in a few rooms that evening. The Foreign Minister ordered a searching investigation. Air raid defence procedures have been tightened up. Wenmakers, who is the man responsible for air raid defence, seemed completely shattered by all this. After we had listened dutifully to his homily, I pointed out the necessity for a revisal of the entire Ministry defence scheme in view of the changed conditions. Our duties, I emphasised, were complicated by the fact that a number of rooms remained locked for security reasons. The doors between houses number 74 and 73 and the front door of number 74 leading to the Wilhelmstrasse were kept locked, which made it very difficult to keep an eye on the corridors.

Wednesday, March 7, 1945

On Tuesday, March 6, General Guderian delivered a talk in the Propaganda Ministry to members of the German and foreign press. He was attended by Dr Dietrich, the Press Chief. Guderian referred to the atrocities perpetrated by the Russians in the occupied German eastern territories and introduced two German officers who had made their way through the Russian lines and now gave eyewitness reports of their experiences. The General then quoted an Army Order issued by Marshal Zhukov which states: 'The time has now come to put an end to the fascist beast in its own lair.' At the end of his talk, Guderian declared: 'I have myself fought in the Soviet Union, but I have never seen any trace of those fiendish ovens, gas chambers and other phenomena which are the product of a diseased imagination. The object is obvious: barefaced lies of this nature are being spread in order to kindle hatred in the heart of the primitive Soviet soldier'.

This speech did not leave a good impression. The whole world now possesses evidence in the shape of photographs, films and eyewitness accounts of the existence of extermination camps such as Maidenek, Auschwitz and similar institutions in territories formerly occupied by the Germans. The German people knows nothing about these things. But it must be assumed that Guderian had been informed of their existence, and this makes it all the more extraordinary that he should have raised the subject in the manner in which he did. One cannot also help wondering how the Chief of the General Staff found time to take part in a propaganda gathering in a moment of such acute military crisis. Grosse, Kronika and Finlay all reported that the German spoken by one of the two officers was far from perfect, a fact which did not encourage them to put much faith in what he told them. This informant from the eastern front claimed to have come across three old women in a farmhouse who, without being asked, opened the door leading into another room, where a fourteen-year-old girl was lying in bed. Seeing an officer's uniform, and taking him to be a Russian, the girl threw back the bedclothes. This 'story' has been repeated in the newspapers. At the same press conference a woman was introduced, who bobbed and described how she had been raped many times, her child had been murdered and she herself had then tried to commit suicide. When she had ended her story, a Scandinavian journalist turned to his colleague and said: 'Watch it – I bet she'll undress next and show us her scars!'

This sort of thing does not make our anti-bolshevist propaganda sound any more credible. Even the Foreign Minister himself admitted at yesterday's diplomatic reception that as propaganda it had misfired. A headline in *12-Uhr-Blatt* reads: 'Captured Americans ask: Bolshevism – what's that?'

Thursday, March 8, 1945

On Wednesday afternoon the Foreign Minister held another of his receptions for diplomats. This time it was the turn of the not-so-senior – the Embassy Counsellors, Press Attachés and so on, and, of course, the German and foreign journalists. From the Ministry, Doernberg, Ruhe, Hewel, Schmidt, Henke, Rühle, Ritter, Gauss, Sonnleithner, Steengraacht and Leithe Jasper were present. They all wore grey uniforms, apart from Henke and Ruhe, who were in black. There were three tea-tables, each with fifteen guests, and the Foreign Minister spent thirty minutes at each of them. Waiters in badly-fitting liveries served. It is rather remarkable that the footmen and diplomats in our Foreign Ministry both wear the same uniform, the only difference being that the former wear silver buttons and the latter gold.

The Foreign Minister dilated on the bolshevik menace in long monologues. Our efforts to reach an understanding with the Soviet Union, had been sincere. He himself, he said, had advised the Führer to make the attempt, when signs became apparent that Russian bolshevism had entered upon a period of evolutionary development. He had set out for Moscow, without knowing exactly what he would be able to negotiate. An hour after his plane had landed at Moscow airport at 5.00 p.m., the negotiations had started and had ended at midnight with the signing of a non-aggression pact. Afterwards he and Molotov and Schulenburg had taken supper with Stalin, who had stood up, glass in hand, and said: 'To the health of Adolf Hitler, whom I have always admired so much'. During the negotiations world politics had been discussed and Stalin had said: 'Up till now we have pelted each other with mud, but that must now be altered.'

The Foreign Minister declared that all had gone well and that a generous agreement, advantages to both sides, had been reached. Then the Russians had demanded the secession of Bessarabia by Rumania. This had been followed by the Vienna arbitration award, under which Germany had given Rumania a guarantee. That same evening he had sent Stalin an explanatory telegram. The latter's answer had been extremely cool. He himself had had the impression that Stalin had become angry at something we had done. The following November Molotov had come to Berlin. The visit had appeared to have gone well, but the political breach had widened. The Russians had demanded a free hand in Finland, Rumania, Bulgaria and the Dardanelles, but the Führer had not been able to accede to these requests. As a result, the Russians had started massing their forces on their frontier, a move which we forestalled with our own counter-measures. This account agrees in many ways with that given by Cafencus, who in his famous book expresses the opinion that it was the Vienna arbitration award that had shattered the newly-founded Russo-German *entente*.

On the military situation Ribbentrop said: 'In the East, militarily, we have had bad luck, because the democracies stabbed us in the back.' Now, he said, everything depended on the ordinary man on the Oder. If he failed to stand firm, then the aspect of the whole world would be changed. After Germany, the Russians would overrun France and Britain and bolshevise the whole earth. Of that he was convinced. Neutrals, he continued, seemed unable to grasp this situation, which they regarded as a figment of German imagination. As regards Sweden, the Foreign Minister said that the

Swedes were so blind that they would applaud the Russians, even when Russian bombs were dropping on Stockholm.

Finally the Foreign Minister touched on the situation in the Balkans. The Führer, he said, had advised Filoff and the other Bulgarian regents to go on fighting rather than to surrender to Russian pressure. If they surrendered, the Führer had told them they would be hanged by the Russians. He, Ribbentrop, had himself directed Beckerle to advise Filoff to take the Führer's warning seriously. With tears in his eyes, Filoff had replied: 'Tell your Chief that he is right. But we cannot change events. We shall be hanged in any event.'

The Foreign Minister expressed his conviction that our determination would carry us through and that we should win the war. The reception ended at 6.15 p.m.

During the Minister's speech I was watching the faces of his audience: servile deference was mixed with incredulity and perfunctory interest.

The former presidential mansion, which has been allotted to Ribbentrop as his residence, is practically unscathed. The present interior decorations were carried out on the instructions of Frau von Ribbentrop, who had the whole house completely transformed when they moved in – an undertaking that took years to complete and cost a great deal of money. The decor *a la* Third Reich, with its marble window-frames and its marble reliefs over the doors, is redolent of a clumsy neo-Biedermeier philistinism. There is no sign of the beautiful modern silver which the Berlin goldsmith Emil Lettre fashioned for the Ribbentrops. Even the reception-rooms have a homely air. The furniture arrangement is just like that in the home of a typical German *hausfrau*. The interior, with its complete lack of character, is rather like a hotel lounge or the saloon of an ocean liner.

Monday, March 12, 1945
Last night we had the twentieth successive night attack by Mosquitoes. The Nollendorfplatz looks more like a bombing-range. Hardly a night passes without a direct hit somewhere in the vicinity of my apartments. Three nights ago No. 15 Derfflingerstrasse was razed to the ground. It almost seems as though the ironwork of the Nollendorfplatz station exercises some magnetic influence on

the bombers' bomb-sights. The chances of receiving a direct hit have increased considerably. As a rule these raids are carried out by about eighty aircraft, and the bombs they drop are heavier and more effective than previously.

The day before yesterday I travelled to Mtincheberg with Hans Flotow, where we parted company. He went to Elisendorf, and I to Buckow, to fetch my dinner-jacket which I had left there. Since the departure of Elly Dohnas, the Schloss reconstructed by Schinkel has fallen into a deplorable state. The beautiful lawns, upon which no one in the old days was allowed to set foot, have been churned up by tanks. The stables to the left of the mansion have been transformed into an army divisional slaughterhouse, where the local inhabitants queue up for such bits and pieces as they can get. The skins of eighty slaughtered head of cattle were drying in the courtyard and giving off a fearful stench. A herd of a hundred and twenty cattle was roaming in the park. The drive is flanked with tank obstacles, trenches and sheds for army transport vehicles. Most of the rooms are filled with iron bedsteads in tiers of three. These provide somewhere to sleep for the refugees from the Oberbruch. Between the rows of beds the bookcases with their superb ceramics have been left where they were, and the lovely pictures are still hanging on the walls. One of the drawing-rooms, which the refugees are using as a wash-house, is crammed with precious French furniture. I saw one old man, wearing muddy boots, stretched out on a Louis XVI *bergère*. The troops billeted there change every few days. The SS, the Army and the Hitler Youth come, steal what they please and depart. Gloria's clothes have all disappeared, the wine-cellar has been looted and is being used as a thieves' storeroom for bales of cloth. The staff have no option but to stand by and watch Buckow being destroyed even before the Russians occupy it.

Instead of the normal hour and a half, it took us seven hours to get to Buckow and five hours to get back. Practically the whole time we were pestered by low-flying Russian aircraft, which were attacking all military vehicles on the road. As I could not get back to Berlin the same day, I stayed at a small hotel where I was served with an excellent dinner. All night long I could hear the roar of gunfire from the front, only twenty miles away.

On Sunday I went to Kerzendorf to say good-bye to the Horstmanns, who have decided to stick it out on their estate to the end.

Except for the Pfuels and Strempel, there is no one left here whom I know. Hans Flotow appeared once more, to take some more things from his house. He is as busy as an ant, removing even the kitchen utensils and glasses, and he seems to be able to carry as much as a mule.

Nowadays, when the evening sirens sound, we usually go to the shelter in the Spanish Embassy. A few Spaniards, among them Buigas, have returned. After the all clear they invited Strempel and myself to have a cognac. We drove home about midnight, slightly tipsy, through the debris-strewn streets.

As I have been detailed to the 'Supreme Staff' of the Foreign Ministry, I am no longer allowed to leave Berlin. Nevertheless, the Minister has granted me five days 'family leave', which I must take before March 20.

The salient feature of the military situation is the crossing of the Rhine by the Americans at Remagen. It came as a surprise to both sides. As the Americans have announced, their original intention had been to establish a bridgehead at Honnef (which they have since done). To their great astonishment the bridge at Remagen fell into their hands undamaged. The German defence unit is said to have surrendered without firing a shot. In the meanwhile, the bridgehead has now become almost ten miles broad and has increased considerably in depth.

We are waiting eagerly to see whether the Americans will now follow the Rhine valley southwards or northwards. They are already talking of being in Berlin before the Russians and talk of joining hands with the Russian armies somewhere in the heart of Germany; they are still three hundred and fifty miles apart.

American war correspondents in the occupied parts of the Rhine-land report that the inhabitants are friendly and servile, obeying American orders in the same way as they were yesterday obeying those of the German authorities. No acts of sabotage have occurred anywhere. Indeed, the people seem to be pleased to have new masters. This seems to confirm the truth of my thesis that the German national character precludes the possibility of any partisan warfare. Much the same sort of reports are coming in from the eastern territories.

On the eastern front, the attack on the capital is taking a long time in coming. Having overrun the area between Frankfurt and Kustrin with their armour, the Russians are now proceeding cautiously. They have established nine bridgeheads over the middle Oder. Some of the armoured divisions operating in this area were withdrawn to execute the thrust through Pomerania which has resulted in the encirclement of the German troops in that area. Two Russian armoured armies are in position between Guben and the Upper Silesian industrial area. They have pushed the front farther westwards and are now in a position to operate with the Bohemian mountain ranges flanking them on each side.

Wednesday, March 14, 1945
The Ministry of Propaganda was hit by a mine yesterday at 9.00 p.m. The explosion destroyed that portion of the Ministry which is situated in Prince Ferdinand of Prussia's palace. The palace was one of the most beautiful in Berlin. It was built in the eighteenth century and was remodelled in the classical style by Schinkel. Goebbels had always been proud of the fact that his house had been practically undamaged by the war in the air. He looked upon it as a good omen. No one was killed, but the Wilhehnstrasse was closed – for the first time in the war – in order to facilitate the work of the fire-brigade and demolition parties. The new Propaganda Ministry building next to the palace can still be used. Today at midday Frau Goebbels arrived, accompanied by three of her children and an Air Force orderly, to view the damage. In her mink coat and green velvet hat, she looked as though she were going to a cocktail party.

Friday, March 16, 1945
Since yesterday the word has been going round that Germany has initiated peace offers. Rundstedt, who was relieved by Kesselring, is said to have made an offer to Eisenhower to lay down his arms. From Stockholm come reports of activity on the part of Hesse.

As regards Rundstedt's alleged offer, the American State Department admits that some such move may possibly have been made. The British Legation in Stockholm confirms that Hesse has tried to establish contact.

Interest in the Foreign Ministry is concentrated on Hesse's action: it has aroused great excitement there. It can be assumed that Hesse was acting on instructions. He went to Stockholm some three weeks ago, returned before it was even known that he had

gone there, and said that his mission had been crowned with such success that he deserved to be received with a bouquet of roses. Madame Kollontay, the Russian Ambassadress in Stockholm, had, he said, expressed a desire to see him before she left for Moscow, but the meeting had not taken place. The Stockholm press has given the affair a certain amount of publicity.

Klosterzella – Tuesday, March 20, 1945

The Government is to leave Berlin after all. In the principal governmental departments, six-tenths of the personnel are being dismissed. The men have been ordered to join the Home Guard, and the women have been advised to 'disappear'. Three-tenths are being moved straight away to the Emergency Headquarters, and the remaining tenth, of which I am one, will constitute the so-called 'Directing Staff' and remain in Berlin. Heribert, who belongs to the second category, has been given the task of finding quarters for Schmidt and the Foreign Press Club in Mülhausen, in Thuringia. Some sections are being transferred to Bad Berka, the diplomats are to go to Wildungen and Supreme Headquarters to Meiningen.

I decided to take advantage of the leave granted to me by the Minister and drive in Strempel's car to Westphalia by way of Thuringia, so that I could visit my family one last time. After having to postpone our departure by a day, we were ready to take the road yesterday evening.

We had just finished packing when the sirens announced the arrival of the Mosquitoes. We drove our two heavily-laden cars to the Spanish Embassy shelter. When the all clear sounded, we returned to Strempel's house, had a quick meal, gathered up the silver and set off at about 11.00 p.m. Henbert took Leila Mecklenburg with him in his Topolino saloon, while I led the way in the open Fiat, which was known as 'the Easter Egg'. Approaching the Avus, we had to make a detour because of unexploded bombs. My umbrella fell out of the car and, astonishingly enough, was retrieved by Heribert and Leila, who had seen it drop. At 1.00 a.m. we were at Zehlendorf. No sooner were we on the Potsdamer Chaussee than I got a puncture. At the same moment the sirens started to howl. During the attack we changed the tyre by the light of the moon. When we set off again, I found that the Fiat would only function on third and fourth gears, the others being jammed fast. While on the *autobahn* near Treunbietzen, we were forced to halt for the third time on account of air raids; the aircraft were swooping straight along the road. We reached the Elbe at dawn and saw gigantic clouds of smoke on the horizon. We passed successfully through a number of strict control-posts and at Halle we left the *autobahn*, which for the last fifteen miles had been littered with the wrecks of cars and lorries shot up by enemy aircraft.

Near Eisleben we came into hilly country, which I found difficult to negotiate without my low gears. We breakfasted at a small inn off supplies we had brought with us, and here – as she confessed the next day – Leila slipped two Pervetin tablets into my Nescafe, to restore my jaded energies and prepare me for the feats of driving endurance to come. Driving through the night in an open car and with the temperature well below freezing had left me so stiff with cold that I changed cars with Heribert. This had the additional advantage that Leila could now perch in the dickey of the sports two-seater and keep watch for low-flying aircraft. Sitting there with her gaily-coloured headscarf in the sparkling, light blue Fiat, she presented so striking a picture of happy, carefree motoring amid the grim devastation of war, that all the peasants stared wonderingly at her as we passed. We had just driven through Wallhausen, a recently destroyed village, when the aircraft arrived. We turned off the road and up a forest track, where we waited and had a picnic meal until the danger had passed – an interlude that was to be repeated half a dozen times during the next few hours.

In the late afternoon we reached Mulhausen, and found that its wooded surroundings harboured a number of old friends from the Ministry – gaunt clerks and weary, strained-looking secretaries, who seemed somewhat lost on this lovely day and in these idyllic surroundings and were damning the orders which had removed them from the bomb-torn but familiar surroundings of Berlin.

Klosterzella – Friday, March 23, 1945
When we drove into the courtyard of Schloss Klosterzella, an old monastery set deep in the forest, we found the owner, Helmut Fries, with the Hammachers and Frau von Goldammer having tea on the terrace. Some officers arrived close on our heels, with orders to requisition the entire estate as a site for V-weapons. Heribert,

however, succeeded not only in persuading the unwelcome visitors to leave us in peace but even induced them to have the broken-down Topolino repaired for us by a mobile Army service unit! This feat justified our imposing ourselves on our host as temporary guests. The Hammachers had arrived in Silesia a few days before, after a three weeks' journey by horse-carriage, having had to flee from their estate, Schloss Lampersdorf, now part of the Steinau bridgehead. In addition to giving shelter to these friends, Helmut had had to find billets for some sixty officials from Crackow, who had installed themselves in Klosterzella complete with the furniture and carpets they had brought with them from Poland, and were now busily employed in burning office files. They have to transport the documents to a designated funeral pyre in a nearby forest clearing, but the only means of transport available to them is a small sledge which would normally have been used for dragging loads through rough country.

Reelkirchen – Sunday, March 25, 1945
The journey to Klosterzella was not exactly easy, but our real adventures lay ahead of us. After a day's rest, I set out for Kassel on Saturday afternoon. The local train from Lengenfeld to Leinefelde, where I had to change, was using peat as fuel, and the showers of sparks from the engine threatened to set fire to the whole country-side. Arrived in Kassel at 1.00 a.m., without a hope of finding any-where to sleep in the completely gutted city. There is a temporary wooden barracks at the station for members of the armed forces, but it was already cram-full. Since my train was not due to leave until 4.18 a.m. and the temperature ruled out any idea of camping on the platform, I made my way to an air raid shelter, the cement floor of which was already occupied by hundreds of night-time occupants. Someone stole my butter ration during the few moments when my eyes were not on my haversack. The skeleton of the ruined city, shimmering in the moonlight, presented a macabre spectacle.

A day which was destined to be unlucky for us started with the non-departure of our train, which should have left at dawn but was now announced for 7.00 a.m. A superb sunrise presaged a perfect day for air raids. The first alarm sounded in Sundern at 8.15 a.m. Two fighter-bombers suddenly swooped down from over the tree-tops, causing us to flee to the shelter of the station buildings. When the danger seemed to be over, the train left the station at a snail's pace. Every time we approached an open stretch of country, the train pulled up while driver and conductors scanned the skies with binoculars, searching for signs of enemy aircraft. Suddenly four fighter-bombers appeared in the distance, flying at a great height and receding from us without changing course. Then, just as we thought we were safe, they wheeled and dived down on our train with all their cannon and guns blazing. Fountains of earth and dust shot into the air. I took up a position on the side of the train away from the shooting, next to a young woman, one of the train's conductresses, beside the open carriage door. Suddenly the girl collapsed and fell out on the permanent way. I started to climb out of the slowly-moving train to go to her assistance, got entangled with my trench-coat, freed myself, fell down again, then stumbled across the rails and into a railway cutting at the edge of the forest. By this time the firing had brought the train to a halt. Dense clouds of steam were pouring from the engine's punctured boiler. Everyone fled to the shelter of the woods, to wait until the planes had departed, so that we could go to the aid of those who had been injured in the attack. The young conductress was fatally wounded, as was one soldier. For the rest, we had got off lightly with three badly wounded and a dozen or so with minor injuries. An army medical orderly who happened to be travelling on the train rendered first aid, but we had to wait several hours before the doctor and stretcher-bearers who had been summoned to the scene arrived in a horse-drawn carriage. While I was helping to bandage the injured, someone noticed that I was myself bleeding heavily. It seems that I had been hit by two bullets, one of which pierced the lobe of my ear and the other grazed my shoulder-blade.

We saw more aircraft, swooping like hawks in search of prey, but we ourselves were left in peace. At about 3.00 p.m. – the attack had started at 8.52 that morning – a relief steam-engine arrived to take the train on to Altenbeken. But we could not shake off the fighter-bombers. We reached Altenbeken at last, at about 4.00 p.m. Just as we drew up, the alarm sounded and everybody was ordered to get clear of the platforms. An hour later, new air raid warnings. Flights of enemy fighters overhead. We all clambered into a special train used for air raid protection, which was driven into the Altenbeken tunnel, where the thick smoke from the engine almost choked us. I ran to the tunnel entrance, and found the evening sunshine twisting the smoke-clouds into fantastic shapes. Just as the train was creeping out of the tunnel, back came the aircraft and drove it back in again. We were indeed thankful when dusk came and we were able to continue our journey to Horn, where I arrived at 7.30 p.m. after spending twenty-four hours on the journey from Thüringen. I then found that the tramway connection to Meinberg was not functioning, and I had to cover the last five miles to Reel-kirchen on foot. All around me, the horizon was glowing and sparkling with gunfire. Overhead, formations of aircraft thunder through the night sky on their way to Berlin. War and the roar of war from dusk till dawn.

Reelkirchen – Friday, March 30, 1945
The fine weather continues. The local Home Guard was mobilised yesterday at 10.00 p.m. The village cinema closed abruptly halfway through the performance. American armoured spearheads in Paderborn. Long columns of lorries going eastwards throughout the night.

Reelkirchen – Saturday, March 31, 1945
All bicycles have been requisitioned. We have been expecting the Americans to arrive for the last twenty-four hours, but so far nothing but a few weaponless convoys and refugees, all in frantic flight. One six-gun battery lumbered through, otherwise nothing but communications vehicles. Dispatch-riders from Marburg report that the Home Guard are tearing down the newly-erected tank obstacles.

Schmidt telegraphed for news of me, but I am unable to reply to him. In Blomberg not even the senior civil authority is allowed to send a service telegram. All means of communication have been requisitioned by the Army. The one thought in all our minds, day and night, is whether this will become a battle zone. We are taking what steps we can. Pictures and porcelain are being stowed away in the cellar. But from my own experience I know that whatever one does always turns out to be wrong. In Belle the authorities have requisitioned the last of the peasants' horses. Tank obstacles are being set up in Butterberg.

April 1945

'Days of intolerable tension' at home: 'danger threatens from all sides' – Shall we be homeless again tomorrow?

Reelkirchen – Wednesday, April 4, 1945

The last few days have been days of intolerable tension. At 2.00 p.m. on Easter Day the roar of gunfire grew to a crescendo. Detmold is said to have been declared a defence zone, and Horn, too. On Monday afternoon, the Metternichs' sixteen-year-old son Peter arrived from Vinsebeck. His District Leader had ordered his category to cross the Weser and report for duty to an army training camp. But since the situation is so confused, he is stopping the night with us and then cycling back tomorrow. He could not possibly have gone on.

There was a violent explosion on Monday night at about 11.00. When I went out I found the whole sky lit up with flares. The next morning I heard that the low-flying aircraft which visits us each evening planned to drop a bomb on the Schloss. We have given the pilot the nickname of *'Kreisleiter'* ('District Leader') because he turns up regularly every day. In Vinsebeck they nickname him 'Johnny the stunt flyer'. Except for a few broken tiles, the house remains undamaged.

For the past few days we have done nothing but pack our belongings and store them in bomb-proof sites. Danger threatens from all sides. The most immediate is the possibility of finding ourselves in the battle area. National Road number One, which runs right past the house, is a magnet in this motorised warfare. If the Schloss, with its moat and ancient walls, and the adjoining villages of Reelkirchen and Herrentrup are incorporated into a defensive scheme, then we are lost. The Americans are using phosphorus shells, against which all extinguishers are useless. As a precautionary measure we have removed all the lumber from the attics.

The second possibility is that the house may be occupied by

enemy troops. Eisenhower has issued a directive that allied troops shall not sleep under the same roof as Germans. So we shall find ourselves in the street.

The third danger comes from the released prisoners of war and the liberated foreign workers.

Last night I evacuated Gini to Vinsebeck by bicycle, and had to grope my way back through a violent rainstorm. In Billerbeck I ran into a formation of German Tiger tanks and armoured troop-carriers.

Sleep is out of the question. The night is filled with tormenting thoughts. The fatherland's situation is so dire, its collapse so terrible, that it is no consolation at all to know that one had foreseen it all, years ago. The more bitterly disappointed our countrymen may be, the more they will have to suffer now, I am afraid. Yet the faith of our youth has even now not been quenched. It is always a source of astonishment to me to see how little our younger generation has been affected by the catastrophe and how willing the young men remained to return to the battle, if only they could find a leader whom they trusted. But any further resistance is futile. The advances made by the enemy armies during the past week have been fantastic. The Russians are fighting in Pressburg and the suburbs of Vienna, the Americans are in Thüringen and the British are at the gates of Bremen. From Berlin one hears nothing but the constantly resuscitated parrot-cry that our moment of destiny – and God knows what else besides – now faces us.

By tomorrow we may well be homeless again, as so often during this war. In a world in which havoc spreads far more swiftly than life can burgeon, to look more than fifteen minutes ahead is pointless.

Index

Arco, Countess Gertrud (Kalle), *née* Wallenberg, 132
Arenberg, Hereditary Prince and Duke, Engelbert Maria (Enka), 76f.
Arenberg, Valerie, Hereditary Princess and Duchess of, *née* zu Schleswig-Holstein Sonderburg-Augustenburg, 76 f.
Ark Royal, HMS, 60
Arnim, Jüergen von, Colonel-General, 55
Arriba, Madrid daily newspaper, the organ of the Falange, 179
Arrow Cross, Hungarian fascists, 214
Ascensio, Restaurant in Rome, 28, 31
Assmann, Dr, Councillor for Indian affairs, German Foreign Office, 26
Associated Press (AP), 216
Atelier, Berlin restaurant, 9
Avenida Palace Hotel, Lisbon, 126
AWAG, Allgemeine Warenhaus Aktien-Gesellschaft (formerly Wertneim) Berlin, 241
Azad Hind, Fortnightly journal published in Berlin by the 'Free India Central Committee', 26

Backe, H., Secretary of State in the Ministry of Food and Agriculture, 249
Bader, General, Commander-in-Chief in Serbia, 51
Badoglio, Pietro, Marshal of Italy, Head of the Italian Government, 32, 86 ff., 93, 98, 111, 118, 121, 129, 134, 169, 175, 215
Barcelot, Sophie, 131 f.
Barcenas, Juan de Las, Spanish Consul in Geneva, 191

Barros, Tobias, Chilean Ambassador in Berlin, 67
Baruth, the estate of Prince Solms-Baruth, 43
Basler, Hilmar, Councillor in the Foreign Office Press Department, 117, 199
Basler Nachrichten, 139
Bastianini, Giuseppe, Secretary of State, Italian Foreign Office, 32
Baworowsky, Count Adam von, 7
BBC, 81
BDM, Bund Deutscher Madel, roughly German counterpart of Girl Guides, 116
Beattie, American journalist, 214
Beatty, Admiral Earl, 81
Beaumont, Count and Countess of, 132
Beck, Colonel Josef, Polish Foreign Minister, 57
Becker, Wilhelm, Berlin hairdresser, 150
Beckerle, Adolf Heinz, German Minister in Sofia, 212, 259
Beck-Frijs, Baroness, wife of the Swedish Minister in Lisbon, 122f.
Behl, Dr Carl, Friedrich Wilhelm, 178
Benazzo, Agostino, Secretary of the Italian Embassy in Berlin, 43
Benckiser, Dr, Nikolas, *Frankfurter Zeitung* correspondent in Budapest, 43
Benes, Dr, 135
Benger, Textile manufacturer, Stuttgart, 29
Benzler, Felix, Minister and Foreign Office Plenipotentiary in Belgrade, 51
Berchtold, Count Leopold (1863-1942) Austro-Hungarian statesman, 204